THE WORD OF LIFE

THE WORD OF LIFE

A Theology of John's Gospel

Craig R. Koester

WILLIAM B. EERDMANS PUBLISHING COMPANY

GRAND RAPIDS, MICHIGAN / CAMBRIDGE, U.K.

Published 2008 by

Wm. B. Eerdmans Publishing Co.

2140 Oak Industrial Drive N.E., Grand Rapids, Michigan 49505 /

P.O. Box 163, Cambridge CB3 9PU U.K.

www.eerdmans.com

Printed in the United States of America

13 12 11 10 09 08   7 6 5 4 3 2 1

Library of Congress Cataloging-in-Publication Data

Koester, Craig R., 1953-

The word of life: a theology of John's Gospel / Craig R. Koester.

p.   cm.

Includes bibliographical references (p.   ) and index.

ISBN 978-0-8028-2938-2 (pbk.: alk. paper)

1. Bible. N.T. John — Criticism, interpretation, etc.

2. Bible. N.T. John — Theology.   I. Title.

BS2615.52.K64   2008

226.5′06 — dc22

2008022118

Scripture quotations from the New Revised Standard Version Bible are copyright © 1989 by the Division of Christian Education of the National Council of Churches of Christ in the U.S.A., and used by permission. Unless otherwise indicated, all other biblical citations have been translated by the author.

For Nancy

Contents

Preface

The author of John's Gospel is traditionally dubbed "the Theologian" because of the way he leads readers into questions pertaining to God. Those who read the Gospel find a well-crafted narrative, which can be appreciated as a piece of literature or as a testimony to the beliefs of an ancient Christian community. But to read the Gospel theologically is to ask, Who is the God about whom Jesus speaks? Who does the Gospel say that Jesus is? And how does the Gospel understand life, death, sin, and faith? Such issues come up repeatedly in the narrative, with each occurrence disclosing different dimensions of these themes. Therefore, thinking through major theological questions means drawing on the Gospel as a whole. This is what this book, *The Word of Life: A Theology of John's Gospel,* attempts to do. A few comments about the project may be helpful for the readers.

There are many ways to explore the theology of John's Gospel. The approach taken here is to work with the Gospel narrative in its present form. Many of the chapters focus on the theological significance of the principal figures in the story: God, the world and its people, Jesus, and the Spirit. Other chapters explore the theological dimensions of key events, like the crucifixion and resurrection. Still others consider themes such as faith, and the Gospel's perspective on the present and future. There are usually several dimensions to each of these topics, and this creates tensions in the Gospel. We will ask how the various perspectives work theologically in the present narrative, and how the tensions contribute to our understanding of the whole.

This approach differs from studies that try to identify the background

ix

of John's theological ideas in the thought of the Old Testament or other ancient sources, and then trace the way the evangelist adapted these ideas in his Gospel. It is valuable to compare and contrast the perspectives of John's Gospel with those found in Jewish and Greco-Roman writings, but this is not the focus of this project. My approach also differs from studies that try to trace the way Johannine theology developed over time. One might try to distinguish early stages of the Gospel tradition from the theological elements that were included later. But again, that is not what I do here. My hope is that careful theological work with the present text will be of value to a broad range of readers, including those who approach the Gospel from other perspectives.

The questions considered in this book come from several circles of conversation. One consists of recent scholarship on John's Gospel. Many interpreters have tried to identify the theological issues that are most prominently addressed in the Gospel. For example, questions about the status of Jesus are explicitly raised and debated in the narrative. Scholars who have tried to reconstruct the social and historical context in which the Gospel was written generally assume that these issues are prominent because they were the focus of actual disputes in the period when the Gospel was composed. This seems plausible, and the first half of Chapter 1 summarizes my understanding of the Gospel's setting and its importance for theology. At the same time, scholars recognize that the Gospel's theological world includes other dimensions, which may be assumed rather than argued in the narrative. The bibliography at the end of this volume lists many of the major studies that have taken up many different theological topics related to John's Gospel. These include God, anthropology, the nature of sin, Christology, the Spirit, eschatology, ecclesiology, and patterns of discipleship. Many of these topics, which have been considered by my colleagues in Johannine studies, have found their way into this volume.

Other questions come from a wider group of readers, who have lived in times prior to our own. The second half of Chapter 1 offers a survey of some of the moments in history when divergent readings of John's Gospel have had an important impact on church and society. These disputes over meaning, which have occurred from ancient times to the twenty-first century, show how differently certain passages of the Gospel can be read. We can learn from this broad history of reading, since we find in it many whose assumptions and perspectives differ from our own. This calls for clarity about the way we approach the text and articulate our views.

Finally, this book tries to take seriously the questions raised by modern readers of John's Gospel, including students, pastors, and many others who ask what the Gospel means. Good theological questions are often easy to ask and difficult to answer. Listening to readers who are non-specialists can help to point the study of John's theology to significant issues.

The chapters in this book are organized in categories that are, in part, based on the major figures in the narrative, as noted earlier. The categories will also be familiar to many students of theology. The hope is that using these categories will make the material within each chapter more readily accessible for readers. Moreover, recent studies of John's theology have often focused on one or more of these major topics, as noted above. Including chapters on these topics helps bring together the fruits of these separate studies, inviting further research and reflection. To be clear, I use familiar theological categories as a way of grouping issues that pertain to John's Gospel. I do not try to provide a systematic overview of the whole field of theology. Rather, this book proposes ways of bringing together different aspects of what the Fourth Gospel says about God, human beings, Jesus, the Spirit, faith, and so on.

This text is written in a non-technical style in order to make the discussion accessible to a wide range of readers. I have chosen a simple style in the hope that non-specialists will be able to follow the discussion, while those who teach and write in the field of New Testament studies or theology may find value in the way the book works through different aspects of John's Gospel. Discussion of detailed interpretive points is included as necessary, especially when there are notable differences of opinion about a given passage. Endnotes are included to suggest further reading on certain issues, but the body of the text is intended to offer a sustained discussion about major aspects of John's theology.

A number of preliminary studies have provided material for some of the chapters. Parts of Chapter 3 are drawn from "What Does It Mean to Be Human? Imagery and the Human Condition in John's Gospel," in *Imagery in the Gospel of John: Terms, Forms and Theology of Figurative Language* (ed. Jörg Frey, Jan G. van der Watt, and Ruben Zimmermann; Tübingen: Mohr Siebeck, 2006). Part of Chapter 5 is from "The Death of Jesus and the Human Condition: Exploring the Theology of John's Gospel," in *Life in Abundance: Studies of John's Gospel in Tribute to Raymond E. Brown, S. S.* (ed. John R. Donahue; Collegeville, Minn.: Liturgical Press, 2005). Some of the material in Chapter 8 is from "Jesus the Way, the Cross, and the World

According to the Gospel of John," *Word & World* 21 (2001): 360-69. Permission to adapt these materials for use in the present book is gratefully acknowledged.

Many people helped to make this book possible. I am grateful to Luther Seminary for a sabbatical leave that allowed me the time to complete this project. The Center of Theological Inquiry in Princeton, New Jersey provided a gracious and supportive working environment. My thanks go out to the director, William Storrar, and to the colleagues and staff at the Center whose comments and questions enriched my own process of reflection. Thanks are due to Nancy Koester and Marianne Meye Thompson for giving the manuscript a critical reading. Their questions and comments have helped me clarify many points. I also want to express my appreciation to Allen Myers and the staff at Eerdmans for all they have done to bring the project to completion.

Abbreviations

<table>
<tr><td>AB</td><td>Anchor Bible</td></tr>
<tr><td>ABD</td><td>Anchor Bible Dictionary</td></tr>
<tr><td>AGAJU</td><td>Arbeiten zur Geschichte des antiken Judentums und des Urchristentums</td></tr>
<tr><td>AnBib</td><td>Analecta biblica</td></tr>
<tr><td>BECNT</td><td>Baker Exegetical Commentary on the New Testament</td></tr>
<tr><td>BETL</td><td>Bibliotheca ephemeridum theologicarum lovaniensium</td></tr>
<tr><td>Bib</td><td>Biblica</td></tr>
<tr><td>BibIntSer</td><td>Biblical Interpretation Series</td></tr>
<tr><td>BZAW</td><td>Beihefte zur Zeitschrift für die alttestamentliche Wissenschaft</td></tr>
<tr><td>CBQMS</td><td>Catholic Biblical Quarterly Monograph Series</td></tr>
<tr><td>ConBNT</td><td>Coniectanea biblica: New Testament series</td></tr>
<tr><td>ETL</td><td>Ephemerides theologicae lovanienses</td></tr>
<tr><td>FRLANT</td><td>Forschungen zur Religion und Literatur des Alten und Neuen Testaments</td></tr>
<tr><td>Int</td><td>Interpretation</td></tr>
<tr><td>JBL</td><td>Journal of Biblical Literature</td></tr>
<tr><td>JETS</td><td>Journal of the Evangelical Theological Society</td></tr>
<tr><td>JSNT</td><td>Journal for the Study of the New Testament</td></tr>
<tr><td>JSNTSup</td><td>Journal for the Study of the New Testament: Supplement Series</td></tr>
<tr><td>JSOT</td><td>Journal for the Study of the Old Testament</td></tr>
<tr><td>LNTS</td><td>Library of New Testament Studies</td></tr>
<tr><td>LS</td><td>Louvain Studies</td></tr>
<tr><td>NIB</td><td>The New Interpreter's Bible</td></tr>
<tr><td>NHMS</td><td>Nag Hammadi and Manichaean Studies</td></tr>
<tr><td>NovTSup</td><td>Supplements to Novum Testamentum</td></tr>
</table>

SBLDS	Society of Biblical Literature Dissertation Series
SBLMS	Society of Biblical Literature Monograph Series
SHCT	Studies in the History of Christian Traditions
SNTSMS	Society for New Testament Studies Monograph Series
SP	Sacra pagina
SPCK	Society for Promoting Christian Knowledge
WMANT	Wissenschaftliche Monographien zum Alten und Neuen Testament
WUNT	Wissenschaftliche Untersuchungen zum Neuen Testament
ZNW	*Zeitschrift für die neutestamentliche Wissenschaft und die Kunde der älteren Kirche*

CHAPTER 1

Introduction

Theology is thinking about God, ourselves, and the world in which we live. To think theologically is to think relationally. God has a central place in theology, yet questions about God are interwoven with those about people and the earth to which they belong. God is not known in the abstract. Similarly, asking what it means to be human leads to reflection on a broader web of relationships with others and with God. John's Gospel is a passionately theological work that opens readers to the world of God and invites them to consider their place within it.

Theological questions can be deceptively simple. Some of these appear in the Gospel itself. As the story opens, John the Baptist sees Jesus and says, "Behold the Lamb of God" (1:36). His message initially generates more curiosity than insight. Two people wonder what he means, so they follow Jesus to learn more. But the first words Jesus speaks come as a question: "What are you looking for?" (1:38). No grand pronouncement; just a question. It seems innocent enough. But one wonders. The people mentioned earlier in the chapter were looking for things too. They asked John the Baptist: "Who are you?" The Messiah? Elijah? The prophet? If not, then, "Why are you baptizing?" (1:19-28). Their specific questions come from the broader issue of what God is doing in the world. John the Baptist points to the Lamb of God, yet the questions linger (1:29).

So Jesus asks those who follow him, "What are *you* looking for?" Their searching can take place at different levels. Perhaps those intrigued by the Lamb merely want a little more information. Or perhaps their search is for something more significant. In any case, the seekers respond to Jesus with a

1

question of their own, "Rabbi . . . where are you staying?" (1:38). Then instead of an answer, Jesus gives them an invitation: "Come and see" (1:39). He could have replied with simple information: "Where am I staying? Go three blocks down, take a left, and it will be the second house on the right, opposite the weaver's shop." But Jesus' invitation to "Come and see" assumes that a genuine answer to their question cannot be given in advance. Insights will emerge from their continued encounter with him. They may also find that they are challenged to look more deeply than they initially anticipated.

Theological reflection on John's Gospel is like this. Perspectives are shaped by a continued encounter with the text. The Gospel is written in a way that invites readers into the story. Its rich images of light and darkness, living water, and the fruit-bearing vine appeal to the imagination. Conversations between Jesus and other people careen between utter confusion and surprising insights. A straightforward statement often has a trap door that swings open to reveal depths of meaning that were only hinted at on the surface. John calls Jesus the Lamb of God. That seems pretty clear. At least until one asks what it means. Then theological reflection begins.

Readers also bring their own questions to the Gospel, yet they are rarely given a pat answer. "What are you looking for?" the Gospel asks. A reader might respond, "What should I do with my life?" and finds that Jesus says, "Follow me" (1:43). Yet this makes one wonder who Jesus is and what it means to follow him. Readers form responses to such questions as they continue following the Gospel's account of Jesus' life, death, and resurrection. They explore the realm of theology.

The Theological Shape of the Gospel

Theology is a creative venture that involves thinking through various issues. To focus specifically on *John's* theology means developing responses to questions about God, people, and the world based on a reading of the Gospel. This theological reading works primarily with the Gospel narrative, but it is also informed by other disciplines. Historical questions deal with the context in which the Gospel was composed. Literary questions pertain to the Gospel's plot, character development, and use of imagery. Before turning to the major theological themes, it may be helpful to make a few observations about the origins and literary form of the Gospel, and the implications for theological interpretation.

Origins of John's Gospel

Where did John's Gospel come from? The concluding verses of the Gospel say that it presents the witness of the disciple whom Jesus loved (21:24). This disciple is never named, but he is beside Jesus at the last supper, is present at the crucifixion and empty tomb, and finally goes fishing on the Sea of Galilee (13:23; 19:26-27; 20:1-10; 21:7). The Gospel was probably completed about A.D. 90-100. A century later, Christian writers were identifying the unnamed author as John the son of Zebedee, one of the twelve disciples. This became the common church tradition. More recently, many interpreters have been content to leave the disciple unnamed, since this is what the Gospel does. We will call him the Fourth Evangelist or John, using the traditional name, but will not assume anything more about his identity.[1]

The witness of this disciple was preserved by a circle of early Christians. The conclusion of the Gospel says that "*we* know that his testimony is true" (21:24). The context implies that he died before the Gospel was completed and that others put the text into its present form (21:20-23). Seams in the narrative give some evidence of editing. For example, the story reaches a fine conclusion in 20:30-31, where the narrator says that Jesus did many other signs that are not written in this book, but these were written in order that readers might believe and have life. Yet the narrative continues with scenes beside the Sea of Galilee and then repeats that Jesus did much more than the Gospel could include (21:25). The double ending might suggest that an early short form of the Gospel was later expanded to its present length. If so, the additional material came from the same body of tradition and was incorporated before the Gospel circulated widely. (The exception is the story of the woman caught in adultery in 7:53–8:11, which does not appear in the earliest manuscripts of the Gospel.)

The present form of the Gospel can rightly be read as a whole. It has a high level of consistency in style and content. A clear and simple style of Greek is used throughout the book. Patterns of misunderstanding, irony, and symbolic language shape the telling of the story. Despite the occasional marks of editing, the present text coheres very well, and we will interpret the Gospel in its present form. Where theological tensions remain, we will ask how they function in the text as it stands.

John's Gospel has much in common with the other New Testament gospels. All of them link Jesus to the village of Nazareth and note his early

connection with John the Baptist. They say he gathered a group of disciples, taught, healed, and fed a large crowd with a few fish and loaves of
bread. Controversies with Jewish leaders created tension, and at some
point he disrupted the merchants in the temple. At the end of his ministry
a crowd welcomed him to Jerusalem. Yet he was betrayed by Judas, arrested, and questioned by the Jewish authorities and by Pilate the Roman
governor. After being beaten, he was executed by crucifixion and his body
was placed in a tomb. The story culminates with his resurrection from the
dead. All four gospels have the same basic plot line.

The Gospel of John also has distinctive content and ways of telling the
story. Many key episodes appear only in John. These include Jesus turning
water into wine at Cana, his encounters with Nicodemus and the Samaritan woman, the healings of the paralytic and blind man in Jerusalem, and
raising Lazarus from the dead. The other gospels present Jesus' teachings
in short pithy sayings, but John includes long discourses that explore Jesus'
relationship to the Father and the world. Instead of parables about the
kingdom of God, the Jesus of John's Gospel says things like "I am the light
of the world" and "I am the bread of life." When recounting the crucifixion, John alone says that Jesus entrusted his mother to the Beloved Disciple and that blood and water flowed from his pierced side. When telling of
Jesus' resurrection, John includes unique elements like the giving of the
Spirit and the appearance to Thomas.

A common way to account for the similarities and differences is to suggest that John knew one or more of the other gospels and wrote his text as a
supplement. The idea goes back to the late second century. Clement of Alexandria (d. ca. 215) claimed that after the first three gospels had recorded
the "physical" things about Jesus' ministry, John composed a "spiritual"
gospel (Eusebius, *Eccl. Hist.* 6.14.5). This fits the way Scripture is read in
many churches, which follow the story line of Matthew, Mark, or Luke during most of the year, while weaving in passages from John at certain liturgical seasons. Many people have the impression that the other gospels present
the history of Jesus, while John offers additional theological commentary.

A more plausible alternative is that John is largely independent of the
other gospels. The evangelist may have been acquainted with one or more
of the other written gospels or with similar traditions that circulated by
word of mouth. If John did know any of the other texts, however, he did
not feel constrained to tell the story in the same way. We will occasionally
compare John to the other gospels to highlight distinctive emphases, but

will not assume that the evangelist knew the other gospels in the form we have them.[2] We will also assume that all four gospels preserve traditions about Jesus and that all of them develop the traditions theologically. It is not helpful to categorize John as the theological Gospel and the others as historical books. This split between theology and history creates problems for the interpretation of all the gospels. Each of them works with traditions about Jesus' life, death, and resurrection, and each of them reshapes the tradition theologically. Our focus is on the distinctive way this takes shape in John.[3]

The historical and social context in which John's Gospel was composed has been reconstructed in various ways. Here we simply note three dimensions that will inform our theological reading of the text. First, the Gospel presupposes that many readers will be familiar with Jewish tradition. The social world described in the Gospel is one in which the followers of Jesus are mainly Jewish. The narrative also assumes that at least some of the readers will also be familiar with Jewish life and thought. John identifies Jesus as the fulfillment of the Law and the Prophets, and expects readers to catch allusions to biblical episodes like the angels ascending and descending on Jacob's ladder (1:45, 51). Jesus' ministry is structured around the Sabbath (5:9; 9:14) and Jewish festivals, including Passover (2:13; 6:4; 19:14), Booths (7:2), and Dedication or Hanukkah (10:22). The evangelist assumes that at least some readers will see the connection between Jesus and the traditions concerning these festivals.

Theologically, the Gospel presupposes important aspects of Jewish tradition. It is understood that there is only one true God (17:3). Whatever the Gospel says about Jesus' heavenly origin occurs within the basic framework of monotheism.[4] Those following Greco-Roman religious traditions typically professed belief in multiple deities, but this is not John's approach. With the Jewish community he acknowledges only one true God. He also assumes that God gives life, has the power to raise the dead, and has the authority to judge people (5:21, 45). This belief in resurrection on the last day, at the end of the age, was shared by many though not all Jewish people in the first century.[5] Finally, John presupposes the validity of the Jewish Scriptures. The identity of God and Jesus is understood in relation to the Law and the Prophets. Quotations and allusions to these texts occur throughout the Gospel. The question is not whether the Scriptures bear witness to the truth but how they do so.

Many of the issues addressed in the Gospel are raised from a Jewish perspective. There are intense debates about whether Jesus is a legitimate teacher and whether it is right to call him the Messiah (7:14-31). Jesus' opponents recall commands from the Mosaic law to show that his claims are false, while the Gospel insists that the Scriptures bear witness to Jesus (5:16, 39; 7:19-24, 41-42, 49). A pivotal question is whether Jesus is a human being elevating himself to divine status, something regarded as blasphemous in Jewish tradition (5:18; 10:30-33; 19:7). In responding, the Gospel draws on Jewish traditions about God's activity and the legal requirement that two or three witnesses be provided to sustain a claim in court (5:19, 31; 8:17). The attention given to these issues and the character of the Gospel's response suggest that conflict between the Christian community and the synagogue was an aspect of the setting in which the Gospel took shape.

Second, the Gospel also envisions a wider circle of readers, who are not of Jewish background. The social world described in the narrative looks beyond the early Jewish Christian community to the wider Greco-Roman world. Ethnic boundaries are pushed outward as Samaritans and Greeks show interest in Jesus (4:39-42; 12:20-21). Jesus speaks of believers who are not of the Jewish "fold" but come into the Christian community from other backgrounds (10:16). He sends his disciples into the world and assumes that they will create a community of believers who no longer live in the same places or have the same ethnic origins, making cohesion within the group a challenge (7:35; 11:51-52; 17:18-23). The Gospel presupposes that its circle of readers will include those who have little familiarity with Jewish tradition. It presupposes a spectrum of readers, rather than just one type of reader. For example, along with the frequent allusions to Scripture and Jewish festivals, the Gospel patiently explains what words like "rabbi" and "Messiah" mean (1:38, 41), that stone jars were used for Jewish purification rites (2:6), and that Jews did not share things with Samaritans (4:9).

The Gospel conveys its message in language accessible to this wider readership. Much of its imagery can be initially understood on the basis of common life experience. For example, linking water or bread to the idea of life would have been familiar to most of the Gospel's earliest readers. An action like footwashing had no special connection with Jewish tradition but would have been understood in similar ways throughout the ancient world. Using these familiar images and practices, the Gospel transforms their meaning in light of Jesus' mission. Some passages also invite engagement with the Greco-Roman philosophical tradition. For example, the term *logos* or Word, which introduces the Gospel, was important in philosophical discourse, as were images of light and darkness (1:1-9). The Greco-Roman connotations of the imagery are appropriated and transformed within John's text.[6]

Certain issues addressed in the Gospel come from the Christian community's encounter with the Roman world. One of these is the question of authority. The way Jesus flees from those who wanted to make him king after he fed them with bread implicitly contrasts him with those who sought to gain authority by winning public approval with free distributions of bread (6:15). The sign above the cross announces his kingship in Hebrew, Latin, and Greek (19:19-20). But Christians have to consider what kind of kingship this is and how it relates to other forms of authority. Jesus' conversation with Pilate the Roman governor helps to define Jesus' power and distinguish it from imperial practice as well as from the patterns of violent resistance that typified would-be rebels against Caesar (18:33-37; 19:12).[7]

Third, the Gospel of John was composed among Christians who understood the Spirit to be active among them. Other early Christian writings give an important place to the Spirit, but in John this takes a distinctive form. According to 14:26, Jesus promised that the Spirit would teach and remind his followers of all that he had said. The process of teaching and reminding involved preserving the tradition of Jesus as well as discerning new meaning within it after his death and resurrection. The dynamic of preserving and interpreting the tradition is explicit in the episodes of the temple cleansing and Jesus' entry to Jerusalem. The Gospel preserves tradition by recounting the basic actions that occurred. Yet the narrator observes that the disciples did not understand these things at first, and that only after Jesus was raised from the dead or glorified were the disciples able to remember and understand what these things meant (2:22; 12:16). Therefore, the Gospel not only preserves tradition but interprets it, showing insights that emerged later. This interplay between preserving and interpreting the tradition characterizes the Gospel as a whole. Early readers of the Gospel would have understood this process to be part of the Spirit's work (14:26).[8]

Theological Shaping of the Narrative

The Fourth Gospel took shape in an ancient context, but its literary design continues to shape the perspectives of readers living in other contexts. The structure of the book, along with its imagery, portrayals of people, use of irony, and other literary devices creates a way of seeing the world and human beings in relation to God. The prologue (1:1-18) introduces this theological vision. The term *logos* or Word dominates the initial verses. Readers learn that the Word was with God, that the Word was God, and that the Word became flesh (1:1, 14). This creates a framework for understanding Jesus' relationship to God. Then, having created this theological framework, the term *logos* fades from view. Elsewhere it is simply used for the spoken word. The basic perspective continues, but the language of God and Word shifts to that of Father and Son (1:14-18) — a theme that runs throughout the book.

The prologue sets the ministry of Jesus in a cosmic framework. The narrative that follows will tell of Jesus encountering people in Galilee, Samaria, and Jerusalem. But in light of the prologue readers can see that the story of Jesus encountering particular people is also the story of God engaging the world. Note that the prologue does not offer a complete summary of the Gospel. Its themes of belief and unbelief, the world, glory, and truth are played out at length, but the passion and resurrection remain implicit. Rather than actually telling the whole story, the prologue establishes a *perspective* on the whole story. It gives readers a transcendent vantage point, enabling them to see things about Jesus that are hidden from the people described in the Gospel. Readers know of Jesus' heavenly origin at the outset, and from that perspective can chart a course through the debates and misunderstandings that emerge during his ministry.

The body of John's Gospel is a drama in two acts. Act I recounts Jesus' public ministry, beginning with the testimony of John the Baptist and ending with Jesus' approach to Jerusalem. It concludes with the evangelist's comments on the unbelief of the crowds (John 1–12). This section encompasses seven miraculous signs, which reveal the power of God in a manner that can be perceived by the senses. These include turning water into wine, feeding the five thousand, walking on the sea, acts of healing, and raising the dead. The author does not give a comprehensive list of Jesus' signs but recounts a number of them in order that people might believe and have life (20:30-31). Conversations and discourses accompany the signs and point to their significance. For example, the disciples' recognition of Jesus as the Messiah (1:29-51) precedes the first sign at Cana (2:1-11). Later, a lengthy discourse about Jesus' relationship to the Father (5:17-47) follows the healings in Galilee and at Bethzatha (4:46–5:16). Similar discourses or conversations precede or follow the remaining signs (6:1-59; 9:1-41; 11:1-44). Verbal commentary is needed because the evangelist recognizes that Jesus' signs can be taken in sharply differing ways.

The Gospel lets readers hear several points of view, not just one. The theological significance of the signs emerges from the clash of different perspectives. When Jesus heals a paralytic and blind man on the Sabbath, some identify him as a lawbreaker. This perspective has internal coherence for many of Jesus' opponents. For them, healing is a form of work; work is forbidden on the Sabbath; therefore Jesus has deliberately broken the law of God and is a sinner (5:16; 9:16a). Yet others point out the problem with this line of thought. Jesus has been empowered to heal, and healing consistent with the will of God. From their perspective Jesus is not a sinner (5:19; 9:16b, 30-33). The evangelist clearly advocates the second point of view, but he must make the case for Jesus over against the contrary interpretation.

Conversations and disputes sometimes open up multiple perspectives, all of which have some validity. The Samaritan woman and the man born blind progressively recognize that Jesus is a Jewish man, a prophet, and perhaps the Messiah (4:9, 19, 29; 9:11, 17, 22, 32). Each of these insights is true, though no one of them fully encompasses Jesus' identity. The different facets work together to create a multidimensional portrait of who Jesus is. At the same time, these perspectives can be misconstrued. The crowds that Jesus feeds recognize that he is prophet and king, but Jesus flees from them (6:14-15). The problem is not that they see him as prophet and king but that they think his kingship derives from public acclaim. Elsewhere it is clear that his power comes from above (18:36).

Act II tells of Jesus' passion and resurrection (John 13–21). As the curtain rises, the writer provides a clue to the meaning of what follows: "Now before the festival of the Passover, Jesus knew that his hour had come to depart from this world and go to the Father. Having loved his own who were in the world, he loved them to the end" (13:1). This enables the audience to see that by washing the disciples' feet and laying down his life Jesus conveys love. The discourses and prayer at the last supper speak of Jesus' departure to his Father, the coming of the Spirit, and the life in the ongoing community of faith (John 14–17). The theme of glory in Jesus' prayer before his arrest anticipates that even in death Jesus will reveal the power of God.

The passion and resurrection narratives continue disclosing meaning through the interplay of perspectives. During a series of hearings, Jesus' opponents seek to show that he is in the wrong, but Jesus maintains that he came to bear witness to the truth (18:37). They argue that he should be put to death for opposing God, yet he says that he goes to his death in obedience to God (18:11; 19:7). His followers rightly understand that crucifixion culminates in death, but they do not comprehend that his tomb is empty because he is risen (20:2). Jesus must encounter them and call them to recognize what has happened.

Imagery plays a major role throughout John's Gospel. Light, darkness, water, and other images contribute to its theology. The challenge is that images typically do not have a single well-defined meaning. They evoke a range of different and often contradictory associations. For example, light comes gently with the promise of dawn, but glares harshly from the noonday sun. It enables people to see, while threatening to expose them to the gaze of others. Darkness can lull the weary into peaceful sleep, while cloaking the movements of a thief. The literary context helps to screen out meanings that are unsuitable while permitting other connotations to shine through.[9]

The major images bring together several levels of meaning, much as a shaft of light encompasses a spectrum of colors. When light strikes a prism, the many hues within it become visible to the eye. All the colors contribute to the quality of the light as a whole. The literary context serves as the prism that enables interpreters to identify the dominant "hues" within an image in the Gospel. For example, Jesus is called "the light of the world" during disputes about his identity (8:12). Bystanders argue over whether he is a teacher, Messiah, or Son of God. The imagery relates to each part of the debate. There were precedents for thinking of a teacher, the Messiah, and God as sources of illumination. Calling Jesus "the light" encompasses all these aspects of his identity (see p. 104).

Ironies in the story contrast what appears to be true with what is actually true. Those who meet Jesus often judge by appearances, but clues within the narrative point readers in the opposite direction (7:24). The Samaritan woman assumes that Jesus is a thirsty Jewish man, who cannot possibly be greater than Jacob, the giver of the well (4:12). Ironically, Jesus is greater than Jacob, for he offers living water (4:11). Theologically, giving attention to irony is crucial since readers are to distinguish truth from appearance. It may seem that the man born with physical blindness is a sinner, yet the evangelist seeks to show that sin is actually manifested in the blindness of unbelief (9:2, 41). Again, as Jesus stands before Pilate's judgment seat his accusers condemn him. Yet in a deeper sense they actually pass judgment on themselves by their rejection of truth (18:37; 19:13-17).

Wordplays also work with two levels of meaning. Sometimes readers are to select one meaning instead of another. People in the story show the comic results of choosing the wrong option. When Jesus speaks of "living water," the Samaritan woman is baffled because she thinks he means water that flows from a spring in the ground. Readers can see that the living water is not flowing water but a metaphor for a heavenly gift (4:11, 14). But elsewhere, readers must see two meanings together. The expression "lift up" refers to Jesus' physical elevation on the cross as well as to exaltation in honor (3:14; 8:28; 12:32). People in the story see the disgrace of crucifixion as the antithesis of divine glory. Therefore, the Gospel must show how both are true at the same time — and this connection is integral to John's theology.

The whole Gospel is written from a post-Easter perspective. Those who know the end of the story can see things that participants in the story do not. One might compare Jesus' disciples to characters in a detective novel, who receive clues to a mystery but cannot determine what they mean. Only in the end does the master detective provide the perspective that everyone needs to make sense of the whole. In John's Gospel, clues from the end of the story are woven into each part of the narrative. The moment Jesus steps into public view in 1:29 he is called the sacrificial Lamb of God. No further interpretation is given, but readers who know the ending can see that it foreshadows his death. Later, Jesus speaks of destroying and raising the temple, and the narrator explicitly says that the disciples only understood this later, as a portent of his death and resurrection (2:22). The post-resurrection perspective also enables the evangelist to make connections with the Old Testament that were not evident during his ministry. John cites the Scriptures to emphasize the truth of Jesus' kingship (12:15-16), to make sense of the unbelief that Jesus encountered (12:38-40), and to show that incidents during the crucifixion fit into God's purposes (19:24, 28, 36, 37).

The evangelist's assumption is that the Jesus who lived and died has been raised and is now a living presence. Accordingly, ordinary categories of time and space are fluid, and it is not always clear whether it is the pre-Easter or the post-Easter Jesus who speaks. While addressing Nicodemus, Jesus speaks as if the Son of Man has already ascended into heaven (3:13). At the end of the last supper, before going to his arrest, Jesus prays as if he is no longer in the world but has already returned to the Father (17:11). The

Gospel relates what happened in the past in order to bear witness to a Jesus and a God who live in the present. The Gospel seeks not only to show who Jesus *was* but to reveal who Jesus *is*.

A History of Theological Questions
from the Early Church to the Present

Exploring John's theology means framing questions and developing responses through a reading of the Gospel. Many of the major questions have been asked by the Christian community in many times and places. Therefore, at this point we will shift our focus from the context in which the Gospel was written to some of the settings in which it has been read and debated. John has played a volatile role in many of the controversies that have shaped Christian life and thought. Its interpretation has not been confined to the classroom but has taken place in the turbulent forums of church and public life. Differing perspectives on the Gospel's theology have been shaped by social and religious currents of the readers' own contexts. Their interpretations of the Gospel have, in turn, influenced the way they have responded to their contexts.

God and the World

The prologue to John's Gospel says that the Word of God brought all things into being (1:1-4). Yet the Gospel also portrays the world as a place of darkness, in contrast to the true light that comes to it from above (3:19). According to John, the people Jesus meets are typically unable to grasp the higher truths of which he speaks. They are from below and he is from above (8:23). They judge by what their senses perceive and seem incapable of understanding the truth he reveals (7:24; 8:15). In contrast, the redeemed do not belong to this world (15:19). They are set free by coming to know the truth (8:32).

These aspects of the Gospel made it appealing to those who embraced the worldview known as Gnosticism. This name is based on the word *gnōsis* or knowledge, since Gnostics claimed to have special insight, a higher form of knowledge than most people had. Some of their most influential teachers lived in the mid- to late second century A.D. They drew ideas from Jewish tradition, Greek philosophy, and Christian teaching. Although Gnostic theology took many forms, it had typical features.

The material world was said to be a realm of darkness and ignorance in contrast to the realm of light and truth above. Gnostics maintained that their true spiritual selves had originated in the Fullness of the higher realm, but they were now imprisoned in the oppressive sphere of matter from which they sought release. The God of the Jewish Scriptures was the Creator of the lower material region of the cosmos. Since the Creator's realm was the material world, he was not a source of salvation. Gnostics thought that the true God was above the Creator. He belonged to the higher realm from which the Gnostics' spiritual selves had originated. Release from imprisonment in the material world was said to come through knowledge of one's true spiritual origin and destiny.[10]

A writer named Heracleon (ca. A.D. 145-180) produced a commentary that interpreted John's Gospel in Gnostic categories.[11] For him the idea that Jesus was a human being, who lived in the flesh, was of no theological importance. Jesus' earthly career was significant only as an illustration of spiritual truth. For example, in his interpretation of John 4:46-54, the Galilean official represents the Creator and his feverish son signifies humanity trapped in matter. Just as the official has no power to save his son, the Creator has no power to save humanity and therefore goes to the Savior seeking help. Although the Savior offers aid, he rebukes the official (i.e., the Creator) for needing signs and wonders (i.e., sense perception) in order to believe. In contrast, the Samaritan woman is one of the spiritual elect, who has simply lost the awareness of her true self. Jesus tells her to call her "husband," who signifies her counterpart in the transcendent realm. This helps awaken her to knowledge of who she is (4:16). Jesus also tells her that she will not worship on "this mountain," which symbolizes the material world, or in Jerusalem, where the Creator is honored. Rather, she has the spiritual knowledge that enables her to rise above the creation and Creator to the truth (4:22-24).

Theological critiques of the Gnostic readings of John were written by a number of ancient authors. They stress several key points: First is the unity of God. The Gospel understands there to be only one God, who is the Creator of all things. It does not suggest that there is a higher God, who remains distant from the world. The goal of salvation is not to go beyond the Creator but to be restored in relationship with the Creator. Second is the importance of the physical world. Although the world is marked by sin and death, it remains God's creation. The drama of redemption takes place in and through events in the created order. God works within the world he has made. Third is the incarnation. The Word of God, which is the source of life, becomes flesh in Jesus of Nazareth. The Word becomes an embodied human being in order to redeem those who are human.[12] These debates show the need to consider how John portrays God's relationship to the world.

The Identity of Jesus

Who is Jesus? People debate this question, in part, because of the complexity of his legacy. His early disciples regarded him as a Jewish teacher from Galilee. He taught in synagogues and ran into conflict with other Jewish teachers. Some acclaimed him a prophet and told of his ability to work miracles. Some thought of him as the Messiah, the anointed king whom God sent to rule his people. Yet his death by crucifixion shattered the usual paradigm of kingship and redefined what it meant for him to reign. "Son of God" was also a royal title, but in light of the resurrection many discerned a deeper sense of what this meant — a more integral connection between Jesus and the God he called his Father.

Answering the question "Who is Jesus?" mattered because people were called to put their faith in him. What was said about Jesus had implications for the way they understood their lives and hopes. If Jesus was a teacher, then he provided instruction for those who needed it. He could move people from ignorance to understanding. But what if the human situation was more deeply flawed? Did Jesus provide something more than instruction? As the crucified and risen king, did he wield the power that delivers people from sin and death? There were many prophets in Israel's history and they brought a word from the Lord. So what set Jesus apart? Did he speak God's word as others did, or did he embody it?

Christian thinking about Jesus was profoundly shaped by intense discussion that took place in the fourth century. The main perspectives were represented by Arius (d. ca. 336) and Athanasius (d. 373), both of whom worked at Alexandria in Egypt. John's Gospel was used by both sides, though in quite different ways.[13] Arius emphasized that God is one (17:3). For him this meant that the Son was of a lower status than the Father. Arius argued that God's Son was a created being, brought into existence by the Father. The Son was qualitatively different from the Father. He was subject to change and development, whereas the Father was eternal. Jesus became tired and thirsty, but this could not be said of God (4:6-7; 19:28). Jesus clearly distinguished himself from God when he said, "the Father is greater than I" (14:28). To call him God's Son meant that he was adopted by God for a special purpose.

Athanasius and others considered this perspective inadequate. Scripturally, they pointed out that "the Word was with God, and the Word was God" (1:1). This same Word became flesh in Jesus (1:14). Therefore, to encounter the incarnate Word is to encounter God. Moreover, the Son not only does the work of his Father but can say, "I and the Father are one" (10:30). If this is true, then the Son is not of a different order than the Father. Athanasius found in John's Gospel a conception of God that encompassed both the Father and the Son. He also saw that Jesus' identity was related to the human need for salvation. For Athanasius, the Word that is God fully identifies with human beings through the incarnation. The Creator descends and takes on mortal human flesh in order that people might be raised to share in God's own life.

Language from John's Gospel shaped the creedal statements that emerged from the controversy. These were formulated at Nicea in 325 and Constantinople in 381. The more developed form of the creed introduces Jesus in the following way: He is

> one Lord Jesus Christ, the only-begotten Son of God,
> begotten of the Father before all ages,
> Light of Light, true God of true God,
> begotten not made, of the same being with the Father,
> through whom all things were made,
> who for us human beings and for our salvation, came down
>   from heaven
> and was incarnate by the Holy Spirit and the Virgin Mary,
> and became human.

Statements about Jesus' death, resurrection, ascension, and future coming complete this section of the creed. Note that Jesus is called the only-begotten *(monogenēs)* Son of God as in John 1:14, 18; 3:16, 18. The creed explains that this means "begotten, not made," emphasizing that the Son is not merely a creature. He is Light as God is Light (1:9) and he is true God (1:1, 18). Where the Gospel says that the Father and Son are "one" (10:30), the creed elaborates by saying that they are of one and "the same being" *(homoousios)*. This metaphysical language shows that the Son is of the same order as the Father and is in no way inferior. Then the creed relates this to human need, saying it was "for us human beings" that he came down from heaven. His incarnation was "for our salvation."[14]

Widely used in Christian worship, the creeds have continued to shape the way John's Gospel has been read. Many modern readers find the creedal tradition faithful to the gospel tradition. Others think it gives too much weight to Jesus' oneness with God, and object that it says nothing about Jesus as a Jewish teacher from Galilee. As we explore John's portrayal of Jesus we will find that the debates described in the Gospel differ from those of the fourth-century church, although some issues overlap. We will also note that the theologians who formulated the creeds worked with metaphysical categories that are not developed in the Gospel. Yet by listening to these older debates we sense the challenge of interpreting the many sides of Jesus in ways that are congruent with the Gospel. John presents a portrait of Jesus that is multidimensional.

The Work of the Spirit

John's Gospel refers to the Spirit as the Advocate or Paraclete *(paraklētos)*. Some of these passages have provoked questions about continuing revelation. At the last supper Jesus tells the disciples, "I will ask the Father, and he will give you another Advocate to be with you for ever. This is the Spirit of truth, whom the world cannot receive," but you "know him, because he abides with you and will be in you" (14:16-17). Later Jesus adds, "I still have many things to say to you, but you cannot bear them now. When the Spirit of truth comes, he will guide you into all the truth" (16:12-13). So what does it mean for the Spirit to lead people into the truth? Does the Spirit bring new revelation that surpasses the old? Or does it essentially unfold the truth of what Jesus has already revealed?

The short book known as 1 John was probably written for a Christian group that knew the Fourth Gospel and grappled with the role of the Spirit. The context was that some members of the community had separated themselves from the rest over questions of faith. Those who left apparently had a highly spiritualized view of Jesus and saw little significance in his humanity. Although the Gospel said that the Word of God became flesh and that Jesus conveyed the love of God through crucifixion (John

1:14; 3:14-16), those who left evidently downplayed these bodily aspects of Jesus' identity and stressed only the higher, more spiritual dimensions of who he was. They apparently thought they were moving to this elevated understanding of the gospel message through the leading of the Spirit.[15]

In the face of this conflict, the author of 1 John affirms that the Spirit abides among believers, assuring them of Christ's presence (1 John 3:24). He also recognizes that there are many spirits in the world and that many claim to speak as prophets, but he points out that their messages may conflict. To discern the work of God's Spirit, he provides a confessional criterion. In the Johannine tradition, it is essential that the Word became flesh (John 1:14). The love of God came through the human life and death of Jesus. Therefore, the author of 1 John says that the Spirit's role is to point people to what is essential for faith. He says that where people confess that Jesus Christ has come "in the flesh" one finds the Spirit at work (1 John 4:1-3). The Spirit does not move people away from the basic tradition that Jesus was human, as the author's opponents thought. Instead, the Spirit brings people to a renewed sense of what Jesus' humanity meant.

John's references to the Spirit later played a role in controversies surrounding a new prophecy movement that emerged in the mid-second century A.D. Its founder was Montanus, who claimed to be inspired by God and spoke from a state of ecstasy. He was accompanied by two women, Priscilla and Maximilla, who also claimed the gift of prophecy. In an oracle attributed to him, Montanus is supposed to have said, "I am the Father, and I am the Son, and I am the Paraclete," using the Fourth Gospel's term for the Spirit (Didymus, *De Trinitate* 3.41). Since the source is rather late, it is not clear whether Montanus actually said this. If so, he may have been speaking for God in the first person. His opponents, however, said that Montanus himself was regarded as the promised Paraclete (Eusebius, *Eccl. Hist.* 5.14.1).

The supporters of Montanus appealed to the Spirit passages in John to show that prophecy did not cease with the apostles but continued among the Montanists. They believed that the Spirit was guiding them into all truth through the inspired utterances of their founder. Some claimed that Montanus had said things that were greater than what Christ had revealed in the Gospel. The sharpest critics of the movement rejected the idea of continuing prophecy and tried to discredit John's Gospel since the Montanists found support in it. Others reaffirmed that the Fourth Gospel should be used in the church, but argued that it did not support the kind of prophesying that characterized the Montanist movement. Citing John

16:14 they argued that the Spirit's work was to glorify Christ, not to move beyond Christ (Epiphanius, *Panarion* 48.11).[16]

The role of the Paraclete-Spirit was later claimed by Mani (d. 276), the founder of the religious movement known as Manichaeism. Born in Mesopotamia, Mani was familiar with forms of Jewish, Christian, and Gnostic teaching. He believed that he received direct revelation through the Paraclete, who enabled him to see the totality of all things. Mani thought that he had become united with the Paraclete in Spirit and body.[17] His message contrasted the forces of light and darkness, and drew on the Gnostic idea that salvation came through knowledge of one's true spiritual origin. Blending various religious traditions into a new synthesis, Mani thought that Jesus, Zoroaster, and Buddha belonged to the line of those who brought enlightenment to the world.

Islamic tradition has also drawn on John's Gospel to show that Muhammad (d. 632) was the Paraclete promised by Jesus. The origins of this idea are not clear. In the Qur'an 61.6, "Jesus son of Mary said: 'O children of Israel, I am God's messenger to you, confirming the Torah which was before me, and announcing the good news of a messenger who will come after me, whose name is Aḥmad.'" The name Aḥmad is used for Muhammad. The passage in the Qur'an does not cite any specific New Testament text. But later Islamic tradition did identify Muhammad as the Paraclete mentioned in John 14:16-17, 26; 15:26; and 16:7-15. From this perspective, Jesus' promise of the Paraclete is fulfilled in Muhammad and the gift of Qur'anic revelation, which completes and surpasses previous revelation.[18]

Christian readers of John's Gospel regularly find that the Paraclete passages lead in a different direction. The Paraclete is identified as the Spirit (John 14:16, 26; 15:26; 16:13), and the Spirit is given to Jesus' followers as a group after his resurrection (20:22). Rather than pointing to a specific person, the references to the Paraclete anticipate the activity of the Spirit in the ongoing life of the community of faith. Exploring the theological dimensions of this theme is important for readers living in an interreligious context.

Faith and Experience

How do people know where God is at work in a person's life? Forms of this question are related to Jesus' conversation with a Jewish teacher named

Nicodemus. Jesus said, "Unless a person is born anew he cannot see the kingdom of God" (3:3). When Nicodemus seemed utterly baffled Jesus added, "Unless a person is born of water and the Spirit he cannot enter the kingdom of God," for "that which is born of the flesh is flesh and that which is born of the Spirit is spirit" (3:5-6). This passage has had a profound influence on two major streams of Christianity. One emphasizes the sacramental aspects of the faith, identifying new birth with the rite of Baptism. The other focuses on the experience of being born again, understood to mean a conscious conversion from sin to committed faith. Each tradition has a significant history.

Sacramental interpretations of the new birth were developed in the early church. The North African writer Tertullian (d. ca. 225) summarized the practice of his time by saying that Baptism provided remission of sins, deliverance from death, regeneration of the person, and the gift of the Holy Spirit (*Against Marcion* 1.28). He explained that in liturgical practice the use of water in Baptism provided cleansing while the Holy Spirit was given immediately afterward through prayer and the laying on of hands (*On Baptism* 1-8).

Cyprian (d. 258), also a North African, took being "born of the flesh" to mean sin, which is washed away by the water, so that the Spirit can give the new or second birth (*To Donatus* 4). Cyprian also regarded Baptism as an essential practice of the true church. Since John's Gospel said that no one enters the kingdom of God without water and the Spirit, those seeking salvation were to be baptized within the established church (*Epistles* 72.1; 73.21). Later, Augustine (d. 430) maintained that since all people are born of the flesh and are sinful, the sacrament of Baptism was rightly extended to infants — something already practiced in the church of his time. John 3 was understood to mean that Baptism gave even newborns the gift of forgiveness, regeneration in the Spirit, and a share in the kingdom (*On Forgiveness* 1.58; *On Original Sin* 2.21).[19]

The language of John 3 has been incorporated into baptismal liturgies, where it remains a familiar part of worship in many churches. In Roman Catholic rites, prayers ask that in the sacrament people "may be cleansed from sin and rise to a new birth of innocence by water and the Holy Spirit." The Anglican *Book of Common Prayer* says that in the water of Baptism, by the power of the Spirit, people are "cleansed from sin and born again." Similarly, some Lutheran baptismal services say, "We are born children of a fallen humanity; by water and the Spirit we are reborn children of God."[20]

The alternative approach relates new birth primarily to preaching and the response of faith. The Protestant reformers of the sixteenth century emphasized the importance of the preached word in the life of faith. John Calvin (d. 1564) moved away from the baptismal interpretation. When reading John 3, he took water as a metaphor for the Spirit. For him the passage emphasized how the Spirit made it possible to receive the gospel.[21] The vivid experience of personal renewal played a larger role for John Wesley (d. 1791), one of the founders of Methodism. Wesley was a member of the Church of England, which commonly linked new birth to Baptism. Through participation in gatherings devoted to a deeper spiritual life, he experienced an intense awareness of the grace of God. Accordingly, in his preaching on John 3 he began to emphasize the renewing qualities of the Spirit's work. Being born again meant coming to an awareness of sin, giving up confidence in oneself, and coming to a sure trust and confidence that one's sins were forgiven for Christ's sake. As a result, one would pursue a godly life.[22]

Preaching and the experiential dimensions of new birth have had a central place in evangelical Christianity. A pivotal figure in the awakenings of the eighteenth century was George Whitefield (d. 1770). Like Wesley he experienced a personal renewal, which seemed to be a definite movement from darkness into the light of grace.[23] Whitefield made new birth the focus of his preaching at large revival meetings in Britain and North America. This pattern continued in the preaching of Billy Graham (b. 1918), whose call to be born again was a hallmark of twentieth-century revivalism. At evangelical events around the world he defined an understanding of new birth that involved a conviction of one's sin, acceptance of Christ as Savior, and the new life that follows.[24]

The rapid growth of Pentecostal churches in the twentieth century added another perspective to the question of new birth. The name "Pentecostal" reflects the movement's emphasis on ecstatic manifestations of the Holy Spirit, like those ascribed to the apostles at Pentecost in Acts 2. The modern movement began in 1906 with a series of revivals in Los Angeles, but it has become a global phenomenon. Many Pentecostals interpret John 3:5 in light of the Spirit passages in other New Testament writings, which refer to speaking in tongues and prophesying (Acts 2:4, 38; 10:44-48; 1 Cor. 12:4-13). From this perspective, evidence that one has been born not only of water but also of the Spirit will come in the form of speaking in tongues and similar spiritual gifts. When reading John's Gospel, we must ask about how much variety there is in the work of the Spirit and experience of faith (see pp. 142-43).

The Particularity of Christianity

Jesus tells his disciples, "I am the way and the truth and the life; no one comes to the Father but by me" (John 14:6). These words are spoken in the context of the last supper in response to the disciples' uneasiness about possible separation from Jesus. When read in a Christian context, the verse has continued to foster a sense of communion with Christ. For example, George Herbert (d. 1633) wrote a poem expressing heartfelt longing: "Come my Way, my Truth, my Life: Such a way as gives us breath; such a truth as ends all strife; such a life as killeth death." Similarly, the devotional classic *True Christianity* by Johann Arndt (d. 1621) relates the message about Jesus as the way and the truth to reflections on the Christian's call to genuine repentance and a holy life.[25]

In an interreligious context the idea that Jesus is "the way" becomes more controversial. Expanding networks of travel and trade brought increased contact between Christians and non-Christians in the nineteenth and twentieth centuries. One major response was the global mission movement, which established Christian congregations and schools in countries around the world. Within this movement Christianity's claim that Jesus is "the way" was understood to mean that the gospel should be extended to people everywhere. However, others questioned whether any religion could make absolute claims. Given the presence of Islam, Buddhism, Hinduism, and other faiths, many came to regard Christianity as one religion among many.

Recognition that the church's teachings evolved over the centuries compounded the difficulty in ascribing absolute truth to Christianity. Philosopher and historian Ernst Troeltsch (d. 1923) concluded that Christianity and all other world religions were subject to cultural change. All shared an impulse toward absolute truth, though their forms were distinct. His view was that Christianity could make no claim to finality, though its beliefs could have value for those who professed them. He said that what is "*a truth for us* does not cease because of this, to be very Truth and Life."[26]

Similarly, John Hick (b. 1922) has proposed that all religions deal with common problems and share a common ethical ideal, calling their followers to transcend self-interest and to be open to a higher reality. For him, the message of John's Gospel is one manifestation of this tendency. Drawing on historical studies of early Christianity, Hick maintains that John's Gospel does not preserve the original teachings of Jesus. Rather, he assumes that in the gospels the early church projects its own developing beliefs onto the figure of Jesus. There is nothing definitive about John's claim that Jesus is the way, truth, and life. This idea simply manifests one stage in the church's evolving belief system. As beliefs continue to change, Hick anticipates that they will move beyond this particularism toward a wider view of reality.[27]

The opposite view reads John's emphasis on Jesus as "the way, the truth, and the life" as a call to the church, a summons to faithfulness. With Hitler's rise to power in Germany in the 1930s, the church was confronted by a competing truth claim. The Nazi ideology made absolute claims about the primacy of the state, race, and culture. Trust and obedience were ultimately claimed by the totalitarian state, with its program of anti-Semitism. Many German Christians were willing to accommodate this belief system. But in 1934, some theologians and church leaders formulated the Barmen Declaration, which began by quoting John 14:6. The declaration reaffirmed the ultimate claim of Christ over against the state, called for trust to be placed in Christ, and rejected other powers that sought to take the place of the gospel.

Theologian Karl Barth (d. 1968) was one of the principal authors of the Barmen declaration. In the words "I am the way, the truth, and the life" he heard Christ calling the church to be faithful in life and death. No human belief system, including the ideology of the state, could be put in Christ's place. This also meant that all forms of religion, including Christianity, stood under Christ. All world religions had forms of worship, morality, art, and social customs. Christianity could claim no privileged position in this regard. Rather, Barth understood that the truth of Christianity rested on the truth of Jesus, the one in whom God made himself known. Christianity has a special place insofar as it points to Jesus, the one in whom God extends truth and life to human beings.[28]

The questions about the inclusive and exclusive aspects of Christianity continue to be debated. Many of them are beyond the scope of this study. Our challenge will be to read John 14:6 within the Gospel as a whole. Exploring its significance in that context can contribute to those working theologically in other contexts (see pp. 209-14).

Venturing Forward

As we bring theological questions to John's Gospel, we will consider several dimensions of its message, seeking to integrate them into a coherent whole. First, we will ask what the Gospel presupposes. We have noted that it assumes there is only one true God, who gives life and raises the dead. We will also find that the Gospel assumes that Jesus is a human being, who dies by crucifixion. No one in the Gospel questions these things. They are taken for granted by Jesus' followers and his foes. Yet even if Jesus' humanity and death are presupposed rather than argued, they are clearly crucial aspects of his identity. We do well to ask how these and other presuppositions work theologically.

Second, we will consider the theological points for which the Gospel must build a case. Everyone may agree that God gives life, but they disagree about whether Jesus can claim this as a precedent for healing on the Sabbath (5:17-18). Again, everyone may agree that Jesus is human, but they dispute whether he can claim to be the Messiah or Son of God. His adversaries charge that he is a mere human being trying to elevate himself to the place of God (10:33). The Gospel must show that the opposite is true: he has come down from God to work as a human being. Similarly, no one questions the fact that Jesus died by crucifixion. What is disputed is what his death means. Jesus' opponents are convinced that his execution is rightful punishment for his rebellion against God (19:7). The evangelist must show that it carried out the purposes of God.

Third, we will explore the implications of what is said. For example, Jesus is called the Lamb of God who takes away the sin of the world (1:29). But there is no overt explanation as to how his death removes sin. To formulate a response to this question, one must work with related themes throughout the Gospel. Similarly, Jesus says that those who follow him do not walk in darkness but have the light of life (8:12). The imagery is appealing, but there is no clear explanation as to what it means. Reflecting theologically on this aspect of discipleship means tracing the theme of light and darkness through the narrative and trying to identify its main facets of meaning.

Our interpretation will try to take account of the whole story. The Gospel shows the problems that arise when people try to understand Jesus on the basis of his public ministry alone. Their triumphant portrait of the miracle-working Messiah disintegrates at the prospect of his death (12:31-

36). Interpreting Jesus' ministry means relating it to the cross and resurrection. The Messiah's victory does not come by avoiding death but by enduring and overcoming it. Conversely, Jesus' death and resurrection are to be understood in light of the preceding ministry. If giving life was central in his acts of healing, feeding people, and raising the dead, then this helps readers see that giving life is what he does through his death and resurrection. Working with the Gospel as a whole will also shape the way we consider the identity of God, the human condition, the work of the Spirit, and the life of faith.

CHAPTER 2

God

The question, "How do people know God?" is at the heart of John's Gospel. The prologue declares that all things came into being through God's Word (1:1-3), which means that the world and its people were made by God for relationship with him. God loves the world and sends his Son to it, yet God remains unseen (1:18; 3:16). He is "from above," while human beings are "from below," and people lack the capacity to peer behind heaven's veil for an unmediated glimpse of God (8:23). Throughout John's Gospel, God's purposes drive the story. Jesus says that he has come to do the will of his Father. He speaks the words God told him to speak and does the works God gave him to do (5:30; 6:38; 12:49). Yet God remains hidden, his presence elusive. In the end even Jesus' followers grow restive and say, "Show us the Father" for then "we will be satisfied" (14:8).[1]

It would perhaps be easier to begin our work with Jesus, who speaks words that can be heard and does actions that can be seen. He touches the sick with hands that can be felt and feeds the crowd with bread that can be tasted. Yet tracing the ministry of Jesus soon brings the issue back to God. The Gospel insists that the point of Jesus' coming is to make the unseen God known (1:18). At the end of his public ministry Jesus says, "Whoever believes in me believes not in me but in him who sent me. And whoever sees me sees him who sent me" (12:44-45). The story climaxes when Thomas encounters the crucified and risen Jesus and confesses, "My Lord and my God" (20:28). The Gospel was written in order that readers might make a similar confession. In the crucified and risen Jesus, they are called to see the face of God.

John writes about God for an interreligious world. He does not offer theoretical arguments for God's existence, since everyone in the story assumes that there is a God of some sort. The problem is that their ideas about God conflict. There are Jews who worship at the temple in Jerusalem and Samaritans who insist that God should be worshiped on a mountain to the north, in Samaria. They agree *that* God should be worshiped, but disagree about how this should be done (4:20). Then there are the Greeks, who on occasion may worship in Jerusalem, but who are known for venerating many different deities at sanctuaries scattered throughout the ancient world (7:35; 12:20). Pilate the Roman governor has his own religious sensibilities. While interrogating Jesus, Pilate is told that his prisoner has been making himself into the Son of God, and the idea that there might be divine involvement in the case makes Pilate afraid. The issue is delicate because Pilate's career depends on good relations with the emperor, who also claims the title "son of god" (19:7-8). John must disclose who God is in the context of competing truth claims.

Questions about God belong to the fabric of human life. If all things have been created by God, then all people are related to God as his creatures. The issue is not *whether* people will relate to God — that is a given — it is whether this relationship will be positive or negative, faith or unfaith. And John's Gospel assumes that the way people understand and relate to God affects their relationships with other people and the world around them. The way they live and work is shaped by the relationships they consider most important. So who is God, according to John's Gospel? And how is God known?

God and the Word

The Gospel begins with God's Word, his act of communicating. The opening lines read, "In the beginning was the Word *(logos)*, and the Word was with God, and the Word was God . . . all things came into being through him" (1:1-3). The Greek term *logos* has a wide range of meanings. It resonates with Jewish traditions about the power and wisdom of God as well as with philosophical teachings concerning the energy that shapes the universe.[2] But the term is often used for the spoken "word" (e.g., 2:22; 4:37; 5:24). A word is a form of address, a means of engagement. To say, "In the beginning was the Word" is to say that in the beginning is God's act of communication. Without communication God remains unknown and unknowable. For the Gospel to say anything about God means that God must first disclose something of himself.

John assumes that God communicates in three ways: First, God is known through *Israel's Scriptures.* The Gospel does not argue this point but presupposes it.[3] The opening lines of the prologue, which were quoted above, use the term "god" or *theos* without further explanation. This could conceivably be problematic, since the same term was used for the deities of various religious traditions in the ancient world, and one might wonder which god John refers to. Yet the prologue's language makes clear that John speaks of the God known in Israel's Scriptures, who is the Creator. The first line of the Scriptures reads, "In the beginning . . . God said" (Gen. 1:1-3). John echoes this by saying, "In the beginning was the Word," who "was with God" and who "was God" (John 1:1). John presupposes that there is only one true God, who has already made himself known through the law and the prophetic writings (5:44; 17:3). When the Gospel speaks of "god" in the singular, it refers to the God of Israel's tradition.

Since the Scriptures already speak of God, much of what the Gospel says about God may seem commonplace. John refers to the creative power of God's Word (1:1-3); he assumes that God has the power to give life and to raise the dead (5:21); and he identifies God as the one with authority to judge all people (5:45). None of this is new information for those who are familiar with the Old Testament. Yet for the Fourth Evangelist, the question of knowing God is not primarily a matter of receiving additional pieces of information. The Gospel depicts people who affirm that what the Scriptures say about God is true, but whose words and actions show that they do not truly "know" God from John's perspective (8:54-55). For John, "knowing" is a relational term. It involves trusting God and showing faithfulness to him. And to bring about such relationships, John says that God makes himself known in another way.

This second form of communication takes place through *Jesus of Nazareth.* In Jesus, God's Word comes to people as an embodied human being. This is the heart of the Gospel. There are many human beings who say things *about* God, but in Jesus the Word comes *from* God in human form. God speaks to the world through the words Jesus utters, the actions he performs, and the death that he dies. In Jesus' life, death, and resurrection, people not only receive information about God, but are granted an encounter with God. And the prologue prepares readers to see the whole story of Jesus as God's act of communicating through his embodied Word.

The prologue defines the relationship of God to his Word as follows: "the Word was with God, and the Word was God" (1:1b). This deceptively simple statement includes two seemingly incompatible thoughts. People normally speak of someone's identity by saying that the person "is." Or else they refer to a relationship by saying that the person "is with" someone else. But in the world of God both are true at the same time. The Word not only is "with" God but "is" God.[4] This paradoxical statement presses readers to think through the way a speaker relates to a word. In ordinary experience, people know that a word can be differentiated from the one who speaks it and that a person who utters a word has an existence outside of that word. Yet there is a deeper connection. To hear a person's word is to hear the person. When a person's word effects something, the person effects something. This is what the prologue is driving at. The Word is differentiated from God and yet is identified with God. Where the Word addresses the world, God addresses the world.

God communicates with the world in order to bring about relationship. This is the reason he sends the Word. The pattern has some analogies at the human level. People generally understand that communication is essential for relationships. Where there is no communication people have no means of coming to know, love, and trust someone else. Where there is miscommunication, relations suffer. Therefore, people foster relationships by the words they speak and the actions they do for others. The same is true of God and human beings. The God who made all things sends his Word in order that people might know him, receive him, and believe in him (1:10-12). To know and believe the Word is to trust the God who sends it.

The challenge is that God must communicate in a form that can be received by human beings. God might choose to speak in the mysterious language of heaven, but his message would not mean anything to the people who know only the dialects of earth. At one point in the narrative, God does speak directly from heaven, proclaiming his glory, yet the bystanders take it to be the rumbling of thunder or the unintelligible speech of an angel (12:28-29). Communication requires that the sender find a way of connecting with the intended recipients. On the human level, a person might speak perfectly clear English, but the words will mean nothing to someone who understands only a dialect from Indonesia. For communication to take place, the speaker must find an alternative way to convey meaning, such as making visible gestures with the hands and using facial expressions. According to John's Gospel, this is what God does. He makes his Word visible as well as audible.

God addresses human beings through the Word that becomes flesh in Jesus of Nazareth (1:1, 14). God sends his Word in the flesh because flesh is what all people share. The flesh is not strange but familiar. This enables God to speak to human beings in genuinely human form. God can do this because he is the one who created flesh in the first place. The Gospel recognizes that human flesh is weak and mortal, yet it is not inherently evil. God made the flesh and can use it as a vehicle for his Word.

But here is the complicating factor. For communication to take place, people must receive what is essentially different (the Word of God) in what is essentially the same as themselves (the flesh). In Jesus, people meet someone who is as human as they are, yet he claims to have come from God and to address them with God's own authority. This provokes a new issue. In the eyes of many people, Jesus seems too human to have come from God. Since they see that Jesus is a living breathing person, they cannot believe that he is from God in any unique way. They insist that he is a human being, who is wrongfully trying to elevate himself to the status of God. They reject the idea that he has come down from God to carry out the work of God in human form. This irony is central to John's Gospel: God reaches across the barrier that separates him from human beings by sending his Word in human form; yet this human form becomes a new barrier, since many people see only the human Jesus and cannot comprehend that he is from God (1:10-11).[5]

The Gospel assumes that God has spoken in Scripture and in Jesus, yet recognizes that both forms of communication can be misunderstood. There are some people in the Gospel who recognize that what Jesus says and does fits well with what God has declared in the law and the prophets (1:45; 5:37-39), but others argue the reverse. They insist that the Scriptures discredit Jesus, since his Galilean origins do not fit the biblical paradigm for a Messiah and his practice of healing on the Sabbath seems to violate God's law (7:41-42; 9:16). This is a major point of conflict in the narrative. Jesus' opponents derive from the Scriptures an understanding of God that sets them against the Word made flesh (8:54-55). Therefore, as we explore the debates in the Gospel, we find that the evangelist will seek to show that the Scriptures bear witness to the truth of God in Jesus, and that Jesus discloses the truth of God in Scripture.

Third, God continues to communicate through the *Holy Spirit* after the ministry of Jesus has ended. The Gospel says that the Spirit comes from the Father and is given to the disciples by the risen Jesus (14:16, 26; 15:26; 16:7). The Spirit is not an independent witness to God, but continues to disclose the meaning of Jesus' words and deeds after the conclusion of his incarnation. God communicated through the Word made flesh, and the Spirit continues to teach and remind people about the significance of what Jesus said (14:26). The Spirit does not bring new revelation but conveys the meaning of what God revealed through the life, death, and resurrection of Jesus (see pp. 152-57). In this process the community of faith continues to discern how Jesus' witness to God is related to what was previously included in the Scriptures. For the Fourth Evangelist, God is known through all three forms of communication noted here. The Gospel focuses on what God communicates through the Word made flesh and understands this in light of the Scriptures and the ongoing witness of God's Spirit.

Creator and Giver of Life

Basic to John's theology is that God has created all things through his Word. Referring to God's Word the prologue says, "all things came into being through him" (1:3a). This too echoes the biblical creation story. The main verb is *egeneto,* which is used repeatedly in the Greek translation of Genesis: "God said, 'Let there be light,' and there was *(egeneto)* light"; "God said, 'Let there be a dome in the midst of the waters'... and it was so *(egeneto)*" (Gen. 1:3, 6-7). Throughout the biblical account of creation, God speaks and things happen; his Word forms the world.

John uses this biblical language to establish a pattern of relationships between God and others. God and his Word are simply present at the beginning. Their existence is taken for granted. By way of contrast, the world comes into being. It is not self-generated or ultimate. It owes its existence to the God who called it into being. The prologue does not speculate about what God might have been doing before creation — though Jesus will later disclose that God's glory and love existed before the world was ever made (John 17:5, 24). Instead, the prologue helps define God's relationship to the world. God is the Creator; the world is created. The world may claim independence, but this is not the case. Its existence depends upon the Word of God.

Emphasizing the scope of creation, the prologue says that without

God's Word "not one thing came into being" (1:3b). This is important given John's sharp distinctions between what is above and below, between heaven and earth (3:12, 31). Readers can get the impression that the earth is inherently evil, unlike the celestial sphere above. John contrasts flesh and Spirit, what is of this world and what is not of this world (3:6; 8:23). Readers may infer that the flesh and the world are intrinsically bad, while the Spirit and the otherworldly realm are good. Yet this is not the view of the Gospel writer.

God is the Creator of all things in heaven and on earth. The world and the flesh are limited and perishable, yet they belong to God's creation and are not essentially evil. The Word can become flesh because the flesh itself is fashioned by God. The created order does not, in itself, yield any sure knowledge of God. Yet upon entering the world, Jesus calls upon things that can be seen and heard and tasted to bear witness to the unseen God who sent him. Water jars filled with wine, bread made from barley, shafts of light striking the eye of a blind man — all become vehicles for revelation. When teaching, Jesus invokes images of flowing water, a shepherd and sheep, a vine and a vinedresser, so that aspects of the creation are used in witness to the Creator and his gifts.

Thus far the prologue has said that the Word of God has given things existence. Now it says that in God's Word was *"life,"* which is something more (1:4). Life is pictured as a light for human beings, and it is central to John's understanding of God's identity and purposes. God "has life in himself," which means that his life is not derived from any other source (5:26). God has life and God gives life. This gives readers a basic sense of who God is.[6] Human beings, in contrast, do not have life in themselves. If they are to live they must receive life from God. This means that in John's Gospel life is understood relationally. To have life is to relate to the God who is the source of all life.

Life has multiple dimensions in John's Gospel. One of these is physical. Those who are alive physically have hearts that beat and lungs that breathe. Since God's Word is the source of physical life, this is an essential feature of the ministry of Jesus, the incarnate Word. He restores the health of a boy dying of a fever, so that the child "lives" (4:50-51). Giving bread to a hungry crowd, enabling a paralyzed man to walk, giving a blind man his sight, and calling Lazarus out of the tomb — all of these reveal the power of the life-giving God.

There is also a dimension to life that goes beyond the physical. To have true life is to know and trust God and his Word. The prologue develops this idea by tracing the coming of the Word into the world. Those who have life "know" God through his Word (1:10). This is a positive form of relationship. Knowing can simply mean that someone has correctly absorbed information, but knowing God is more like knowing a person. It involves a recognition of identity, a discerning of the truth about someone. Knowing has a cognitive dimension, yet it is not limited to this. To know God through his Word is to "receive" him, as one welcomes a person into one's home (1:11). It is to "believe" in the Word, which means trusting God himself (1:12).

The Gospel recognizes that there may be disjunction between the different facets of life. Physically, all people receive life from God, yet that does not mean that everyone has the life that comes through faith. People who can breathe and move have the capacity to turn away from their Maker. They can reject the Word of God that brought them into being and refuse to believe in him (1:10-11). They can receive the gifts of food and healing that sustain the body, while repudiating the giver (5:14-16; 6:26-36). All people are related to God as his creatures, yet faith is life-giving in a way that alienation from God is not. People can be alive physically and yet dying relationally.

The Gospel also recognizes that true life begins while the heart beats and the lungs breathe, yet it has a future that extends beyond physical death. Therefore, true life is often identified as "eternal life" (e.g., 3:15; 4:14; 5:24). Eternal life begins now, in faith, and it continues beyond death through the promise of resurrection. Life in the present can be called "eternal," as faith brings people into relationship with the eternal God. People are not inherently immortal, and even those who believe will die. Yet the relationship with God is not terminated by death. God does not abandon believers but gives them a future through resurrection (see pp. 130-32, 179-82).

Human beings are created with a need for life, and they pursue what they think will bring it. So if life comes from God, as the Gospel says it does, then questions about life are ultimately questions about God. This inherent need for life makes the matter of God inescapable. The issue is not whether people will seek life — that is a given — the issue is where their pursuit of life will take them and how this relates to what God is doing.[7] The human side of the issue will be the focus of our next chapter. Here we focus on God's actions and what they reveal about his identity.

The Sender

God's will for relationship is reflected in the theme of "sending" *(apostellō, pempō)*. According to the Fourth Gospel, God sends John the Baptist, Jesus, and the Holy Spirit into the world to carry out his purposes. Sending is a form of engagement. Through his emissaries, God engages the world he has made. In the climactic scenes following Jesus' resurrection, the disciples are also "sent" into the world and empowered by the Spirit (20:21-22). The pattern of sending ultimately gives shape to Christian discipleship. We will find that as God sends others, he goes with them. God does not send others into the world in order that he might remain comfortably absent from it. God is in the middle of things, so that even in the face of conflict Jesus can affirm that the "one who sent me is with me; he has not left me alone" (8:29; 16:32). Sending is an action of the God who is present, not a God who is absent.

Offering Life — Confronting with Truth

Sending presupposes that God is separated from the world and yet engaged with the world. A gap stands between God and human beings, and for a genuine relationship to exist this gap must be overcome. The separation is usually depicted in spatial terms: God is associated with heaven while people belong to the earth. God is above while human beings are below. But the spatial imagery describes what is essentially a relational issue: human estrangement from God. The problem is not that God lives in one part of the universe while human beings inhabit another. Rather, it is that people are estranged from their Creator (see pp. 59-74).

Rather than accepting separation, God engages the world. He sends emissaries in order that the world might know the One who made it. God entrusts those whom he sends with two main tasks: The first is to bring the message of salvation and life. Those who are sent are to call the world to faith, so that relationships with God might be restored and people might have life. This is the primary purpose of the sending. The second task is confrontational. Those whom God sends are to tell the world the truth about itself. They reveal the world's estrangement from God and bring its sin to light. They confront the world in order to startle people into awareness of their situation, so that they see their need for the life God offers. The two aspects of the sending work together when people recognize their own need and receive God's gift of life. But the sending also leads to judgment when people refuse God's gift and insist on remaining alienated from him.

The interplay between offering life and confronting with truth is evident in scenes featuring John the Baptist, who is one of those "sent" by God. The prologue says that God sent John to be a witness (1:6-8). A witness speaks in contexts where the truth is disputed. If everything is clear, there is no need for testimony. In the opening scene of the Gospel, a delegation comes to John with questions about his identity and his reasons for baptizing. John lets them know that he is not the one who will ultimately carry out God's purposes (1:19-21). Then he tells his questioners about themselves. He says that they are unable to recognize the one who will carry out the work of God, even though that one already stands among them (1:26-27). This reveals their limitations. The next day John goes further. He points to Jesus, calling him "the Lamb of God, who takes away the sin of the world" (1:29). The goal of John's witness is that people might believe through him (1:7). Faith is the primary purpose for which he is sent. Yet as John bears witness to the Lamb, he also attests to the sin of the world, which must be taken away. To believe that God has sent the Lamb means believing that the world has a need for its sin to be removed. John is sent to tell people the truth about their own separation from God and about what God is doing to overcome it.

John the Baptist also appears later in the Gospel, where some complain that people are now going to Jesus rather than coming to John. So John testifies that he was "sent" to prepare people for the Messiah (3:28). This is the positive side of his message. John compares himself to the best man at a wedding, who helps with arrangements, but steps aside when the bride comes to meet the groom. John testifies that Jesus is the messianic bridegroom. Therefore, people are to go to Jesus (3:29-30). According to this passage, God has "sent" Jesus to be the giver of life (3:34). People receive life from God by believing in Jesus, since faith is the relationship that is life-giving.

The counterpart to this is John's warning that those who do not believe thereby repudiate life and embrace God's wrath (3:36).[8] This is the only reference to "wrath" (orgē) in the Fourth Gospel. Wrath is God's judgment against human rejection of him. People were created for life with God, and when they turn away from life God finds it outrageous. There is no suggestion that God might simply remain indifferent toward human beings. God loves the world and his will is to give it life, so when the world repudiates God's gift, it makes alienation the norm. If God's will is for relationship, then his judgment on human animosity toward him can only be negative.

When we turn to the ministry of Jesus, we find that the interplay between offering life and confronting with truth also characterizes his work. The Gospel says that Jesus is "sent" by God, but in a manner that differs from that of John the Baptist. God sends John in order to call people to faith, but God sends Jesus to be the focus for faith. In Jesus, God's communication takes embodied form. To believe in this embodied Word is to believe in the God who sends it. Similarly, to reject the message is to reject its divine Sender. Therefore Jesus can say, "Whoever believes in me believes not in me but in him who sent me" (12:44).[9] It is clear that God sends Jesus in order that people might believe and have life: "God did not send the Son into the world to condemn the world, but that the world might be saved through him" (3:17). Yet the need to continue confronting the world with truth persists. And when the world rejects the one whom God sends, it brings judgment upon itself (3:18-21).

God sends Jesus to perform actions that give life and reveal who God is. Jesus says, "We must work the works of him who sent me while it is day" (9:4). Then he heals a blind man to show what kind of work he means. Many of the works God sends Jesus to do are called "signs" because they display God's power in a manner accessible to the senses. The Gospel says that signs reveal God's glory or *doxa,* using a term that suggests majestic radiance. The signs that show God's glory reveal his power and presence. The signs also help to show people who God is. Power can be revealed in many forms, but the signs reveal power in ways that give life. Jesus feeds people, heals the sick, and calls Lazarus out of the tomb. This exercise of creative and life-giving power reveals the character of God (11:4, 40).

People respond to the signs in different and often contradictory ways (see pp. 163-70). Those who perceive the signs through the eyes of faith respond positively and have their faith confirmed, but many either misinterpret the signs or respond negatively to them. Since Jesus heals on the Sabbath, many insist that he violates God's law, which says that no work is to be done on the Sabbath. From their perspective, God cannot have sent Jesus, since Jesus' actions run contrary to the will of God. From the perspective of a believer, the signs may reveal the life-giving power of God, but those who do not see things this way oppose what Jesus is doing and reject what he offers — and this brings them under judgment.

Jesus' preaching works with this movement between giving life and the need to confront the opposition. A good example is found in a debate that takes place in the temple. Jesus' opponents find what he says about himself and his Father to be incomprehensible (8:12-20). When replying, Jesus makes specific reference to the sending motif. He says, "the one who sent me is true, and I declare to the world what I have heard from him" (8:26). So what has Jesus heard from God? Part of what he says in this context is clearly confrontational. He tells his opponents, "You are from below, I am from above; you are of this world, I am not of this world," and "I told you that you would die in your sins" (8:23-24a). God has sent Jesus into the world to tell it the truth about sin and death. His words are disturbingly blunt — and this is evidently the point. What Jesus says is designed to unsettle his hearers. But this is not his last word.

Jesus continues speaking and says that his hearers will die in their sins "unless" they believe (8:24b). The word "unless" is like a window bringing light into a darkened room. It means that separation from God need not be final. "Unless" extends the prospect of change, and the shape this change takes is faith. Jesus says that sin is overcome and relationships restored when people come to believe in him, or more specifically, to "believe that I Am" (8:24b). The expression "I Am" recalls the traditional biblical name of God (Exod. 3:14; Deut. 32:39; Isa. 45:18). To believe that Jesus is "I Am" is to believe that in him God encounters people. God sends Jesus to call people away from unbelief and toward the God who made them. If telling his hearers the truth about themselves is part of Jesus' message, the other part is the offer of life that comes through faith.

Images of God in the Preaching of Jesus

As Jesus is sent, he bears witness to God by using richly metaphorical language. At the close of his ministry he tells the disciples, "I have said these things to you in figures of speech *(paroimiai)*. The hour is coming when I will no longer speak to you in figures, but will tell you plainly of the Father" (16:25). To use figurative language is to speak of one thing in terms appropriate to another. Jesus will use images that are both similar to and different from God. This means that listeners must discern analogies between things that are otherwise dissimilar.[10] For example, Jesus calls God his Father, yet the Gospel makes clear that God does not beget children in the way that a human father does (1:13). Therefore, the expression must be taken in another way (see pp. 47-52). This pattern continues each time an image is used for God. People must distinguish what the image does and does not say about God.

Jesus' listeners and even his disciples find his figurative speech confusing, and want Jesus to speak more plainly (10:6, 24; 16:29). Yet Jesus cannot speak of God directly. God is different from the world, which is why Jesus uses figurative speech. The imagery is not designed to obscure meanings that can be plainly stated but to communicate the mystery of the unseen God in earthly forms.[11] Here we will consider the way God is portrayed in several passages, noting the continued interplay between the themes of life and judgment.

First, God is like a *craftsman*. Jesus makes this tacit comparison during a dispute over his right to heal on the Sabbath. He says that he can heal because his Father "is still working" (5:17). In what follows Jesus describes a scene that was familiar in many towns and villages. A father would work at a trade and teach it to his son. If the father was a potter he would work at his wheel, forming clay into jars, cups, dishes, and other items. When a boy was young he would play in the shop, watching his father do this work. As the boy grew older the father would give him some clay and show him how to mould it into a simple bowl. The boy would develop his skills by watching the father and learning to do what the father did. In time the father would entrust the son with certain responsibilities, which he was expected to carry out. Giving the son a trade was what a father would do out of love.

Jesus alludes to this pattern by saying that "the Son can do nothing on his own, but only what he sees the Father doing; for whatever the Father does, that the Son does likewise. The Father loves the Son and shows him all that he himself is doing" (5:19-20a). Here the Father is like a master craftsman, instructing his Son.[12] And what is God's trade? To raise the dead and give them life (5:21). Since giving life is what God does, this is what he sends Jesus to do by acts of healing. In the immediate context Jesus gives life by healing a boy of a fever and raising a lame man to his feet (4:50; 5:8). The Son's actions carry out the life-giving work of the Father. Another aspect of God's work is judgment. God is the judge of all the earth (Gen. 18:25), but now he has now entrusted this part of the business to Jesus. "The Father judges no one but has given all judgment to the Son" (John 5:22). If Jesus pronounces judgment on the unbelief of those he meets, he is carrying out the responsibilities the Father has given him (5:14, 38).

Later in this passage, God becomes a *witness* who is drawn into court. Jesus finds himself accused of wrongdoing, since he claims that he can work on the Sabbath because God does so (5:17). During a legal hearing witnesses were commonly summoned in order to testify on behalf of the prosecution and the defense. According to the law, two or three witnesses were needed to sustain a charge in court (Deut. 17:6; 19:15). As part of his defense, Jesus must summon witnesses to testify on his behalf. The problem is the peculiar nature of the case. The plaintiffs charge that Jesus is a human being trying to elevate himself to divine status, which is sin (John 5:18). Jesus counters that he is not acting in opposition to God. Rather, he has been sent by God and works in obedience to God.

So has God sent Jesus or hasn't he? As the defendant, Jesus understands that he needs to call God to take the witness stand on his behalf. The problem is how to get God to appear in court. The challenge is daunting, yet Jesus does introduce two forms of testimony from God. One concerns the kind of work that Jesus is doing. Jesus points out that he is giving life, not destroying it. Anyone can take life away, but giving life is exactly what the Creator does. By empowering Jesus to give life through healing, God testifies that he has indeed sent him. (5:21, 36). The other form of testimony is God's written deposition. In the Scriptures God testified that he would send someone to speak on his behalf. Moses set it down in the record, and Jesus assumes that his opponents have read the text (Deut. 18:18; John 5:37-39, 46). Jesus expects his opponents to agree that God has spoken through the Scriptures. What must be argued is that Jesus is the one to whom the Scriptures point. If what Jesus says is true, then those who reject Jesus reject God's own testimony. After all, the Scriptures include an affidavit saying that God will hold people accountable for their unbelief (Deut. 18:18; John 5:45).

Another passage portrays God as a gracious *host at a banquet,* though the actions visible to the eye are performed by Jesus. He invites a great crowd of people to recline on the grass, which was a common posture at a banquet. It means they are to lie down on their sides, propped up by their left arms, with their right hands free to hold the food. No one has asked Jesus to provide a meal. As host he assumes the initiative (6:4-5, 10). Taking five loaves of barley bread, he gives thanks and distributes it to the people. Then he does the same with two fish. The guests are allowed to eat as much as they want, as was proper. Then Jesus has the leftover fragments gathered up, and they fill twelve baskets (6:12-13). As a good host he is generous but not wasteful with food.[13]

Jesus' interactions with the crowd depict, in miniature, God's interactions with the world. After Jesus has conveyed a message by his actions, he comments on its meaning in the discourse that follows. God is identified as the host of the meal. By giving bread to the crowd Jesus attests that God gives bread to the world (6:32-33). More startling is that Jesus is identified as the bread God offers (6:35). This alters the perception of God's action. Barley bread gives life physically, but bread in the form of a person gives life relationally. God gives Jesus to the world in order to bring people into renewed relationship with himself. This is life in the theological sense.

God's will to preserve life is expressed in Jesus' act of gathering up the fragments "that nothing may be lost" at the end of the banquet (6:12). It is the will of God that Jesus "lose nothing" of all that has been given him, "but raise it up on the last day" (6:39). By giving Jesus, God provides the "bread" or means of relationship that sustains faith. To believe is to have life with God now, and this relationship has a future through the promise of resurrection. Jesus' actions and the words that interpret them convey the will of God in visible and audible form.

Finally, Jesus depicts God as a *vinedresser*. A vineyard is planted with vines, each of which has a main stalk from which the branches grow. During the growing season a worker examines the vines and removes any lifeless branches that bear no fruit. These are piled at the edge of the vineyard and later burned. The worker also prunes away the excess growth that detracts from the vine's ability to produce large clusters of grapes. At the harvest, the vinedresser rejoices at the fruit that the vine yields.

Jesus identifies himself as the vine, his followers as the branches, and God as the vinedresser. Love is the fruit that the vinedresser desires (15:1-17). On the surface the imagery is placid, yet closer inspection discloses actions of God that seem remarkably severe: "He removes *(airō)* every branch in me that bears no fruit. Every branch that bears fruit he prunes *(kathairō)* to make it bear more fruit" (15:2). We might expect the acts of cutting to depict God's stance toward the unbelieving world, but here they portray his relationship to the followers of Jesus. They are the branches being tended by the Father. The assumption is that sin is not limited to the outside world. It persists even within the Christian community.[14]

So what does it mean for God to remove a branch? A fruitless branch has already lost its vital connection with the vine. The complete absence of fruit shows that the branch is no longer drawing life from the stalk. Note that there is no speculation about what might cause a branch to become separated from the vine. The imagery does not suggest that God initiates a person's separation from Christ any more than a vineyard owner causes a branch to wither on the vine. Rather, removing the branch finalizes the separation that has already occurred. This corresponds to the idea that people place themselves under divine judgment by separating themselves from the love that the Father provides through the Son (3:16-18). The passage assumes that the vinedresser will determine when a branch's relationship to the vine has ended. Final judgment belongs to God rather than to members of the community.

The alternative to being removed *(airō)* is to be pruned *(kathairō)*, which seems only somewhat better. After speaking about the faithless being cut off, Jesus now speaks about the faithful being cut back. One might find some assurance in the fact that pruning is God's corrective judgment rather than a final condemnation. At least the branches remain in the vine. But one wonders what pruning means. Initially one might assume that God "prunes" people by subjecting them to painful experiences in order to strengthen their faith. If taken this way, the passage would mean that people are to shoulder their afflictions, believing that God has sent them hardship for their own good. But this is not what Jesus says about God the vinedresser.

Jesus describes God's action with a word that has a double meaning. The term for pruning *(kathairō)* also means cleansing, and cleansing is God's response to human sin. In John's Gospel sin is rooted in unbelief. And the vinedresser prunes away sin through words that identify sin and call people to faith. This is why Jesus goes on to explain that the disciples have already been "pruned" or "cleansed" *(katharoi)* "by the word" that he has spoken to them (15:3). Pruning does not describe the various kinds of suffering that believers experience. Rather, it depicts the way that God the vinedresser addresses sin through the words of Jesus.

The vinedresser's goal is that the branches bear fruit, and the fruit that God desires is love. For the branches to show love, they must receive love, and this comes from Jesus the vine (15:4, 9). Sin or unbelief interferes with fruitbearing because it saps away the strength of the relationship between the vine and the branches, between Jesus and his followers. Therefore, the words that God has given Jesus to speak can act as a cutting tool to remove sin. When Jesus' words identify and confront sin, they cut to the heart of a relational problem. The words do this to make the branches draw more fully on the love that the vine offers, so that they might bear the fruit of love in relationships with others (see pp. 195-96).

God of the Cross and Resurrection

Thus far we have focused on the way God is made known through Jesus' words and signs. It would be easy to stop here, before considering the crucifixion, which brings violent death into the story. It might also be natural to move quickly to the resurrection, treating the crucifixion as a tragic end to Jesus' career, which God soon rectifies by raising him from the dead. Yet the crucifixion raises pointed questions about God, and the Fourth Evangelist does not allow readers to evade them. The Gospel's presentation of God involves both the cross and the resurrection. We will see that according to John, Jesus goes to his death because his opponents condemned him and the power of Satan was operative (see pp. 70-72, 76-80). Yet this raises major issues. If Jesus' death is the result of human sin and demonic evil, does that make the cross a victory for sin and evil? Ultimately a reader is expected to say no, since Jesus is raised from the dead. But if life wins in the end, then why is Jesus crucified at all? Is it because God is unable to prevent it? Does God get caught off-guard by his opponents? Or does God play a role in the crucifixion? John's understanding of the crucifixion and resurrection has multiple dimensions, which will be considered below (see pp. 108-32). Here we will concentrate on God's role in the process.

Restraining Evil

The crucifixion is, in part, the result of human opposition to Jesus. During Jesus' ministry his Jewish opponents insist that he violates the will of God by healing on the Sabbath. He also uses the expression "I Am" for himself in a manner that recalls the name of God. To Jewish hearers, this sounds like blasphemy (8:58-59). By calling God his Father, they argue that he is elevating himself to divine status, making himself equal with God, which is sin (5:17-18; 10:33). Moreover, by restoring the dead man Lazarus to life, Jesus seems to be fomenting a popular movement that could lead to a disastrous revolt against Rome (11:48). In order to prevent this from happening, Jesus' opponents determine to kill the one who gives life to the dead.

One might want to ask why God allowed Jesus' opponents to put him to death. But before getting to that question, the Gospel writer addresses another: Given the intensity of the opposition, why was Jesus able to continue working for so long? One might have expected him to be put to death much sooner. Here the evangelist suggests that God's hand restrains evil during Jesus' public ministry. This is reflected in the theme of the "hour" appointed for Jesus' death. Although Jesus' words and actions provoke angry responses from many people, the Gospel says that no one could arrest him because his "hour" had not yet come (7:30; 8:20).

The evangelist understands that there is a divinely appointed hour for Jesus' death, and until that time Jesus can work with impunity.[15] For example, when Jesus decides to go to Judea, where people want to stone him, he says "Are there not twelve hours in the day?" (11:9). In antiquity the day was always divided into twelve equal parts, winter and summer. The first hour was at dawn, the sixth hour at noon, and the twelfth hour at sunset. Each day had a fixed number of hours. The implication is that Jesus has a "day" or fixed span of time in which to work.

The Gospel tolls Jesus' hour at the beginning of the passion (12:23, 27; 13:1; 17:1). Night falls when the day of his ministry ends and the betrayer departs into the darkness (13:30). Behind the scenes God has held back Jesus' adversaries, but at the appointed hour he allows their will to take its course. Only when God's timing permits it can they arrest Jesus and bring him to trial. During the interrogation, Pilate claims to have the power to do as he wishes with his prisoner. Yet Jesus replies that Pilate has no inherent authority to do as he pleases. He can act against Jesus only because it has been granted from above, from God (19:11).

References to the Scriptures being fulfilled by the events surrounding Jesus' passion also reveal that God knew there would be hostility to Jesus and wove this into his plans. The evangelist observes that when Jesus' public ministry ends there is widespread unbelief among the people. He says this fulfills what Isaiah said: "Lord, who has believed our message" and "He has blinded their eyes" (Isa. 53:1; 6:9; John 12:37-40). To be sure, these fulfillment passages do not suggest that God wills unbelief. According to John, God does not blind people by immersing them in darkness. Rather, human blindness occurs when God sends them the *light* (9:5, 39). The evangelist does not quote the Scriptures to relieve people of responsibility for rejecting the truth and light that Jesus brings. Rather, they show that the unbelief is divinely foreknown. This is underscored when Jesus later says that his words and actions leave people without excuse for their unbelief, for the Scripture said, "They hated me without a cause" (15:22, 25; cf. Pss. 35:19; 69:4).

The betrayal is also brought within the sphere of God's purposes through the citation of Scripture. Referring to the betrayer, Jesus cites the

Scripture passage, "The one who ate my bread has lifted his heel against me" (Ps. 41:9; John 13:18). He later refers again to the betrayer by saying that none of those whom God gave him was lost, "except the son of destruction, in order that the Scripture might be fulfilled" (17:12). The use of Scripture has sometimes been taken to mean that Judas was predestined for his role as betrayer and doomed to destruction because God willed it. English translations sometimes render "son of destruction" *(ho huios tēs apōleias)* as "the one *destined* to be lost" (NRSV) or "the one *doomed* to destruction" (NIV). But note that the English words in italics do not appear in Greek, and adding them actually runs counter to the theology of the Gospel. The expression "son of destruction" means that Judas belongs to destruction and that his actions are characterized by destruction. The reason is that he is allied with the powers of destruction, just as the comparable expression "sons of light" is used for those who belong to the light and are allied with the light because they believe in the light (12:36). There is no suggestion that God destines Judas for destruction.

Popular treatments of Jesus' passion sometimes assume that God needed a betrayer to carry out his purposes, and that Judas happened to be the unlucky person God selected for the task. Yet the idea that God wills the betrayal does not fit the wider context. Throughout the Gospel Judas is given the same favor that the other disciples receive. Jesus includes him among his twelve disciples, even though Judas is already a devil (6:70-71). He washes Judas's feet even though Judas remains unclean (13:10-11). He even feeds Judas, only to have Satan enter him (13:27). The betrayal is explicitly said to come from the devil, not from God (13:2).

In John's account, Judas and other agents of evil can best be understood in light of two theological questions. First, were the powers of evil able to thwart the will of God? John insists that the answer is "no." He says that Jesus knew from the beginning who would betray him and that Judas departs only after Jesus gives him leave to do so (13:27). We will see that at the time of the arrest Jesus subdues the opposition by uttering the divine "I Am," and he secures the release of his disciples before going along willingly with the soldiers. According to the Fourth Gospel, it is clear that the powers of evil do not prevent God's purposes from being accomplished (see pp. 117-20).

The second question is: Was God responsible for the betrayal? After all, Judas fulfilled the Scripture, so perhaps the betrayal was ultimately God's doing (13:18). The evangelist's response, however, is again "no." The Gospel consistently ascribes betrayal to the powers of evil, and says that at each juncture Christ responded to evil with graciousness. None of this suggests that Judas was a victim of a malicious God who destined him for his role.

The Fourth Evangelist asks a different question: *Given the presence of evil, how will God deal with it?* God was not the source of the evil that led to betrayal. Evil is simply a given. So given that evil is present and active, what will God do with it? John will trace the way God directs the forces of evil so as to accomplish his own saving purposes. Satan may work through Judas and others to carry out evil intentions, but these hostile actions are ultimately harnessed for good, since Christ's crucifixion becomes the means for manifesting God's love to the world.

Giving Love and Life Through Crucifixion

The Gospel takes us more deeply into God's role by saying that God commanded Jesus to lay down his life. The context is the passage about the good shepherd, who lays down his life amid thieves and bandits, rather than fleeing like a hired hand. He says, "I lay down my life in order to take it up again. . . . I have power to lay it down, and I have power to take it up again. I have received this command from my Father" (10:17-18). But why would God command Jesus to do this?

God's purpose is indicated in the third chapter of the Gospel where Jesus says, "just as Moses lifted up the serpent in the wilderness, so must the Son of Man be lifted up, in order that whoever believes in him might have eternal life" (3:14-15). This passage indicates that Jesus "must" *(dei)* be lifted up in crucifixion. Yet this divine necessity must be properly understood. Crucifixion is not the goal of God's action; God's purpose is not to have Jesus put to death. Rather, Jesus must be crucified *in order that* people might believe and have life. Faith and life constitute the goal. The cross is a means to that end. For life to be received, people must be brought to faith, and the crucifixion is integral to God's design for doing this.[16]

The saying in John 3 reveals how something resulting from opposition to God can be transformed into a means of giving life with God. Both the serpent on the pole and the Messiah on the cross display the results of human sin and alienation from God. The serpent recalls that people of Moses' time sinned by speaking in mistrust against God and Moses in the wilderness. The result was that God sent poisonous serpents among them, and many died. The serpent on the pole was a visible reminder of sin and

God's judgment upon it (Num. 21:4-7). By analogy, the people of Jesus' time sinned by acting in unbelief against the Messiah and having him put to death. Jesus' opponents "lift him up" to die by crucifixion. This makes the crucified Messiah the visible result of sin (John 8:28; 12:32-33).

At the same time, both episodes show God transforming the result of sin into a means of giving life. In the Old Testament story, Moses puts a bronze serpent on a pole so that people can see it. When they turn to the serpent on the pole, they are confronted with what is killing them. Yet in so doing they receive life by being restored to health (Num. 21:9). In John's Gospel it is Jesus who hangs on the pole or cross. When people turn to him they are confronted with the results of the sin that is killing them. Yet as they turn to the crucified Jesus, they receive eternal life.

People receive eternal life by being brought to faith. Throughout John's Gospel, faith is the opposite of sin. Where sin brings death by alienating people from God, faith brings life by drawing people into relationship with God. When defining the idea, Jesus simply says that "this is eternal life, that they may know you, the only true God, and Jesus Christ whom you have sent" (John 17:3). According to the Fourth Gospel, eternal life is a present reality for those who believe, for in faith people come to know God and so pass from death to life (3:18; 5:24). Physical death remains a reality for people of faith, yet the life that faith brings is called "eternal" because it is a life lived in relationship to the God who is eternal. It begins now in faith and continues beyond the death of the physical body through the power of the resurrection (11:25-26).

By conveying the divine love that evokes faith, the crucifixion gives people eternal life. Jesus explains that the Son of Man was lifted up because "God so loved the world that he gave his only Son, so that everyone who believes in him may not perish but have eternal life" (3:16). In the Fourth Gospel the world is dominated by the evil ruler of this world, and the world's stance toward God is unbelief. Therefore, if people are to receive eternal life, their estrangement from God must be overcome. The crucifixion does this by communicating God's love for the world that hated him. It conveys the love that moved God to give his Son for a world that rejected him. And when the love of God calls forth faith, it overcomes the world's hostility by bringing people back into relationship with the One who made them.

The Fourth Evangelist recognizes that the crucifixion is the product of human sin and satanic evil, but he insists that this does not make the cross a victory for sin and evil. It is God's will to turn the power of falsehood toward the revelation of truth, the power of hatred toward the revelation of love, and the power of death toward the giving of life.

Bringing Life out of Death Through Resurrection

The love God gives through Jesus' crucifixion is a source of life now, for it restores human relationships with God, but the problem of death remains. Those who receive the love of God in faith still face the prospect of dying. So if their relationships with God are to have a future, death itself must be overcome. This is what resurrection does for Jesus and for those who follow him.

God commanded Jesus not only to lay down his life but to take it up again (10:17-18). This means that Jesus' resurrection is the will of God. By commanding Jesus to take up his life, God empowers Jesus to do so. The idea is that God's command gives Jesus the ability to do what God asks. It is analogous to the way Jesus commands a paralyzed man to rise and to take up his mat and walk (5:8). It is also like the command Jesus gives to the dead man Lazarus, whom he tells to come forth from the tomb (11:43). The command gives the recipient the power to perform it.

God's will for resurrection also extends to Jesus' followers. Jesus says, "This indeed is the will of my Father, that all who see the Son and believe in him may have eternal life; and I will raise them up on the last day" (6:40). The promise of resurrection means that the relationship with God that begins in faith has a future. It is not terminated by death. If God's command brings Jesus through death to life, Jesus will also bring his followers through their own deaths to life. The promise of resurrection does not mean that either Jesus or others will avoid death. Rather, it means that they are brought through death to life, for Jesus' resurrection defines the shape of the resurrection hope for those who follow him.

Resurrection is the culminating chapter in John's witness to God. The prologue identified God as the Creator, who brought all things into being through his Word. It also told of God sending the Word to people in embodied form. The resurrection shows that hope itself is to be understood in an embodied way. Jesus died and rose as an embodied person. His body is not discarded but resurrected and transformed, according to the final scenes in the Gospel, where he comes to his disciples. Believers too live embodied lives. To be sure, it is common to assume that death means the end of embodied life and that future hope means a person's spirit is set free for life in heaven. But God creates people as embodied selves; God sends the Word in embodied form; and God gives the hope of an embodied future through the promise of resurrection. We will see that resurrection is not simply a resumption of bodily life with its physical frailties. Rather, resurrection involves the transformation of the whole person that God has made. It is the hope the Creator extends to those he has created and redeemed (see pp. 179-82).

The Father

Jesus calls God his Father throughout his ministry, but we have saved this theme until the end of this chapter because God is identified as the Father of believers only at the end of the Gospel (20:17). For many readers "Father" is a familiar and meaningful way to refer to God. The Lord's Prayer addresses God as "our Father," the creeds express the church's faith in God the Father, and blessings given during worship often speak of God as Father. Others find that "Father" is a problematic expression because it might suggest that God is a male, thereby distancing God from women. It might also imply that God resembles the autocratic fathers of ancient households or the flawed human fathers known in every age. Given the disparate connotations of the word, we must explore the specific traits that John ascribes to God as Father.[17]

The Father of Jesus

God is primarily the Father of Jesus in John's Gospel. Throughout his public ministry, Jesus calls God "the Father" or "my Father." By referring to God in this way, Jesus identifies God in relational terms. A father by definition has children. No one is a father in isolation. Among human beings, one learns what kind of a father someone is by asking how he relates to his children, and the same is true of God. One comes to know God as Father by asking how he relates to Jesus his Son, and then how he relates to the wider community of people who are his children.

There are three major dimensions to God's identity as Father in John's

Gospel: He is a source of life, one who loves his children, and someone worthy of honor and obedience.[18] Each of these has analogies to human fatherhood, which helps to make the term "father" meaningful when used for God. Yet analogies always involve similarities and differences. If God is like a human father in some ways, he is different from a human father in others.

First, God the Father is the source of life for Jesus his Son. Jesus says that "just as the Father has life in himself, so he has granted the Son also to have life in himself" (5:26). Life characterizes who God is. To say that he has life in himself means that his life is not derived from any other source. As Father, God also gives life to his Son. In this sense the term "father" fits God, since a father is a source of life for others. The Gospel, however, distinguishes the way God gives life from the way that ordinary fathers do. According to the prologue, human beings beget children through blood, human desire, and the will of a man. But this is not true of God. Referring to God as Father does not suggest analogies at the physical level (1:12-13). In John's Gospel, "begetting" is often a metaphor for God bringing people to faith. Generating faith fits the Father's relationship to believers, but it does not fit his relationship to Jesus, which is unique.

Jesus is the "only" Son *(monogenēs)* of the Father (1:14, 18; 3:16, 18). God may have many "children" *(tekna)* but only one Son. The Gospel does not say how the Father gives the Son life, only that he does so. Moreover, the Father gives the Son life in a unique way. He enables the Son to have life "in himself," just as the Father does (5:26). This cannot be said of God's other children. If the Son is given life from the Father, this means that the Son is not a second source of life, alongside God. Yet the Son shares fully in the life of the Father, for he too has life in himself. This is what makes it possible for the Son to give life to others. He has received it and shares in it fully, as his Father does.

The Gospel assumes that the relationship of Father to Son existed before the world was made (17:5). Yet the prologue announces this unique relationship at the point of the incarnation. The author initially speaks of God and the Word (1:1-2), but after saying that the Word became flesh, he begins speaking of the Father and only Son (1:14).[19] This is appropriate because the ministry of Jesus the incarnate Son will involve giving people the life that he has received from his Father. This theme is made clear in the Bread of Life discourse. Jesus says, "Just as the living Father sent me, and I live because of the Father, so whoever eats me will live because of me"

(6:57). As the living Father, God is source of life for Jesus and then through Jesus for others. The Father gives life to and through the Son.[20]

Second, love is central to the Father's relationship with the Son. The Father gave love to the Son before the foundation of the world (17:24). This love was at work before the incarnation. It also fits the relationship of the risen and exalted Jesus to God, since the Gospel says that he is now "close to the Father's heart" (1:18). The image is like that of a banquet, where people recline around a table. The one who receives special favor lies with his head on the chest of his father, who is the host. The Gospel uses this familiar image to depict the Father's love for the Son in a manner that can be understood to some extent by human beings. At the same time, it emphasizes the unique character of this relationship. The Father loves the Son in a distinctive way, and this has implications for understanding Jesus' ministry.

Love is what binds the Father to the Son, and this love is what the Son extends to others. Although words for love convey a sense of intimacy and depth of feeling, John understands love primarily as a bond of commitment. It is what will enable Jesus to carry out the will of his Father. There is mutuality in the love between the Father and the Son. If the Father loves the Son it is also true that the Son loves the Father (3:35; 14:31). But the character of God can also be seen in that God also loves the world — and in this case the love is not mutual. God loves a world capable of hating him (3:16, 19-20), which means that God's love is more than a feeling. It is his commitment to the world. And it is out of such committed love that God sends the Son, whom he loves, to bring love into the world that is alienated from its Maker.

The Father shows his love for the Son by giving him responsibilities and the power to carry them out. The Gospel says that the Father loves the Son and puts all things into his hands, showing him all that he himself is doing (3:35; 5:20). The authority the Father gives to the Son expresses his love, and the Son uses this authority to convey love. If the Father has put all things into his hands, the Son uses his hands to wash the feet of his disciples in love. Here, love is expressed in an act of self-giving service (13:1-5). But readers find that the most radical expression of love is the crucifixion, when the Son lays down his life to convey God's love to the world.

The crucifixion both fractures and reconstitutes the familiar patterns of fatherly love. At one level the crucifixion is utterly inexplicable on the basis of love. Ordinarily, a father who loved his son would do everything possible to protect the child from harm. No loving father would allow his son to be treated this way. Yet God is no ordinary Father and Jesus is no ordinary Son. John finds that in the end, the only thing that explains the inexplicable is love. If God truly loves the world as well as the Son, then the only way to bring the world back to relationship is by communicating love to it. And God does this in the crucifixion. The Son is *able* to bring love into the world because he receives love from his Father (3:35; 10:17). The Son is also *willing* to bring love into the world because he himself loves the Father (14:31; 15:9-10). Love is what the Father and Son share, and this love is what is given to human beings — through the life and death of Jesus. The reason is that the love that comes from God makes it possible for people to relate to both Father and Son and to become part of a community that is shaped by their love (17:23-26).

Third, the relationship of Father and Son involves honor and obedience. Honor has to do with the value that someone has in the eyes of another. To honor one's father means holding him in high regard. In this sense genuine honor is an expression of love. To love one's father means showing him respect — and the reverse is also true. A father who loves his children will respect them too. Obedience can be an expression of honor, so that honoring one's father means doing what he asks. But at the human level this becomes problematic if the obedience is coerced rather than coming from respect. Therefore, the Gospel grounds the Son's obedience to the Father in the love and honor that constitute the relationship.

The Father gives the Son commands concerning what to say and do (10:18; 12:49). There is no suggestion that the Son gives commands to the Father. Yet the Father gives these commands out of love and also gives the Son the authority to carry them out. This shows complete confidence in the Son (13:3; 17:2). By carrying out the Father's wishes, Jesus honors his Father and expresses his love for him (8:49; 15:10). Jesus can say that "the Father is greater than I" (14:28) since the Father is the source of life and love for the Son, and the Son in turn keeps the Father's word and commandments. Yet this is not a simple hierarchy since the Father grants that the Son has life "in himself" as the Father has it. When the Father gives the Son a command, he also puts all things into the Son's hands. The mutuality of love is reflected in the Father's desire that the Son be honored as the Father is honored (5:23).[21]

The Father himself gives the Son divine glory, which honors the Son — and more. The Father gave the Son the majesty of divine glory before the world was made (17:24). The incarnate Son glorified or honored the Father on earth by obediently carrying out the works his Father gave him to do (17:4). He also revealed the power of divine glory by healing the sick and raising the dead, and finally revealed the glory of divine love by laying down his life. Yet the Father who raises the dead continues to glorify the Son by bringing him again to the heavenly glory, which he shares in love in his Father's presence (17:5).

The Father of Believers

God is called the Father of believers after Jesus' death and resurrection. Outside the empty tomb Jesus tells Mary Magdalene, "Go to my brothers and say to them, 'I am ascending to my Father and your Father, to my God and your God'" (20:17). The assumption is that people know God as their Father through their relationship to Jesus. This is also the first time that Jesus refers to the disciples as his brothers. If he and his followers have the same Father, then they are members of the same family. This will have implications for the way Christian community is understood (see pp. 197-98). Because God's role as Father is shaped by his bond with Jesus the Son, these same traits are extended to those who follow Jesus.[22]

First, God the Father is the source of life for believers. This is anticipated in the prologue, which speaks of people becoming children of God (1:12-13). The Gospel recognizes that all people are physically begotten through the natural processes associated with blood, flesh, and human desire. But to be born or begotten of God means believing in the Word of God, who gives life. Through this birth into faith, people become children of God. All people come into being through God's Word and are related to him as his creatures (1:4). Yet some people reject the Word while others receive and trust him (1:10-11). A relationship of faith is life-giving in a way that a relationship of animosity toward God is not. Therefore, to believe in God's Word is to be in a life-giving relationship with God, and this is what it means to be God's child in the Johannine sense. We have already seen that the Father gives life through the Son (5:21; 6:57). Later we will also find that giving life is the work of the Spirit, which is the means by which people are begotten from above and given new birth (3:3-5). This new birth is faith, and to continue making people his children through faith is the ongoing work of God (see pp. 137-43).

Second, the Father relates to his children in love. God extended his love to the world through Jesus his Son. As people come to love Jesus, they love the Father who sent him. That is what it means to be a child of God. Jesus says, "If God were your Father, you would love me, for I came from God" (8:42). The love that comes from the Father and the love the faithful show to the Father are not separable topics. Both involve the Son: "the Father himself loves you, because you have loved me and have believed that I came from God" (16:27). Here again love can connote intimacy and depth of feeling, yet it cannot be reduced to emotion. Love is the bond in which people live.

Love from the Father is essential for the children because they are called to give their love to others. This is remarkably unsentimental. The Father's love for the Son was not his private possession but was brought into the world through the incarnation and extended through Jesus' ministry and crucifixion. Those who receive love from Jesus are called to love one another. And expressing love within a community is anything but simple. The Gospel recognizes that faith creates relationships, yet human foibles and failings remain a part of every believer's life — this is evident in the all-too-human side of the disciples in the Gospel. Given this challenge, Jesus assures those who love him and seek to keep his word that "the Father will love them" and be present with them (14:23). The love the Christian community receives from the Father and Son is not its private possession but is to be given as a witness to the world.[23] Where believers love each other the community is "one." This is not an end in itself. Jesus says that love is shown within the community "in order that the world may know that you have sent me and have loved them even as you have loved me" (17:23; see pp. 200-202).

Finally, relationships with the Father are characterized by honor and obedience. The Father gave Jesus commands concerning what to say and do. Jesus in turn gives a command to his followers: Love one another (13:34). To love Jesus is to keep his commandment, and those who do so experience the love of the Father (14:21). In their obedience to Jesus they glorify the Father by making his love known (15:8-10). Jesus loved by serving, even washing feet, which by ordinary social standards was considered degrading. Yet his Father regarded him with honor and glorified him. Jesus' followers are called to serve as he did. They do so knowing that though their service may not be valued by the world, it is valued by God. Jesus gives them the promise, "Whoever serves me, the Father will honor" (12:26).

CHAPTER 3

The World and Its People

The question of what it means to be human has long occupied philoso-
phers and poets, theologians and social scientists. People have a perennial
need to understand who they are as individuals and members of a wider
human community. John's Gospel is a promising place to pursue this question because it presents readers with portraits of human beings who span
the social spectrum, from the highly placed leaders that dominate public
affairs to the hapless beggar sitting on the street. To be sure, none of the
figures in the Gospel actually discuss what it means to be human. Their debates usually focus on the identity of Jesus, and whether he is from God
and is doing the works of God, or whether he is a deceiver and blasphemer.
Jesus often responds by using imagery to describe his heavenly origin and
mission, calling himself the light of the world, the source of living water,
and the bread that comes down from heaven.

As the narrative unfolds, however, the question of identity comes full
circle. People may ask who Jesus is, but their encounters with Jesus also
disclose who they are. If he is the light, then the world lies in darkness; if he
gives the living water, then people must be thirsty; if he is the bread, then
people must hunger. Each of the main images for Jesus has a correspond-
ing image for human beings, and this allows us to ask what the Gospel
might say about what it means to be human. The way that images for people are related to those for Christ reflects an underlying theological perspective, which is that people are to be understood relationally: In John's
Gospel human life is seen in relation to Christ and to the God who sent
him.[1]

The Gospel reveals things that are broadly true of human beings through its portrayals of particular people. Nicodemus is a good example. The setting is Jerusalem, where many are attracted to Jesus because of the signs he performs. Here the narrator makes this broad statement about the people: "Jesus did not entrust himself to them, for he knew all people and needed no one to testify concerning human beings *(anthrōpoi)*, for he himself knew what was in human beings *(anthrōpoi)*" (2:24-25). Then, in the next verse, the narrator directs readers to a test case: "Now there was a human being *(anthrōpos)*," whose name was Nicodemus (3:1). What Jesus knows about human beings in general will be reflected in his encounter with one human being in particular: Nicodemus.[2]

On one level, the Gospel depicts Nicodemus as a unique individual. He is a Pharisee and ruler of the Jews, who is present in Jerusalem and can be called a teacher of Israel. He has his own identity (3:1, 10). On a second level, Nicodemus is also a spokesperson for a wider group. He appears to be alone when he comes to Jesus, but speaks in the plural when he says, "Rabbi, *we* know that you are a teacher who has come from God" (3:2). Jesus also addresses him by using the Greek plural, which we might translate, "you people." He says, "you people do not receive our testimony" and "you people do not believe" (3:11-12). What is true of Nicodemus as an individual is evidently true of a wider circle of people who share his views. On a third level, the Gospel indicates that Nicodemus and his group also have traits that are typically human. The final part of the passage extends the horizon outwards by speaking broadly of "the world" and the human beings *(anthrōpoi)* within it (3:16-21). As Nicodemus comes to Jesus "by night," he serves as the spokesman for a world enmeshed in "darkness" (3:2, 19).[3]

The evangelist recognizes that people have distinctive identities and life stories. In addition to Nicodemus there is a woman with five husbands, a royal official in Galilee, a man blind from birth, and other people. No two of them are alike. John also knows that unique individuals belong to groups. The Gospel includes people who are Jewish, Samaritan, or Roman, and come from different strata of society. They share certain traits in common with the groups to which they belong and raise issues of importance to their groups, like the difference between Jewish and Samaritan worship practices (4:20). Finally, the Gospel shows that the people in one group often have traits in common with those in other groups. There are issues that are not distinctly Jewish or Gentile but are predominantly human problems, such as sin and death, belief and unbelief.

In what follows, we will begin with the theme of life, which is introduced in the prologue, repeated throughout the Gospel, and expressed again in the Gospel's statement of purpose: The author wrote in order that people might believe and have life (20:31). Then we will look at the issues that threaten life. These are multidimensional. We will begin at the physical level with questions about suffering and death, and then consider the issues of relating to God that are suggested by metaphorical use of hunger, thirst, and darkness. Next we will move to the Gospel's understanding of sin, which raises questions about human accountability and human bondage. Then we will explore the problem of evil, which is a force at work within the human sphere. Each level discloses an aspect of the human situation, and together they give a sense of "the world" portrayed in John's Gospel.

Created for Life

The Gospel sets human beings in the context of creation. The opening lines say that "all things came into being" through God's Word (1:3). People exist because of this creative activity of God. The basic term for a human being is *anthrōpos* or person (2:25; 9:1; 17:6).[4] And to be a person is to share in flesh or *sarx* (17:2). Flesh is the means of human procreation (1:13), it is limited and cannot generate relationships with God (3:6), and it is also subject to death. But flesh is not inherently evil; it belongs to the creation. People also have a heart, which is linked to the emotions (14:1; 16:6), to the will and intentions (13:2), and to understanding (12:40). And people have a *psychē*, which is sometimes translated "soul," but is better understood as "self." The *psychē* gives a person life, consciousness, and emotion (12:27), but it is not immortal. John does not work with a dualistic view of human beings, which distinguishes the mortal flesh from an immortal soul. To die means laying down one's *psychē* (10:18; 12:25; 13:37), just as it means giving up one's flesh (6:51). The whole person includes flesh, heart, and self *(psychē)*.

God gives people "life" *(zōē)* through the action of his Word. The prologue says, "That which has come into being in him was life, and the life was the light for human beings" (1:3-4). As noted earlier, human life has a physical dimension: the beating of the heart and breathing of the lungs. The people who are alive in the bodily sense also have a need to relate to God in faith. This is integral to the Gospel's understanding of true life, as we noted in the previous chapter (see pp. 30-32). People do not have life in themselves. They must receive life from an outside source. The idea that human beings are created in this way means that they have an inescapable need for the life that comes from God. People may or may not be aware of this need, and may seek to meet their need for life in ways that actually take them away from God, but the Gospel assumes that the *need* for what brings life is inescapable. It is built into the structure of human existence.[5]

"Life" is a central theme for John, though the concept is never fully defined. Instead, the characteristics of "life" are suggested by the Gospel's imagery. Life is described as light, which is associated with knowing God and his Word (1:4, 9-13). It also connotes truth and love rather than falsehood and hatred (3:19-21). Elsewhere Jesus says, "Whoever follows me will not walk in darkness but will have the light of life" (8:12). To walk in the light is to have a sense of direction, in contrast to those who walk in darkness and do not know where they are going (12:35). Light conveys a sense of purpose rather than futility.

When Jesus says that he has come to provide abundant life, he pictures himself as a gate to a sheepfold. Here life connotes a sense of belonging. Those who enter through the gate become part of a flock or community of people. Jesus traces the movement of life from the sheepfold or gathered community out into the world and back again. This sense of relationship to God and a community of people is part of a life that is truly abundant (10:7-10). The centrality of the need for life is evident in the way the Gospel continually returns to the theme, speaking of the living water that springs up to eternal life (4:14) and the bread of life, who gives life to the world (6:33, 35). Jesus identifies himself as the resurrection and the life (11:25) and the way, the truth, and the life (14:6). The reason that the Gospel was written was that people might have the life for which they were created (20:31).

The Problem of Death

Life is an issue for the Gospel writer because there are forces that interfere with it and threaten to bring it to an end. In the physical sense people are subject to illness, which can take life away. Sickness and death are prominent in the Gospel narrative, where people turn to Jesus for healing. Moreover, in the relational sense people have a need for God that they cannot meet from within themselves. Metaphors of hunger, thirst, and darkness depict this need. Ironically, this need for life can turn people away from God and lead to "death" in the sense of final separation from God. This is the antithesis of the life God offers. We begin with physical life and then move to its wider relational aspects.

Physical Suffering and Death

John's Gospel often pictures people in situations of physical need. A royal official has a son who is dying of a fever, prompting the man to travel half-way across Galilee seeking help (4:46-47). A man who cannot walk has been ill for thirty-eight years, and now lies beside a pool in Jerusalem, along with other blind, lame, and paralyzed people (5:2-5). Another man, blind from birth, sits on a street in Jerusalem, begging in order to make a living (9:1, 8). In the case of the official's son, the illness threatens to bring about a sudden death. In the other two cases, paralysis and blindness diminish life more slowly, but in each episode, the physical problems are real.

If God is the giver of life, one may wonder why illness exists or why one person becomes ill and another does not. Yet the Gospel does not offer theological explanations for these questions. Instead, the Gospel reframes the issue. This is done most directly in the story of the man born blind. When the disciples see the blind man sitting along the street in Jerusalem, they ask, "Rabbi, who sinned, this man or his parents, so that he was born blind?" (9:2). Their assumption is that physical suffering must be a form of divine punishment. There was biblical warrant for assuming that a person could suffer because of the sins of his parents, since God warned that he would visit "the iniquities of the fathers upon the children to the third and fourth generation" (Exod. 20:5). Other passages insisted that God would not make a child suffer for the sins of the parents, but would punish each one for his or her own sin (Ezek. 18:20).

Jesus, however, *turns away from speculative questions about the cause of the blindness to ask what might be done with the blindness.* He says, "Neither this man nor his parents sinned" (John 9:3). The disciples want to know what caused the man's condition, but Jesus says that none of their perspectives fits the situation, and he refuses to offer an alternative explanation. To be clear, Jesus is not saying that the beggar and his parents are sinless people. The point is that the man is not being punished with blindness because of some specific transgression. Jesus does not categorically reject the idea that God might ever punish someone for sin, and John's Gospel does assume that sinners are subject to judgment (3:36; 5:29). Similarly, Jesus does not deny that human actions might bring negative consequences, since people do perform actions that injure themselves and their children. The idea is that suffering is not always a penalty for some wrongful act.

Instead of looking backwards to determine what caused the blindness, Jesus simply accepts it as a given. And given the blindness, whatever its cause, Jesus looks ahead to what he might do about it. Many English translations obscure the shift by paraphrasing what seems to be an incomplete sentence: "Jesus answered, 'Neither this man nor his parents sinned; *he was born blind* so that God's works might be revealed in him'" (9:3 NRSV); or "'Neither this man nor his parents sinned,' said Jesus, 'but *this happened* so that the work of God might be displayed in his life'" (9:3 NIV). The words in italics, which do not appear in Greek, are added by the translators. The problem is that they wrongly imply that God caused the blindness so that Jesus could use it to reveal divine glory. Moreover, the NRSV even omits the contrastive word *alla* ("but") that appears in Greek and is essential to the meaning of the sentence.

The best way to approach the passage is simply to follow the Greek wording, recognizing that the sentence begins in 9:3 and continues in the next verse: "Neither this man nor his parents sinned, but in order that [*all' hina*] the works of God might be revealed in him we must work the works of him who sent me while it is day" (9:3-4a).[6] Jesus does not explain the cause of the blindness. He simply accepts it as a given and declares that he will deal with it in order to do God's work of healing.

The same pattern occurs later in the Gospel, when Jesus' friend Lazarus becomes seriously ill. Lazarus's sisters send a message to Jesus, who is quite some distance away, saying, "Lord, he whom you love is ill" (11:3). Their comment is significant because it assumes that those who are loved by Jesus can and do become terminally ill. The Gospel even emphasizes that "Jesus loved Martha and her sister and Lazarus" (11:5). It seems clear that the illness is not an act of divine hostility toward Lazarus. Then Jesus says, "This illness does not lead to death; rather it is for the glory of God" (11:4). Note that there is no speculation about the cause of the illness. Jesus does not say that God caused the illness in order to use it as an occasion for revealing his glory. Instead, he simply accepts the illness as a given and will work forward from there to bring glory to God by giving life.

The Gospel does not attempt to explain why some people are healed and others are not. It is not that those who believe are always restored to health while those who do not believe suffer illness. The royal official shows signs of faith (see p. 166), but the invalid at the pool of Bethzatha does not, as we will see (p. 67). Jesus is free to heal where there is faith, and free to heal where there is no faith. His acts of healing set him on the side of life over against death. Yet the Gospel assumes that death remains an issue for all people, including the followers of Jesus. The message of resurrection actually presupposes that death is real. The promise of resurrection is not that people escape dying, but are given life through and out of death — something that must be considered further below (see pp. 179-82).

Relational Hunger, Thirst, and Darkness

Many episodes in the Gospel show that the physical dimensions of human need point to needs that are of another order. The images of hunger, thirst, and darkness are based in human experiences of deprivation. All of them recognize the need for things that come to people from outside themselves. Those who hunger, thirst, and are in darkness require food, water, and light from external sources. If the needs expressed in hunger and thirst are not met, they eventually culminate in death — and death is often signified by darkness. This pattern enables the images of thirst, hunger, and darkness to function as metaphors for the human need to relate to God in faith. The Gospel uses these images to show that people have an inherent need for God, yet it also discloses that the need may take people away from God and prompt them to seek life in other ways.

We begin with the image of *hunger,* which takes on theological meaning in the story of the feeding of the five thousand (6:1-15).[7] Jesus has the crowd lie down on the grass, then feeds them with five barley loaves and two fish. After everyone has had enough, the disciples gather up twelve baskets full of leftovers so that nothing is lost. The Gospel presents this as a sign that functions on two levels: On the physical level this sign recognizes that people need food for their bodies. Jesus does not tell hungry people to ignore their need for daily bread; rather, he meets this need by giving them food and collecting twelve baskets of leftovers. They have all they need to sate their physical hunger. On another level Jesus also assumes that people hunger for relationship with God, and this hunger presupposes a human separation from God that must be overcome.

The problem becomes evident when the well-fed crowd pursues Jesus the next day in the hopes of acquiring yet another free lunch. In responding to Jesus this group collapses the two levels of the sign into one. They reduce the need for a relationship with God to a need for more bread. Having eaten their fill of the loaves, they simply seek more loaves. They seek a material solution to their relational problem. Therefore, Jesus tells them, "Do not work for the food that perishes, but for the food that endures to eternal life, which the Son of Man will give you" (6:27). To some extent this comment observes that material food does not endure. The ordinary bread that people eat each day spoils, and even the manna that God gave people in Moses' time deteriorated in a matter of hours. Those who tried to hoard the manna in the wilderness found that it melted away in the heat of the sun (Exod. 16:20-21).

The comment also warns that those who make perishable food the ultimate object of their life have set a direction that will end in their own deaths. The passage plays on the different dimensions of the meaning of death. The perishing that Jesus warns about goes beyond what is physical; it involves final separation from God. This kind of death is the counterpart to eternal life. The Fourth Gospel assumes that eternal life begins in the present, as people relate to God in faith. It also recognizes that people of faith do die. Their hearts stop beating and the lungs no longer breathe. Yet the relationship that begins in faith is not terminated by death, and in this sense people of faith do not die, since they are not cut off from God and have the promise of resurrection (John 6:33, 39). The crowd in John 6, however, fixes its attention on finite and perishable food in ways that turn them away from the divine giver. When this pattern of alienation is allowed to take its course, it leads to final separation from God, which is death in the ultimate sense.

The solution to this problem would seem to be obvious: People must redirect their attention to God and his gifts. After all, Jesus says, "I am the bread of life. Whoever comes to me will not hunger and whoever believes in me will not thirst" (6:35). The crowd grumbles when he says this, but the point seems clear: People are to come to Jesus. What complicates matters is that people are evidently not capable of doing what Jesus says. He tells his hearers, "No one can come to me unless the Father who sent me draws him" (6:44). This makes a surprising judgment on the human condition. Human beings not only do not come but apparently *cannot* come to the bread of life. Jesus' startling statement is made without qualification.

When he says that "no one" can come he includes all people. When he says that no one "can" come, he points to a fundamental inability of human beings to come. In human terms, coming to Jesus is impossible.

Jesus goes on to say, however, that people *can* be drawn to him by God's action. Human beings cannot overcome the barrier separating them from the source of life, but God can overcome the barrier. The bread of life must not only be received by faith, it must evoke faith; and when the divine gift evokes faith, human separation from God is overcome, and people are brought to life with God.

The image of *thirst* is closely related to that of hunger.[8] It is introduced in Jesus' conversation with the Samaritan woman (4:1-15). As the story opens, Jesus sits beside a well and the woman comes to draw water. On an ordinary physical level, the situation assumes that people need water. A lack of water makes people thirsty, and thirst makes them seek water in order to live. It is natural that the woman comes to the local well with her jar, looking for the water she needs for daily life. Jesus initially asks her for water, saying "Give me a drink" (4:7). But then he abruptly shifts the conversation to the level of thirst for God. He says, "If you knew the gift of God, and who it is that is saying to you, 'Give me a drink,' you would have asked him and he would have given you living water" (4:10).

The playful turn in the conversation makes one wonder who really is thirsty. The woman comes looking for ordinary water and is now told about the water that quenches a thirst she did not even know she had. Jesus' offer seems ludicrous, since he does not even have a bucket to carry the water. So Jesus says, "Everyone who drinks of this water" from the well "will be thirsty again, but those who drink of the water that I will give them will never be thirsty," for it will "become in them a spring of water welling up to eternal life" (4:13-14). The woman asks for the water, though she seems to have no idea what it is — she seems to think of it as a plumbing miracle, which will eliminate the need to haul water from the well each day. Readers, however, can see that Jesus speaks of thirst as the need for God and of living water as the gift that brings people into relationship with God (4:10).

The conversation shifts to the woman's personal life, but soon the question of God resurfaces. After Jesus speaks about the woman's various husbands, she identifies him as a prophet and asks whether worship should take place on the nearby Samaritan mountain or in Jerusalem. The text suggests an analogy between the woman's daily life and her people's worship life. Just as she keeps coming to the well for water, her people keep coming to the mountain to worship. When speaking about water, Jesus referred to the gift that the woman did not know, and when speaking about the mountain he says that her people worship what they do not know (4:10, 22). The problem is not that the Samaritans refuse to worship — they do worship — the problem is where their worship leads them.

Jesus says, "You worship what you do not know; we worship what we know, for salvation is from the Jews" (4:22). From a Jewish perspective, Samaritan worship is directed away from God, not toward him. Although Jews and Samaritans shared some common traditions, going back to Jacob and his predecessors (4:12), it was said that Samaritan worship included other deities, which had been introduced into the region centuries before (2 Kings 17:29-41). Their practice was considered a departure from true faith. To say that they worship what they "do not know" means that something has taken God's place. Similar expressions were commonly used for various kinds of false worship: "All who make idols are nothing . . . their witnesses neither see nor know"; indeed, "they do not comprehend . . . they cannot understand" (Isa. 44:9, 18).[9] Samaritan practice may reflect the *need* to worship God, yet it has led them away from God.

What is remarkable is that Jesus does not say that the Samaritans should redirect their worship from their own mountain to Jerusalem. Apparently, the problem cannot be resolved by a shift in geographical focus. Rather, Jesus says that it is God who "seeks" people to worship in spirit and truth. And he anticipates that people will be brought to true worship through the Spirit, which is the "living water" that God will send (John 4:23-24). Through the agency of the Spirit, God engenders the faith that issues into worship that is true (see pp. 203-6).

Thus far the thirst for God has been a Samaritan issue, yet several chapters later the image of thirst is used for those who worship in the temple in Jerusalem. The setting is the feast of Booths or Tabernacles *(Sukkoth)*, a festival that recognizes the need for water. The festival commemorates the forty years that Israel sojourned in the desert during the time of Moses. At that time the people were desperately short of water, and God commanded Moses to strike a rock so that a stream flowed from it in the desert (Exod. 17:1-7). Remembering this, pilgrims came to the temple in Jesus' time, as prayers for rain were offered. The festival occurred at the end of a long dry season, when it was clear that people needed showers from heaven to sustain life and productivity in the coming year. The priest poured water from a golden pitcher onto the temple's altar as a visible petition that God would send rain on the land, providing life and growth during the coming year.[10]

On the last day of the festival Jesus says, "If any one thirst, let him come to me," promising to give people living water (John 7:37-39). People at the festival presumably know their need for rainwater, but Jesus speaks of another kind of thirst. The need is like that expressed by the Psalmist: "My soul thirsts for God, for the living God. When shall I come and behold the face of God?" (Ps. 42:2; cf. 63:1; 143:6). The difference is that the psalmist is aware of the need for God, whereas the people in John's Gospel do not express their longing in this way; Jesus is the one who names their thirst. It seems odd to speak to people in the temple this fashion. After all, when Jesus was in Samaria he affirmed that "we worship what we know, for salvation is from the Jews" (John 4:22). But apparently this does not mean that everyone who comes to the temple knows God. What reveals the problem, from the perspective of the evangelist, is their negative reaction to Jesus. If the worshipers knew God, they would presumably welcome Jesus, whom God has sent. But this is not the case. Jesus has come to do the works of God, yet they cannot comprehend where Jesus has come from or where he is going, and from a Johannine perspective this means they do not know God (7:28).

The Gospel depicts Jews and Samaritans in the same way, as people who thirst. Because they have the same need, Jesus offers them the same gift: living water, which in John's Gospel is an image for the Spirit of God and the revelation that Jesus provides (see pp. 143-46). Underlying the image of thirst is that people have a need that must be met from a source outside themselves. People do not have the capacity to meet physical thirst with what they have within themselves. Similarly, their thirst for life with God must be met by an outside source. It must be met by divine action through the work of Jesus and activity of the Spirit.

Finally, we come to the image of *darkness*.[11] Like hunger and thirst, darkness can identify a need, in this case the need for light. Yet the image of darkness encompasses several dimensions. These are suggested in the prologue, where the light of life is given by God's Word. The "light shines in the darkness and the darkness did not overcome it" (1:5). On one level darkness connotes not knowing, since it is the opposite of the Word that brings knowledge of God. On a second level the darkness connotes sin and evil, since it is opposed to God and his Word. On a third level the darkness connotes death, since it is the opposite of the light of life.

Theologically, all three levels will be important. The prologue also shows that darkness can act as a power that actively seeks to overcome the light (1:5). The narrative will show that darkness does not overcome Jesus, who is the light of the world, but darkness can overcome others, much as travelers on a road are engulfed in darkness when night falls over them (12:35-36). What is peculiar is that no one wants to be hungry or thirsty, but people may want to remain in darkness. As it surrounds them, people may embrace it, take refuge in it, and find comfort in its shadows. And one wonders how this can be.

The Gospel explores human darkness in its account of Nicodemus, the Pharisee and ruler of the Jews, who visits Jesus in Jerusalem. Nicodemus comes to Jesus "by night" (3:2). The darkness may simply describe the setting, yet it also suggests something about Nicodemus's character. Initially the darkness suggests that Nicodemus lacks understanding. He is "in the dark" about the ways of God, yet he is not aware of this and thinks that he knows more than he really does. When meeting Jesus, Nicodemus says, "Rabbi, *we know* that you are a teacher who has come from God, for no one can do these signs that you do unless God is with him" (3:2). Nicodemus seems to be in the know, but is he?

Jesus' quick responses expose the limits of Nicodemus's understanding. He says that no one can see the kingdom of God without being born anew (3:3). Although Jesus speaks of divine things, Nicodemus plods along on the earthbound level, incredulous at the thought of an old man crawling back into the womb to be born physically all over again. Jesus contrasts physical birth with birth from the Spirit, then likens the Spirit to the wind, whose origin and destination are beyond human knowing (3:4-8). Nicodemus's attempt to understand this grinds to a halt as he is forced to ask, "How can these things be?" And Jesus points out that Nicodemus, who initially claimed to know so much, really does not comprehend the ways of God (3:9-10).

Jesus speaks to Nicodemus as an individual, but expands the scope of his comments when he says that no human being has the inherent ability to see or enter the kingdom of God (3:3, 5). The assumption is that all people begin at a point outside the kingdom and that those born of the flesh do not have the capacity to enter the kingdom on their own. The "kingdom of God" is another way of speaking about the life in relationship with God that is depicted later in this chapter (3:14-18). The kingdom is where eternal life is found. People enter through faith, and faith is not self-generated. Faith is the new birth that comes through an encounter with the love of God, which comes to people from outside themselves, through God's gift of the Son and the working of the Spirit (see pp. 137-43).

The passage describes Jesus as the light, who has come into the darkened world, and one would assume that people would welcome the gifts he brings. But the Gospel recognizes that this is not necessarily the case. It describes a situation in which some people are drawn to the light and others are repelled by it. Some come to the brightness and others flee to the shadows (3:16-21). If people come, it shows that they have found that not knowing is confining and that sin is oppressive. By way of contrast, those who reject the light prefer the darkness. They find the truth to be unwelcome, preferring not to know. Rather than experiencing sin as oppressive, they find it appealing. For them the darkness is comfortable, as it is for the thief who works during the night so as not to be seen (Job 24:13-17). They have the illusion that in the darkness they are protected from judgment. Yet according to John the reverse is true. By embracing the darkness that alienates them from God, people actually place themselves under judgment; and by rejecting the light of life, they travel toward the darkness that ends in death (John 3:19-20).

John's Gospel recognizes that human beings are complex and subject to conflicting impulses. Some passages picture thirsty people, who have a need for the life that comes from God and who search for something to meet this need. Hunger reflects a similar idea, and the Gospel shows how the hunger to overcome one's separation from the source of life can produce a misguided impulse to fix attention on material gifts rather than on the divine giver. Darkness depicts people embracing what alienates them from God, turning the lack of knowledge into a new certainty and unbelief into a new faith. People are both estranged from and attracted to God. They need what they reject, yet have a propensity to reject what they need. And this problem takes us to the Gospel's understanding of sin.

The Problem of Sin

Sin, in John's Gospel, is first a relational concept. It is unbelief or alienation from God, and it is therefore the antithesis of faith.[12] Throughout the Gospel, people relate rightly to God by believing in Jesus, the one whom God sent. If faith involves knowing God, trusting God, and being faithful to

God, then sin is the opposite of faith. It means not comprehending the truth about God and Jesus (8:24; 16:9), and not knowing the truth about oneself. It is a blindness to one's own condition, a pretension to see clearly even when one cannot see (9:39-41).

This primary sin of unfaith is expressed in the many "sins" or wrongful actions that people commit. John does not speak of sins primarily as transgressions of a moral code, but he does assume that human actions reflect underlying commitments. Faith in God rightly leads to faithfulness in relationships with other people, just as alienation from God is expressed in unfaithfulness in other relationships. Sin is depicted as opposition to God and Jesus, and this is evident in animosity toward those who belong to Jesus (3:20; 7:7; 15:22-24).

Sin is closely linked to death, and John's Gospel traces this process in two ways: First, sin can move people to take away life from other people. This is most evident in Jesus' opponents. Because they do not believe him, they denounce him and manage to have him put to death. Their unbelief results in his crucifixion. Second, sin ultimately leads to death for the sinners themselves. In John's Gospel, death is a process. If true life is lived in relationship with God, then those who are hostile to God separate themselves from the source of life. Their relationship with God dies, even while their bodies are still functioning. As this separation continues, it can eventually become permanent; so that sin culminates in the death that is final separation from God (8:21, 24).

Unbelief and Its Effects

The Gospel presupposes that there were problems in people's relationships to God before Jesus' ministry began. The noun "sin" *(hamartia)* is first used by John the Baptist, who introduces Jesus as "the Lamb of God who takes away the sin of the world" in 1:29. It is precisely because of sin that the Lamb is sent to take it away. Because of this, it is startling that the Gospel can also say that Jesus *provokes* sin. When speaking to his disciples at the last supper, Jesus speaks of opposition from the unbelieving world and says, "If I had not come and spoken to them, they would not have sin; but now they have no excuse for their sin" (15:22). Again, "If I had not done among them the works that no one else did, they would not have sin. But now they have hated both me and my Father" (15:24).

These sayings do not mean that the world was sinless until Jesus came. Rather, they indicate that Jesus brings the underlying problem in the world's relationship to God into the open. If Jesus is from God, as the Gospel says he is, then those who reject Jesus show their alienation from the God who sent him. Their negative response to Jesus gives definition to the relational issue, so that it can be identified specifically as "sin."[13] Those who linger in the darkness might claim they cannot be faulted if they have never been shown the light. But in Jesus the light has come. Therefore, by its hatred for Jesus, the world shows its true character and no longer has an "excuse" or pretext for its sin (15:22). By its portrayal of specific people, the Gospel shows how encounters with Jesus "expose" the problem of sin so that it can be seen by the readers (3:20).

The verb "sin" *(hamartanō)* is first used in the story of the invalid in 5:1-16. The setting is the pool of Bethzatha in Jerusalem, where many people with physical ailments come in the hope of a cure. Among them is a man who cannot walk, who has been lying beside the pool for a long time. At the outset nothing is said about sin, belief, or unbelief. Jesus simply approaches him and asks whether he wants to be healed. Rather than giving Jesus an affirmative answer, however, the man complains that he has no one to put him into the pool when the water is mysteriously troubled.

The man's preoccupation with the water is closer to a belief in magic than to what the Gospel considers a belief in God. He seems to assume that those who enter the water at the right moment will be healed automatically and that latecomers will not be helped. From his perspective, everything depends on a well-timed entry into the pool. This belief seems to have little connection with the God of Israel, who does not limit his favor to those who have the best sense of timing. To be sure, the scribes who later copied the Gospel improved the man's image by ascribing the movement of the water to an angel of the Lord, which brings some vestige of God into the picture (5:4). But the verse about the angel is not included in the best ancient manuscripts, and it has rightly been deleted from most modern translations. As the text stands, there is no mention of God in the healing process connected with the pool.

Despite the man's unresponsiveness, Jesus tells him to take up his mat and walk, and immediately the man is healed (5:9a). This means that his physical problem is resolved by the action of Jesus. So having been healed, the man does get up and leave (5:9b). Yet other problems remain unresolved. The man quickly runs into trouble with the Jewish authorities, who reprimand him for carrying his mat on the Sabbath. Without missing a beat, the man tries to evade responsibility by saying that he is only doing what he had been told, since his healer had directed him to carry the mat. Unfortunately, the man had not bothered to learn his healer's name (5:10-13).

Jesus identifies the issue when he finds the man and tells him, "Do not persist in sin, so that nothing worse happens to you" (5:14). The man's sin is his persistent unresponsiveness to his healer, and Jesus warns that by continuing in this pattern of unbelief he will encounter something worse than a reprimand for a Sabbath violation. Carrying the mat brought the man under the judgment of the Jewish authorities, but unbelief brings him under the judgment of God, which is something "worse." Yet despite the warning the pattern continues, and the man reports his healer to the authorities, who begin persecuting Jesus (5:15-16). In the case of the invalid, sin is brought to light as he persistently seeks to protect his own interests, even when this means putting his healer at risk of persecution. His unbelief is expressed in action.

John's understanding of sin is further developed in scenes where conflicting viewpoints are introduced. Jesus' opponents work with an understanding of sin that is based on their interpretation of the Jewish law. From their perspective, Jesus himself is the sinner because he seems to violate the commands of God. Jesus cures the invalid at Bethzatha on the Sabbath and later does the same for the man born blind (5:16; 9:14). The disputes that erupt show readers the issue. According to Jewish law, people are to refrain from working on the Sabbath (Exod. 20:8-11). The Pharisees regard healing as a form of work, and according to tradition people are not to heal on the Sabbath unless a person's life is in danger. Since this is not the case with the man's congenital blindness, Jesus could have waited a day to heal him. Moreover, when curing the blind man, Jesus had made mud from spittle, but kneading was forbidden on the Sabbath.

Some of the Jewish authorities conclude that Jesus must be a sinner, since his actions violate the Sabbath laws, but others counter that a sinner would not have the ability to do such a healing (John 9:16). The problem is that a lawbreaker should not be able to do miracles and a miracle-worker should not break the law. The incongruity of the whole affair makes them doubt whether a healing has taken place, so they question the man's parents in the hope of discovering that he had not been blind in the first place. Then they can throw the case out of court. But the parents testify that the man was born blind and now can see. This puts the issue back in the lap of the Pharisees (9:18-23).

Now that the healing has been authenticated, the Pharisees speak with one voice: They declare that Jesus is a sinner *(hamartōlos)* because he violates the law as they understand it (9:24). As the evidence for the healing becomes increasingly clear, the Pharisees become increasingly strident in their denunciations of Jesus as a sinner. Their point of view has its own logic, but the continued exchanges with the beggar disclose its flaws. The Jewish leaders first rule that Jesus must be a sinner and only later bother to ask how the healing was done (9:26). Yet issuing a verdict before completing an investigation violates the legal tradition that the Pharisees are seeking to uphold, which undermines their position. Dissatisfied with the beggar's reply, they declare that they do not know where Jesus is from, a remark that is intended to discredit Jesus (9:29). But from the perspective of the evangelist, this actually discredits the Pharisees by showing that they act on the basis of ignorance, not insight. In order to condemn Jesus for a breach of Sabbath law they must accept the fact that Jesus has healed, while suppressing the point that he did so by the power of God. The beggar points out the incongruity: If the power to heal really comes from God, then the Pharisees are effectively saying that God promotes sin by empowering Jesus to violate the law by curing a man of blindness. And for him, this makes no sense.

The opposite view, which is that of the Gospel writer, is that sin is exposed when people reject Jesus. The idea is that Jesus does not sin by healing on the Sabbath. Rather, his opponents reveal their sin — their unbelief — by denouncing Jesus for healing. If God gives life on the Sabbath, then healing on the Sabbath is congruent with God's purposes. It does not violate the law (5:17-24; 7:19-24). Giving sight to the blind is something that is done by an agent of God, not an opponent of God. So Jesus cannot be condemned as a sinner (9:31-33). The Gospel assumes that Scripture bears witness to Jesus (5:39) — and there are passages that speak of God's servant opening the eyes of the blind (Isa. 42:6-7). The issue is not whether the law is valid, but whether the Pharisees' interpretation of it is legitimate. The evangelist assumes that if God is active in Jesus' healings, then those who invoke the law against Jesus show that they do not understand God's purposes. The Pharisees, however, remain adamant; and they put their unbelief into action by declaring that the beggar who defends Jesus must also be a sinner. Then they put him out of their community (John 9:34).

Now Jesus says, "I came into this world for judgment, so that those who do not see may see, and those who do see may become blind." The Pharisees reply, "Surely we are not blind, are we?" And Jesus responds, "If you were blind, you would not have sin. But now that you say, 'We see,' your sin remains" (9:39-41). At the beginning of this episode, Jesus identifies himself as the light of the world (9:5). The light shines with increasing intensity as Jesus enables a blind man to see, and the truth of the healing is repeatedly verified by the man and his parents. But the light of truth is like the light of the sun. Its radiance enables some to see, yet it can blind those who stare into it without blinking. This is the situation of the Pharisees. The clearer the truth becomes, the more firmly they reject it. Their blindness to the light of Jesus reveals blindness to the God who sent him. This manifests the sin of unbelief. The Gospel assumes that the problem was there before Jesus came. His opponents' estrangement from God did not begin when he first performed the healing. But their negative response to the light Jesus brings means that their sin "remains," and it is exposed for the readers to see.

Sin and the Crucifixion

The dynamics of human sin led to Jesus' crucifixion, according to John. In the story of the passion we find the Gospel revealing sin through its portrayal of both Jewish and Roman leaders. This shows that sin cannot be limited to Jewish or Gentile circles. It is a human problem. Modern readers of the passion narrative often concentrate on its social and political dimensions, tracing ways in which Pilate and the Jewish authorities maneuver through society's structures of power in order to secure their own aims and safeguard their own interests. And there clearly are political factors. John observes that the Jewish leaders see Jesus as a potential rebel against Roman rule, a figure whose popularity threatens to make the Romans take military action against the Jewish people. Therefore, to prevent the movement from growing, they determine to put Jesus to death (11:47-50). The problem is that under Roman rule they are not allowed to carry out the death sentence themselves, which means they must collaborate with the Roman governor to have Jesus executed (18:31). They tell Pilate, "Everyone who makes himself king opposes the emperor" (19:12), and Pilate soon hands Jesus over to be crucified.[14]

In John's worldview, however, these political dynamics manifest an underlying theological reality, which is the power of sin. John seeks to show that Jesus' kingship cannot be understood in ordinary political terms, since Jesus does not "make himself" a king and does not allow other people to do so. After Jesus feeds the five thousand, the people try to make him king, but he flees; and when crowds later welcome him with palm branches and acclaim him King of Israel, he hides himself from them (6:15; 12:36). During his trial, Jesus tells Pilate that his kingdom is not of this world, meaning that his power comes from God above, not from human beings below, which is why he does not allow his disciples to follow the earthly practice of using violence to prevent his arrest (18:10-11, 36). The implication is that those who reject Jesus reject the power that comes from God above, and this is what the Jewish authorities do, according to John. When Pilate asks whether he should release King Jesus, they reject this idea and ask instead for Barabbas the insurrectionist *(lēstēs)*, a figure associated with the violence of the world (18:40). While turning away from Jesus, whose power comes from above, they embrace the power of the world below.[15]

The disclosure of the Jewish authorities' estrangement from God continues when they tell Pilate, "We have a law, and according to that law he ought to die because he has made himself Son of God" (19:7). This charge marks the culmination of disputes that have developed throughout the Gospel. Jesus healed on the Sabbath, claiming to do so because God his Father worked on the Sabbath. He used the expression "I Am" for himself in ways that had divine overtones, and claimed to be one with the Father. His Jewish listeners regarded these as blasphemous attempts to make himself God, which warranted death under the law (5:17-18; 8:58-59; 10:30-33). Therefore, the evangelist regards their desire to have Jesus crucified as a matter of unfaith, a refusal to believe that Jesus had come from God.

The conflict reaches its climax when Jesus and the Jewish authorities come before Pilate's judgment seat. Having previously supported the release of Barabbas the insurrectionist, the Jewish leaders now seem to change course by telling Pilate that they are loyal subjects of the empire, who have no king but Caesar (19:15). From a political perspective, this tactic is at least partially successful, for Pilate hands Jesus over to be crucified. But from the Gospel's theological perspective, affirming Caesar's exclusive lordship means rejecting God's lordship. Having denounced Jesus for trying to make himself Son of God, the Jewish leaders support the claims of the emperor, the man who was called "son of god" since he occupied the throne of his deified predecessors.[16] On one level it seems inconsistent for the Jewish leaders initially to support an insurrectionist and then to claim loyalty to Rome. Yet on another level their actions show a consistent alienation from God, since they repeatedly reject the king who has come from above in order to embrace the powers of the world below, whether in the form of Barabbas or Caesar.

We now turn to Pilate the Roman governor, who plays a different political role in the story. It is not always clear whether readers are to see Pilate as a weak and indecisive figure or as a powerful and shrewd administrator (18:29–19:22).[17] At first he might appear to be merely ineffectual, since he proposes releasing Jesus only to have the Jewish leaders block his action by demanding Barabbas instead. After having Jesus scourged, Pilate seems to assume that the Jewish authorities will be satisfied, but they tell Pilate to go even farther by crucifying Jesus. Pilate tries to evade responsibility for judgment, then becomes afraid when he hears Jesus called Son of God. He vainly tries to release Jesus only to be told that this would undermine his friendship with the emperor. Yet the appearance of weakness might be deceiving, since Pilate's actions finally serve Roman political interests quite well. He does not agree to crucify Jesus until the Jewish authorities reaffirm their loyalty to the emperor, and the sign Pilate puts above the cross simply calls Jesus the King of the Jews, which disturbs the Jewish leaders because it gives the impression that the Romans are executing an actual Jewish king. Pilate's refusal to change the sign suggests that he is quite content to give the impression that he is crucifying Jewish national aspirations along with Jesus.

Beneath Pilate's political maneuvering, however, the evangelist discerns another factor: the power of sin. Pilate asks, "What is truth?" and even though he does not wait for an answer, readers soon learn that Pilate knows the truth in at least a limited sense. He knows that Jesus is not guilty, which is true, and he declares Jesus' innocence three times (18:38; 19:4, 6). Pilate also has pretensions of being powerful, claiming that he has the power to release Jesus and the power to crucify him (19:10). Yet when Pilate is given the opportunity to exercise his power, he knowingly hands over an innocent man to be crucified. By his action he rejects the truth, and rejecting the truth is sin. Socially and politically, Pilate and the Jewish authorities have different interests, but beneath their differences the evangelist discerns a common human reality: the presence of sin, the power of unbelief.

Sin and Bondage

For John, sin is a form of power that can hold people in its grasp. It does not express human freedom but takes away human freedom. In John 9, the sin of the authorities is described as blindness, as a darkness that makes it impossible for them to see that God is active in Jesus the healer or that the man born blind is telling the truth when he says that Jesus is from God. What is more, the authorities have the illusion that they can see the truth. They are blind to their own blindness; they act in unbelief while assuming they are acting on the basis of truth (9:40-41). In the passion narrative, the Jewish authorities and Pilate are all caught up in dynamics that eventually make them say and do things they would not have anticipated. One wonders how much freedom they really have.

The Gospel sometimes speaks of sin as a form of slavery or bondage. At one point Jesus tells a group of people in the temple, "If you continue in my word you are truly my disciples; and you will know the truth, and the truth will make you free" (8:31-32). The saying presupposes that people need to be made free, which means they are currently not free. If the truth gives people freedom, then falsehood holds them captive. These words — "the truth will make you free" — have been etched on the walls of universities and great libraries, inspiring students to pursue various fields of higher learning. But in the Gospel this saying has to do with Jesus' word concerning himself and his Father, and with the truth that overcomes human estrangement from God.

Jesus' listeners object that they do not need to be made free because they are children of Abraham and have never been in bondage to anyone (8:33). Historically, of course, their comment is not true. Abraham's children were repeatedly in bondage. The first time was in Egypt, where they were enslaved by the pharaohs. Later, they were taken captive by the Babylonians, who conquered Jerusalem and exiled the people from their homeland. Finally, the Romans had conquered the land, and Jesus' listeners were living under Roman domination. Those claiming never to have been in bondage cannot see the truth about their own history. In this context their unwillingness to acknowledge slavery in the historical sense reflects an inability to recognize slavery in the theological sense.

Jesus replies, "Very truly I tell you, everyone who commits sin is a slave to sin" (8:33-34). The idea is that actions reveal a person's character. Those who commit sin show that they are not freely acting on the basis of what is true, but have been taken prisoner by falsehood and are now forced to live on the basis of untruth. The enslaving power of sin might be compared to addiction, where a chemical distorts the way people see reality and overpowers their will, taking away the freedom to do something other than what the addiction demands. The relationship to the chemical becomes the primary relationship, damaging all other relationships. And the irony is that those who are being enslaved have the illusion that they are free to live as they choose.

The power of sin, in John's Gospel, is similar. The people who meet Jesus insist that they are free, and if this is true, then they have no need of the freedom he offers. If Jesus persists in offering them freedom, then they are bound to reject him because they know he cannot be telling them the truth. Jesus says that "if the Son makes you free, you will be free indeed" (8:36), but his listeners do not believe this. Their unbelief drives their actions, so that by the end of the chapter they are ready to stone Jesus. Rejecting the offer of freedom reveals the depth of their bondage.

The Problem of Evil

Enslavement to sin brings us close to another aspect of the human condition, which is oppression by the power of evil. Much of the Gospel focuses on the way people interact with Jesus and each other, yet behind the scenes is another power, which is hostile to God and seeks to exert its influence over the world. John assumes that human beings are accountable for their own unbelief and actions. Yet he also recognizes that there are dimensions of evil that go beyond the merely human. To understand the world and its people, therefore, we must explore the role of this sinister force.

Satan

John calls this transcendent power of evil Satan (13:27), the devil (13:2), the evil one (17:15), and the ruler of this world (12:31). In the other gospels the devil sometimes appears in vivid personified form, tempting Jesus to turn stones into bread, to cast himself down from the temple, or to gain worldly power by worshiping him (Matt. 4:1-11; Luke 4:1-13). Evil spirits seize control of people, and Jesus performs exorcisms to liberate them from demonic power (Matt. 8:28-34; Mark 3:22-27; Luke 9:37-43). In John, however, the devil is not fully personified. He lurks in the shadows, carrying out his designs through human agents. This does not exempt people from responsibility for their actions. John recognizes that there is a power that transcends human sin and aligns itself with human sin in opposition to God. People have a will of their own, but Satan bends it toward his own ends. Jesus tells a group of hostile listeners, who seek to kill him, that "your will" is to do what the devil desires (John 8:44). Significantly, John includes no accounts of Jesus casting out demons from those he meets. The single "exorcism" is the crucifixion itself, since that is where Jesus casts out the demonic ruler of the world (12:31; see pp. 117-20).[18]

There are three principal characteristics of Satan's activity in John: The first is deception. The devil is called a liar and the father of lies. The Gospel says that there is no truth in the devil and that when he lies he speaks according to his own nature (8:44). Falsehood is a form of power, for by convincing people to believe a lie the devil can move people to carry out his designs. John assumes that God is true and that Jesus speaks the truth he received from God. By way of contrast, the devil spins a web of deception, seeking to trap people with the idea that Jesus is misleading them and that they do not need the gifts God offers.

Second, the devil is implicated in the world's hatred of God, Jesus, and the Christian community. God loves the world and sent his Son as the expression of his love (3:16). Therefore, those who belong to God love Jesus, whereas those allied with the devil do not (8:42-44). Insofar as the devil rules the world, hatred characterizes his realm. Jesus tells the world the truth about its evil, and the world hates him for it (7:7). And since God is the one who sent Jesus to testify, the world's hatred for Jesus is hatred for God (15:23). Moreover, Jesus called people to faith, and the unbelieving world hates believers too. He tells his followers, "If you belonged to the world, the world would love you as its own. Because you do not belong to the world, but I have chosen you out of the world — therefore the world hates you" (15:19).

Third, the devil wields the power of death. He was a murderer from the beginning and seeks the death of those who oppose him. The adversaries of Jesus show the influence of the devil by seeking to kill Jesus for speaking the truth (8:44, 59). Later, Satan instigates the betrayal that leads to Jesus' crucifixion (13:2, 27). When Jesus goes to the garden where he is arrested, he is met by a company of armed troops that serve as the agents of the ruler of this world (14:30-31; 18:1-3). God may give life through his Word, but the devil seeks victory by bringing about death.

John refers to the devil as the ruler of this world, while recognizing that God is the superior power. God creates and gives life, but Satan does not. Therefore, the devil is an intruder into God's world (12:31; 16:11). The relationship of Satan to God is like that of darkness to light. Light has a power that darkness does not. The evil one cannot overcome the power of God any more than darkness can extinguish light (1:5). In this clash of powers, the devil uses the weaponry of falsehood, hatred, and death, yet Jesus defeats him with truth, love, and life (see pp. 117-20).

At one point Jesus says his opponents have the devil as their father (8:44). This does not imply that some people are created by God and others by Satan. The Gospel assumes that all things come into being by the Word of God, not by some other power (1:3). If people are not created as children of the devil, they become children of the devil by allying themselves with evil in opposition to God. People can become children of light by believing in the light (12:36). By way of contrast, they can become children of the devil by embracing falsehood, hatred, and the desire to impose death on others. John's worldview is not static — a point we will consider further under the question of human freedom below.

The Gospel's pointed reference to the children of the devil appears when Jesus is debating with a group of Jewish people. Historically, this has led some to demonize Jewish people in general and has been used to justify violence against them. This is exactly wrong. The Gospel is clear that Jesus and his opponents are both Jewish; they share the same heritage and are all together in the Jerusalem temple. The passage cannot be used to demonize an ethnic or religious group. More importantly, deception, hatred, and violence are what Jesus opposes. Therefore, those who claim to follow him cannot engage in hatred and violence without turning against Jesus himself. In this passage Jesus engages in a sharp debate, but when it comes to throwing stones, Jesus does not participate (8:59). This passage provides no warrant for violent behavior against those with whom one disagrees.

Evil in Action

Satan's work is manifested in Judas, one of Jesus' disciples. This is sobering for Christian readers because it shows that evil is not confined to the Jewish or Gentile adversaries of Jesus; Satan works even among Jesus' own followers. Judas is first mentioned at the end of the Bread of Life discourse, where Jesus says, "Did I not choose you, the Twelve? Yet one of you is a devil" (6:70-71). Calling Judas "a devil" points to his propensity for evil without fully identifying him as an agent of "the devil." The Gospel assumes that Judas already is a devil, but it offers no explanation as to how Judas got that way. The evil within him is simply taken as a given. Note that Judas already is a devil, yet Jesus chooses him just as he chooses all twelve disciples to be members of his inner circle. If Judas is a devil, it is not because Jesus deprived him of his favor. Rather, evil is resistant to the graciousness Jesus shows.

One might question whether Judas is in any way representative of the way the power of evil works among human beings, since his role as betrayer is so singular. Yet the Gospel links Judas to the wider circle of people who reject Jesus. The author initially mentions Judas after Jesus has announced that he will give his own flesh for the life of the world, an idea many found difficult to accept. Then the Gospel says that "Jesus knew from the first who were the ones that did not believe, and who was the one that would betray him." After this "many of the disciples turned back and no longer went about with him" (6:64, 66). What readers see happening in Judas has similarities to what they see happening in others who turn away. The forces at work in Judas can and do work in others as well.

The devil takes more direct action by designating Judas as the one to betray Jesus. In John's account of the last supper, Judas is a participant in a conflict between transcendent powers. When introducing the supper, John says that God puts all things in the hands of Jesus, who is God's agent. At the same time, the devil puts betrayal into the heart of Judas, who is the agent of the evil one (13:2-3).[19] The encounters between Judas and Jesus at the supper disclose the nature of the conflict. Jesus washes the feet of all his disciples, a gracious action that shows his love for them, yet readers are told that Judas remains unclean. This continued uncleanness points to a hardened resistance to the love Jesus offers (13:1, 10-11). Later, Jesus dips a piece of bread into the dish and gives it to Judas as a way of identifying him as the betrayer. Although giving someone food was a common way to show favor, Satan immediately enters Judas, so that they are united in purpose and action (13:27). Earlier it was said that those whose deeds are evil love darkness, and Satan's ally goes out to do evil under the cover of night (3:19; 13:30).

The scope of Satan's activity widens as Jesus tells the remaining disciples that "the ruler of this world is coming"; then he directs them to get up and depart from the supper (14:30-31). When they finally leave and go to the garden, they are met by Judas and others, who serve as agents of the ruler of this world (see pp. 117-20). Satan is not explicitly mentioned in the remainder of the Gospel, but given what has already been said, readers might detect his handiwork in the scenes leading up to the crucifixion. The devil works through falsehood, and the evangelist has prepared readers to see that the accusations made during Jesus' trial are false. He is charged with doing evil, although he is innocent (18:30, 38); with seditiously making himself a king, although his kingship comes from above (18:37; 19:12); and with unlawfully claiming to be Son of God, although God is the one who sent him (5:19-30; 19:7). By condemning Jesus, his opponents reject the truth he brings, showing that they have come under the influence of falsehood. Moreover, the devil wields power by bringing death, and those who condemn Jesus serve as the agents of death.

The Question of Human Freedom

The Gospel portrays a world that is troubled and complex. People are created for life in relationship with God, yet are separated from God. They have a need for God, yet are resistant to God. Human beings are sinners, who are accountable for their own unbelief and actions, and who need to be reconciled with the God from whom they are estranged. Yet they are also held captive by sin and are oppressed by the powers of evil at work in the world, so that they need to be set free. These tensions and contradictions characterize the human context into which God sends the Son to atone, liberate, and bring life (see pp. 109-23). But given this portrayal of the situation, what can be said of human freedom?

Freedom, in John's Gospel, is freedom for relationship. This freedom to believe is the result of God's action. Faith is not self-generated; it comes from God's encounter with human beings. People are said to thirst and hunger for God, and these images presuppose that people cannot meet their own need for relationship. They are freed to eat and drink — or to believe — when God comes to them in Jesus the living bread and in the Spirit's living water. Similarly, people engulfed in darkness do not have the ability to see. The coming of the light creates the freedom to see and believe.

Human resistance to God also means that God must turn alienation into trust and hatred into love. The Gospel speaks of God drawing people to Jesus and Jesus drawing people to himself (6:44; 12:32). The assumption is that people not only need an opportunity to believe but need a positive reason to relate to God in this way. God calls forth love in human beings by extending love to them through the gift of his Son, who lays down his life for them (3:16). God evokes faith by giving people a Word that can be trusted, the Word that comes in human form to tell the world the truth about itself and about the life that comes from God (12:44-50).

The Gospel also recognizes that some people respond to Jesus with faith and others with unbelief. Interpreters have wondered whether this means that God has decided that some people will believe and that others will not. After all, the Gospel says that those whom God has "given" to Jesus will believe and have eternal life, which might imply that God has decided not to give faith and life to others (6:39, 65; 17:2, 6). Jesus can say that those who are "from God" and belong to his sheep will respond favorably to his word, while others will not (8:47; 10:26). Moreover, at the end of Jesus' public ministry the Gospel says that he performed many signs, yet people did not believe in him. In fact "they could not believe," because he "has blinded their eyes and hardened their heart, so that they might not look with their eyes, and understand with their heart and turn — and I would heal them," as Isaiah said (12:39-40; cf. Isa. 6:10).[20]

These passages assume that faith comes from God's engagement with human beings, but they do not suggest that God wants some people to reject him. Consider the way the quotation from Isaiah is used. God does not blind people by depriving them of the light. Rather, according to John, people become blind because God gives them the light. This was clear in the story of the man born blind, for as the light of truth shone more brightly, the authorities were less and less able to see it (John 9:1-41). Blindness comes as God gives them the light, and their hearts are hardened as he gives them the truth.

If unbelief is not what God wants, then one might conclude that the difference between belief and unbelief is essentially a human affair. According to this view, God presents the light and truth in Jesus, then leaves it up to people to determine what they want to do with it. This rightly recognizes that the human situation is dynamic rather than static.[21] The Gospel speaks expansively of anyone and everyone who comes to faith, assuming that many can and will believe (3:16, 33, 36; 4:14; 6:48). The author depicts a context in which people can move from unbelief to faith. Jesus may say that his opponents do not belong to his sheep, yet he continues to call them to faith, which means that their unbelief need not be final (10:26, 38). While recognizing human blindness, Jesus urges people to believe in the light while they have opportunity to do so (12:36). The problem with understanding faith in exclusively human terms is that it does not deal adequately with the depth of human resistance to God or with the way God continues to draw people.

In the end, John's Gospel does not explain why some people believe and others do not. Rather than speculating as to the reason that some refuse to believe, the Gospel focuses on what it would take for them to come to faith. God enables people to see who he is through the light of Jesus. If some become blind, the way for their perception to be altered is, paradoxically, through continued exposure to the light. Similarly, God evokes faith through his Word of truth and love. If some reject him, the way for this to change is by continued encounter with the Word of truth and love, through the work of God's Spirit.

The World

The dimensions of the human context, which have been considered above, are reflected in John's use of the term *kosmos* or "world."[22] The prologue speaks broadly when saying that the world was brought into being through the Word of God (1:10). In the broadest sense, the world is God's creation. It has a beginning (17:5, 24), and is the sphere in which life is lived. But the Gospel most often focuses on the human world, on the people whom God has made. In many cases the Gospel speaks of the Jewish world. This is the immediate context in which much of Jesus' ministry takes place. He is told to go to Jerusalem to show himself to the world (7:4). When summarizing his activities he says, "I have spoken openly to the world; I have always taught in synagogues and in the temple, where all the Jews come together" (18:20). For Jesus, being in the world means being among Jewish people. Yet the Gospel extends this horizon to include other groups in "the world." When Jesus goes to Samaria, to non-Jews, he is acclaimed as "Savior of the World" (4:42). By saying this, the Samaritans show they are part of the world to which Jesus has come. Later, as Jesus approaches Jerusalem, a crowd bearing palm branches welcomes him; and the Pharisees say, "the world has gone after him" (12:19). The narrator immediately adds, "Now among those who went up to worship at the festival were some Greeks" (12:20). The Gospel's sense of "the world" includes ever-widening circles that encompass Jews, Samaritans, and Greeks.

This "world" to which Jesus comes is also alienated from the God who made it. This is evident in the resistance Jesus encounters from his Jewish opponents. Before going to Jerusalem, Jesus says that the world hates him because he testifies that its works are evil (7:7). After he arrives, he tells the Pharisees who reject his testimony, "you are from this world, I am not of this world," and he warns them of the consequences of sin (8:23). Some Jews persecute Jesus for healing on the Sabbath, and Jesus later says that this exemplifies "the world's" animosity toward him and his followers (5:16; 15:18-20). Yet the Gospel does not limit the issue of sin to any one group of people.[23] As we noted earlier, Nicodemus is a Jew and a Pharisee, but he reflects tendencies that are true of "the world" and "human beings" *(anthrōpoi)* more broadly (2:23-25; 3:1-2, 16-21). Jesus came into the world to bear witness to the truth, and the truth is rejected by Pilate the Roman governor as well as by Jesus' Jewish opponents (18:37-38; 19:16). All of them come under judgment during Jesus' trial (see pp. 70-72). Sin is a human problem.

Similarly, the power of evil is at work throughout the human world. The devil is active among Jesus' Jewish opponents, as well as in Judas, who is one of Jesus' own followers (8:44; 13:2, 27). Before the passion, Jesus expands the scope of the issue still further when he speaks of the evil one as "the ruler of this world," who is coming (12:31; 14:30; 16:11). And as his opponents come to arrest him, readers find that they include Judas his erstwhile disciple, as well as Jewish police and Roman soldiers (18:3). The influence of the evil one is not limited to one group.

John's ominous portrayal of "the world" gives depth to his understanding of the love of God and the work of Jesus. The "world" in John's Gospel is not characterized by soft summer breezes and the graceful light of dawn, by meadows filled with flowers or gentle waves upon the shore. It requires little effort to love a world like that. But in John's Gospel God loves the world that hates him; he gives his Son for the world that rejects him. He offers his love to a world estranged from him in order to overcome its hostility and bring the world back into relationship with its Creator (3:16).

CHAPTER 4

Jesus

Jesus, according to John, is the Word of God made flesh. With its elegant and soaring prose, the Gospel's opening lines tell of the Word, through whom God made all things, coming into the world as a human being (1:1, 14). The Word is God's way of communicating, and the Gospel traces the way this takes place in Jesus of Nazareth — in the words he speaks, the actions he performs, and the death he dies. The story unfolds through controversy. Readers may know from the outset that Jesus is the Word of God, but those whom Jesus meets during his ministry do not. Some are intrigued by him and follow, while others are initially impressed by his miracles but later find his claims to have come from God to be incomprehensible or blasphemous.

Questions about Jesus are familiar to modern readers, who continue to differ in their beliefs about who he is. Some call him Son of God, Savior, and Lord; others think of him as a teacher and example of compassion; still others view him as an iconoclastic prophet confronting worldly powers. In John's Gospel we meet a Jesus who is a paradox. He is clearly human yet is one with God. He is a rabbi who proves to be a king, a healer who gives life by dying. The Gospel portrays Jesus by using a number of familiar categories, yet in the end readers find that Jesus cannot be confined to any one of them.

We will explore Jesus' identity in several steps. Instead of starting with the prologue's elevated statements about the preexistent Word, we begin where people in the Gospel begin, with Jesus' humanity. Everyone Jesus meets, whether friend or foe, rightly assumes that he is a human being.

They call him a teacher, a Jew, or simply a man. Next, some identify Jesus as a prophet, which seems natural since Jesus speaks on behalf of God and performs miracles like those of Old Testament prophets; and others go further, calling him the Messiah, the king who will reign in righteousness. Finally, we will consider Jesus' oneness with God. Jesus refers to God as his Father and to himself as the Son. He uses "I Am" for himself in ways that recall the name of God, and when speaking of himself as the Son of Man, Jesus claims to reveal the glory of God.

This progression follows the Gospel's statement of purpose. John wrote in order that people might believe that the human being named Jesus is also the Messiah and the Son of God (20:31). What is crucial is that each dimension of Jesus' identity is true and that no single dimension, when taken alone, gives a complete picture. The phenomenon is like a musical chord. When a musician strikes several notes at the same time, the result is multidimensional sound. Each note makes its own contribution, and without a particular note, the chord is incomplete. John's presentation of Jesus asks that we listen for the chord, for the human, messianic, and divine tones that together give a multidimensional sense of who Jesus is.[1]

John tells the story of Jesus in retrospect, including insights into Jesus' life and work that only emerged after his death and resurrection (2:22; 12:16). He recognizes that Jesus' words and actions were interpreted in conflicting ways, and at the end of his public ministry he was widely misunderstood (12:34, 37). Given the sharply differing perspectives that emerged during and after Jesus' lifetime, one might wonder whether trying to understand him is worth the effort. Yet the Gospel encourages readers to grapple with Jesus' identity for at least two reasons: One is the promise that those who come to believe in Jesus will find life in his name (20:31). If this is true, then those who seek life will want to know who the giver of life is. The other reason is that Jesus calls readers to a way of life. To believe is to follow, and those who embark on this path will want to understand who it is that beckons them.

Human Being and Teacher

Jesus' humanity is a helpful place to begin, since everyone in the Gospel agrees that he is a human being. Those he meets may disagree on what kind of a person he is, but no one questions the fact that he is truly human.

Theologically, this is basic to the Gospel's message. What is at stake in affirming the humanity of Jesus is the reality of God's love and the nature of Christian discipleship. If Jesus is not truly human, then how can he show love by dying? And if he is not human, how can ordinary human beings follow him?

The Jewish Man from Nazareth

"Flesh" or *sarx* is the Gospel's most uncompromising way to speak of Jesus' humanity. The first chapter says that human beings are born through blood, the will of a man, and the will of the flesh (1:13). The language is physical and tangible, and having described ordinary human birth in this way, the Gospel says that God's "Word became flesh" (1:14). The verb "become" or *ginesthai* is startling in its directness. There is no suggestion that God's Word merely appeared to be human or assumed a few human features. To become flesh is to become human, completely.[2]

"Flesh" is limited and mortal. It is what all human beings share (17:2). In his conversation with Nicodemus, Jesus contrasts human flesh with the Spirit of God (3:6). The flesh belongs to the worldly sphere, where mortal life is lived, whereas the Spirit brings life eternal. John refers to flesh differently than does Paul, who sometimes equates flesh with sinful desires (e.g., Gal. 5:19). In John, human flesh is known for its limitations. It is earthly rather than heavenly. To be flesh is to be subject to misunderstanding and liable to death (John 6:63; 8:15).

Jesus speaks of dying as the act of giving his flesh. He tells the crowd that what "I give for the life of the world is my flesh" (6:51). In what follows, Jesus speaks of those who eat his flesh and drink his blood, using disturbingly graphic terms to underscore the reality of his death (6:53-56). Many readers hear echoes of the traditional language of the Lord's Supper, and we will explore this question below (see pp. 207-9). But many also recognize that the primary level of meaning concerns crucifixion, which is the way Jesus' flesh is given and his blood is shed.[3]

Jesus is also a man or human being, that is, an *anthrōpos*. This connects him to other people, who are identified in the same way. Some human beings or *anthrōpoi* are afflicted with suffering: the Galilean official with a dying son, the paralytic beside the pool, and the man blind from birth (4:46; 5:5; 9:1). Among human beings one finds a truth-teller like John the

Baptist as well as the unreliable crowds and the sinners who slink into the darkness (1:6; 2:25; 3:19). The human realm is where death takes away life and falsehood undercuts truth. Yet Jesus enters the fray as an *anthrōpos*, a man who is allied with truth against deception (8:40). Those who respond favorably understand that he is a man who speaks the truth and heals (4:29; 9:11). Those who oppose him agree he is a man, but they argue that he is a lawbreaker who deserves to die (9:16, 30; 11:47, 50).

And Jesus does die. During the interrogation after his arrest Jesus is scourged, which involves being beaten with whips that tear the victim's skin and muscle. His captors ridicule him by wrapping him in a royal cloak and placing a crown of thorns on his head. Acclaiming him king, they promptly degrade him by slapping him (19:1-2). Then Pilate brings Jesus out to his adversaries, declaring, "Behold the man!" (19:5). One might wonder whether Pilate speaks contemptuously of Jesus as a mere man rather than a king, or whether he hopes that the beating Jesus received will satisfy the crowd so that he can release "the man." But in either case what Pilate says is profoundly correct; the one who stands before them is truly a human being.[4]

Jesus' humanity is important for several reasons: First, Jesus fully identifies with people, especially in their suffering. He is misunderstood, hated, and condemned; and when his followers encounter these things, they know that Jesus has experienced them too (15:18, 20; 16:2). Jesus is troubled at the prospect of betrayal and death (12:27; 13:21), and yet he offers encouragement to those who are similarly troubled at being separated from him (14:1, 27). Mary of Bethany wept at Jesus' feet after the death of her brother Lazarus, and Jesus himself is disturbed and troubled at the scene. He does not disparage Mary's grief. Instead, he weeps also (11:33-35).[5] Throughout the Gospel he invites the thirsty to come and drink, but when dying he says, "I thirst" (19:28; cf. 4:13-15; 6:35; 7:37). He may say this to fulfill the Scriptures, but that does not make his thirst any less genuine.

Second, Jesus gives the love of God in human terms so that it can be received in human terms. People show love by what they give for others, and the most complete form of love is expressed in the most complete form of giving, the giving of one's life for the sake of others (15:13). For Jesus' love to be real, the death he dies must be real; and for his death to be real, his humanity must be real. Moreover, Jesus dies bodily and is raised bodily, and through his resurrection he extends the promise that others who die will also rise (see pp. 179-82). Finally, Jesus commands others to love as he himself loved, making his death the source and norm for Christian discipleship (13:34; 15:12). Because his love comes to people in human terms, Jesus can call them to convey it to others in human terms (see pp. 110-12).

The problem is that Jesus' humanity seems to negate the other claims made about him.[6] The man Jesus is from Nazareth in Galilee (7:41; 18:5, 7). Yet this has nothing to do with traditional messianic expectations. Philip claims that Jesus of Nazareth fulfills the messianic promises in the law and the prophets, but his friend Nathanael brings him up short: "Can anything good come out of Nazareth?" (1:45-46). The question is logical, since the Old Testament never mentions Nazareth. The sign above the cross repeats that the crucified king is from Nazareth (19:19), yet if Jesus is to be recognized as the messianic ruler, it will have to occur despite his connection with Nazareth, not because of it.

The man Jesus is also Jewish. He teaches in the temple in Jerusalem, preaches in synagogues, and assumes the truth of the Jewish Scriptures. Yet why should he matter to non-Jews? The Samaritan woman at the well is initially put off by Jesus' Jewishness. Yet instead of downplaying his ethnic background, Jesus affirms that his people worship what they know and that salvation is from the Jews (4:9, 22). For Samaritans to call Jesus the Savior of the world, they will have to recognize that the one who brings salvation from the Jews also extends it to all peoples.

Many who meet Jesus are incredulous at his claim to have come from God. The idea that he is from heaven seems absurd, since people in Galilee know that he is a local boy and they are acquainted with his parents (6:42). Moreover, his habit of calling God his Father sounds like a blasphemous attempt to claim divine status (5:18; 10:33). Their objections are well taken. The human attempt to take God's place is the height of sin. Therefore, the Gospel must show that the opposite is true. According to John, Jesus is not a man elevating himself to divine status but the one who has come down from heaven to make God known in a human life.

Finally, Jesus' human death by crucifixion calls everything about him into question. When Jesus speaks about being "lifted up" in death, his listeners object that the Messiah is supposed to remain forever. So how can he be the Messiah if he dies (12:33-34)? His opponents conclude that by putting Jesus to death they can show that his pretensions of being the Messiah and Son of God are merely a sham (19:7, 12). In response, the Gospel must show that his death actually discloses the true character of his kingship and relationship to God.

The Teacher

The disciples call Jesus their rabbi or teacher, and continue doing so even after they acclaim him Messiah and king (1:38, 49; 4:31; 9:2; 11:8, 28). Jesus uses the title for himself and considers teaching to be an integral part of his public role (13:14). When questioned by the Jewish authorities prior to his death, he says that he has taught in synagogues and in the temple, where all Jews come together (18:19-20). Traditionally, a teacher has a special role in society, but not necessarily an exclusive one. Many people serve as teachers (3:10, 26). And John says that Jesus steps into the position of a teacher, even as he stretches and refashions the role to give it new meaning.[7]

Everyone agrees that Jesus teaches. But is his teaching legitimate? Some Jewish leaders, like Nicodemus, think that the signs Jesus performs demonstrate that he is a teacher from God (3:2). Although rabbis were not expected to do miracles, some sages were reputed to be wonder workers, and Nicodemus puts Jesus in this category (*m. Taʿanit* 3:8; *b. Ber.* 34b). Others argue that Jesus' miracles discredit him, since he heals a paralyzed man on the Sabbath, when no work is to be done. From their perspective, breaking the Sabbath law makes Jesus an opponent of God, not a teacher from God (John 5:16).

Jesus meets the traditional qualifications of a teacher from an unexpected angle, according to John. First, a Jewish teacher was expected to have studied with a recognized master. Therefore, when Jesus teaches in the temple, some wonder where he received his education. The implication is that he lacks formal training and therefore is not a legitimate teacher (7:14-15). Jesus replies that he has indeed had proper instruction and is not fabricating his own ideas. He says that he has studied with the best, with God himself (7:16-18). As a qualified teacher, Jesus has learned from a recognized master, but unlike other teachers, he is not dependent on those steeped in the tradition. His master teacher is God.

Second, a teacher was to pass on what he learned by speaking and acting in ways consistent with the Jewish law. Therefore, Jesus invokes the tradition to show that he is passing on what he received from God and doing so with integrity. His detractors object that healing a paralyzed man on the Sabbath violates the law. Yet Jesus replies that they perform circumcision — a form of surgery — on the Sabbath in order to keep the law. (A boy was to be circumcised on the eighth day after birth, even if this fell on the Sabbath; Gen. 17:12.) If they perform surgery on the Sabbath, how can they fault Jesus for healing (John 7:21-23)? Moreover, the law says "You shall not kill," yet they are angry enough to want Jesus put to death (7:19; Exod. 20:13).

John understands that Jesus' teaching is consistent with the Jewish law, rightly understood, though it is not derived from the law. His authority is from God and the Scriptures bear witness to this (John 5:39). An example of his distinctive use of Scripture is set in a synagogue, where Jesus teaches and is addressed as a rabbi (6:25, 59). He develops a message using rabbinic modes of biblical interpretation, but the result is extraordinary. Paraphrasing Scripture, his listeners say, "it is written, 'He gave them bread from heaven to eat'" (6:31; cf. Exod. 16:4). Jesus then explicates each part of the passage.

Jesus' hearers relate the words "he gave them" to what Moses did in the past, when he gave the people the bread called "manna" as they sojourned in the desert. Using a rabbinic technique, Jesus gives an alternative reading of the passage. He says that the real subject of the sentence is God, not Moses, and that the gift is given in the present, not the past: It was "not Moses who gave you the bread from heaven, but it is my Father who gives you the true bread from heaven" (John 6:32).

Like a rabbi, Jesus continues interpreting by taking up the words "bread from heaven." But unlike a rabbi, he relates these words to himself, saying, "I am the bread of life" from heaven (6:35-38). An ordinary Jewish teacher might identify the bread with the law, which God gave to be a way of life for Israel (Deut. 8:3).[8] In Jesus' teaching, however, the bread is Jesus himself; the law bears witness to this. As the bread, Jesus gives life to the world by giving himself — his flesh — through crucifixion. By this act of self-giving, people are drawn to God and sustained in a relationship with him (John 6:39-40).

Jesus completes his teaching by taking up the words: "to eat." On a primary level, to eat is to believe. If God is the giver and Jesus is the bread, then one receives the gift by faith. Throughout the chapter Jesus teaches that whoever believes has eternal life. Saying that the one who "eats" has eternal life is another way of making the same point (6:35, 40, 47). Possible connections to the Lord's Supper are considered below (see pp. 207-9). Here the point is that when teaching, Jesus makes use of the Scriptures and rabbinic modes of interpretation, but in the end the Scriptures bear witness to what God is doing in Jesus himself.

At the last supper Jesus maintains his role by telling the disciples, "You call me Teacher and Lord — and you are right for that is what I am" (13:13).

But he alters the role when he adds, "So if I, your Lord and Teacher, have washed your feet, you also ought to wash one another's feet" (13:14). Socially, the person who washed someone else's feet was in the inferior position, usually a slave. It was conceivable that a student might wash the feet of the teacher, but not the reverse.[9] Yet Jesus does not undertake a simple role reversal in which the teacher assumes the position of the student and the student becomes the master. He remains Teacher and Lord, and his disciples are to do what he has done (13:15). The idea is not that the master should refrain from serving, i.e., from washing feet. Rather, the disciples *should* serve by washing feet, following their master's example (see pp. 110-12).

Then Jesus says, "I give you a new commandment, that you love one another. Just as I have loved you, you also should love one another" (13:34). The command to love is not new. The law says that people are to love their neighbors as they love themselves (Lev. 19:18), and the traditional task of a teacher was to offer instruction on how to keep the commandment. Jesus, however, issues a new commandment. In so doing he makes the love he gives to others — through footwashing and laying down his life — the source and norm for discipleship (see pp. 193-95). His commandment to love is consistent with the law, but it is not derived from the law. It comes from a teacher who embodies the Word of God.

Prophet and Messiah

The next dimension of Jesus' identity concerns his role as prophet and Messiah. These aspects of his identity, which are intensely debated in the Gospel, are theologically important for two reasons: First, they have to do with the integrity of God. According to the Scriptures, God promised to send a prophet and messianic king. Therefore, if God has integrity, those promises must be kept. Second, a prophet or Messiah wields special power. The way Jesus develops these roles reveals how readers can interpret his use of power and understand the power of God.

The Prophet

John assumes that prophets are people sent by God and empowered by the Spirit. Prophets were known to speak words from the Lord and to work miracles. Many such prophets were recognized in Israel's tradition (John 1:23, 45; 6:45; 12:38). During his ministry, Jesus calls himself a prophet (4:44) and is identified as a prophet by others (4:19; 6:14; 7:40; 9:17). Since the term "prophet" is familiar, it helps make some of Jesus' unique characteristics intelligible.

Jesus can be considered a prophet because he communicates what he has heard from God. He knows people and the ways of God to a degree that ordinary people do not. When meeting the Samaritan woman at the well, he tells her to bring her husband, but she replies that she has no husband. Jesus says that this is true, since she has had five husbands and is living with a man who is not her husband. The woman immediately recognizes that he is a prophet and asks him about worship — a topic suitable for a prophet (4:19). Jesus tells her that the hour is coming and has already arrived when true worshipers will worship in Spirit and truth (4:23). His message is not limited to interpreting earlier traditions about worship. He makes a direct prophetic statement about God's action in the world.

The miracles Jesus performs are appropriate for a prophet. Moses was known for the signs and wonders he performed in Egypt, and for feeding people with manna in the desert (Deut. 34:10-12). The prophets Elijah and Elisha also worked miracles by healing the sick, feeding the hungry, and calling the dead back to life (1 Kings 17; 2 Kings 4–5). Jesus is specifically called a prophet after feeding a large crowd with five loaves and two fish, and after healing the man who was blind from birth (John 6:14; 9:17), though his other acts of healing and raising Lazarus from the dead also are analogous to those of Israel's prophets. To some extent Jesus fits the prophetic role.

Calling Jesus a prophet also relates to the question of God's integrity, since the hope that God would send a unique prophet — "the prophet" — comes from the promises God made in Scripture. At the beginning of the Gospel, a Jewish delegation asks whether John the Baptist is the Messiah, Elijah, or the prophet (1:19-21). Their search for the Messiah is based on God's promise to establish a royal heir on David's throne (2 Sam. 7:12). Their question about Elijah recalls that God promised that Elijah would return to deliver people from divine wrath (Mal. 4:5-6). Finally, their interest in "the prophet" is grounded on God's promise to raise up a prophet like Moses (Deut. 18:15-18). The Baptist states flatly that he fulfills none of these roles, and he then directs attention to Jesus.

Jesus is clearly the Messiah, according to John (1:41). Is he also the prophet like Moses? Concerning this figure God said, "I will put my words in the mouth of the prophet, who shall speak to them everything that I command," and whoever "does not heed the words that the prophet shall speak in my name, I myself will hold accountable" (Deut. 18:18-19). Since the Scriptures say that God made this promise, people can expect God to keep it. And Jesus claims this role by echoing the passage from Deuteronomy. He says that Moses wrote about him, that he has come in God's name, and that those who reject him are accountable to God — all of which fits what is said about a prophet like Moses (John 5:39-47).[10]

Some people recognize this aspect of Jesus' identity, calling him "the prophet who is to come into the world" after Jesus feeds them with bread as Moses had done (6:14). Their perception is partly right, but things go awry when they try to "make" this prophet into a king on their own terms, so that Jesus flees (6:15). Others call Jesus "the prophet" after he says he will give them living water, much as Moses provided water in the desert (7:37-40; Exod. 17:6). Again, their perception is partly correct. The twist is that the water will flow from the side of Jesus during his crucifixion, as a harbinger of the Spirit's living water, which will be given by the risen Jesus (John 19:34). In the end the category of "prophet" is fluid and relates to the question of whether Jesus is the Messiah (4:18, 25; 9:17, 22).

The Messiah

The title "Messiah" or *Christos* in Greek means "anointed one." In Israel's tradition it was used for kings, who were anointed with oil when they assumed the royal office. Many kings fell far short of the ideal, and after Jerusalem was conquered in 587 B.C. the land was ruled by a succession of foreign powers. Hope for "the Messiah" was based in part on God's promise to raise up an heir to David's throne, who would build the kingdom and rule in righteousness (2 Sam. 7:12-13).[11] The Jewish delegation in John 1:20 is looking for the Messiah, and the Gospel will show that God's promise is fulfilled in Jesus. At the same time, any understanding of messiahship must encompass Jesus' crucifixion, since the placard above the cross proclaims his reign to the world (John 19:19-20).

The kingship theme is introduced when John the Baptist points to Jesus as the sacrificial Lamb of God and two of his disciples follow, curious to learn more (1:35-36). They soon declare, "We have found the Messiah" (1:41). The next day Philip echoes this confession by telling his friend

Nathanael, "We have found him about whom Moses in the law and also the prophets wrote, Jesus son of Joseph from Nazareth" (1:45). Although Nathanael is skeptical, he goes to Jesus who says, "Before Philip called you, while you were under the fig tree, I saw you" (1:48). In an astonishing turnabout, Nathanael acclaims him "Son of God" and "King of Israel" (1:48-49). The title "King of Israel" connects Jesus with promises concerning the royal messiah. Here the title "Son of God" is also messianic, since the Scriptures say the heir to David's throne will be a "son" to God (2 Sam. 7:14; Ps. 2:6-7).

Nathanael's story is playful, but it makes a serious point. Jesus fulfills God's promises. He is king on God's terms. Philip directs attention to the Scriptures, and Jesus points out that Nathanael was called by a friend while sitting under a fig tree (John 1:48). This recalls that the prophet Zechariah promised that God would send the messianic Branch of David (Zech. 3:8). He would be the righteous ruler foretold in the law and other prophets (Gen. 49:10; Zech. 6:12-13; Jer. 23:6; 33:16). According to Zechariah, a sign of the Messiah's coming was that a man would *"call his neighbor* under a vine and *under a fig tree"* (Zech. 3:10). This is what occurred when Philip called Nathanael under the fig tree. Nathanael's experience bears out the biblical promise, enabling him to recognize Jesus as the messianic Son of God and King of Israel.[12]

The Messiah was not commonly expected to be a miracle worker — at least this is not well attested in Jewish sources. But Jesus' signs help confirm his messianic role. The disciples who call him Messiah and King accompany him to a wedding at Cana. After the wine runs out, Jesus has the servants pour water into six stone jars, which were ordinarily used for cleansing rituals. When the steward tastes the water, he discovers that it has become wine (John 2:1-11). The link with messiahship is suggested rather than stated. Readers have already learned that Jesus fulfills the law and the prophets. Accordingly, his action at Cana seems to recall that the law spoke about the messianic ruler, who was to come from the tribe of Judah. Of him it was said, "Binding his foal to the vine and his donkey's colt to the choice vine, he washes his garments in wine and his robe in the blood of grapes" (Gen. 49:10-11). At Cana, Jesus takes up the idea that the messianic ruler will cleanse with wine by transforming the water that was ordinarily used for cleansing into fine wine. Again, the biblical prophets promised that when God restored Davidic rule, he would pour out his favor on Israel, so that "the mountains will drip sweet wine, and all the hills shall flow with it" (Amos 9:11, 13; cf. Joel 3:18; Isa. 25:6). Jesus' actions fit this promise, since the quantity of wine he produced was enormous.

If Jesus is the Messiah on God's terms, this poses a challenge to those who want to make him king on their own terms. When Jesus feeds the crowd with bread and fish, people initially think he is a prophet like Moses, which is correct as far as it goes (John 6:14). But things go seriously wrong when they want to seize Jesus and "make him king," so that Jesus flees from them (6:15). For them to "make" Jesus king would mean that his power would rest on their acclaim; his authority would derive from the whims of the public. Yet according to John, Jesus' power comes from God above, not from earth below. He meets human needs, but on God's terms, not the world's.

What qualifies Jesus to be the Messiah? This is the focus of public debates about his origin later in the Gospel. Some of the bystanders insist that the Messiah must be of unknown origin, so that "when the Messiah appears, no one will know where he comes from" (7:27). This expectation is not found in the Old Testament but is reflected in Jewish tradition (*1 Enoch* 48:6). The idea seems to discredit Jesus. Since everyone knows that he is from Galilee, he is clearly not qualified to be the Messiah. Or is he? Jesus points out that he has come from God, but the bystanders do not know this (John 7:28). This gives the story an ironic twist. Since Jesus' origin *is* unknown to his detractors, readers can see that he actually meets the qualifications for Messiah.

Others voice a contrary form of messianic expectation. Instead of insisting that the Messiah's origin must be unknown, they argue that his origin should be known: He is to be a descendant of David and come from Bethlehem (7:42; 2 Sam. 7:12; Mic. 5:2). The Gospel does not make a direct response to this group or include stories of Jesus' birth in Bethlehem. Nevertheless, John assumes that readers will know that Jesus fulfills the Davidic promises — the disciples have already discovered that Jesus is the Messiah promised in the law and the prophets (John 1:41, 45, 49). Given this general perspective, readers can be expected to infer that Jesus must fulfill any particular promise concerning the Messiah, including the one concerning Bethlehem. Moreover, the debates in John 7 are full of irony. The crowds make erroneous judgments based on surface appearances, even though readers can see that on a deeper level the opposite is true (7:24). According to this pattern, Jesus' detractors insist that he does not have the proper Davidic qualifications, but readers recognize that he actually does.[13]

In the end, the debates discredit Jesus' opponents, who seem incapable of agreeing who the Messiah should be. One group insists that his origin should be unknown and the other argues that his origin should be known, that is, Davidic. Their disagreements make one wonder how any Messiah could satisfy the public's demands. Yet strangely, readers can see what those in the story cannot: Jesus meets these seemingly incompatible requirements. In one sense his origin is unknown to the bystanders, since he comes from God and they do not know that. In another sense his character is Davidic, since he is the one in whom the promises of the royal Messiah are realized.

Jesus' connection to Galilee remains a problem, however. The authorities declare that anyone who searches the Scriptures will find that no prophet is to arise from Galilee (7:52). One might point out that prophets like Elijah and Elisha worked in Galilee, but the Gospel moves in another direction. Those who search the Scriptures find that Galilee is linked to the Messiah's light, which will illumine "Galilee of the nations." For "the people who walked in darkness have seen a great light; those who dwelt in a land of deep darkness, on them light has shined," for "to us a child is born, to us a son is given; and the government will be upon his shoulder, and his name will be called Wonderful Counselor, Mighty God, Everlasting Father, Prince of Peace" (Isa. 9:1-2, 6). This light-bringing figure will be the heir to David's throne (Isa. 9:7). Jesus claims this promise by saying, "I am the light of the world. Whoever follows me will not walk in darkness, but will have the light of life" (John 8:12). From the perspective of the Gospel, the link to Galilee does not discredit Jesus but identifies him as the fulfillment of God's promise to bring Galilee the light.

After calling himself the light of the world, Jesus validates his claim by healing a man born blind, whose eyes then see the light (9:1-12). The man declares that Jesus is a prophet — with the subtext that he is also the Messiah (9:17, 22). The episode suggests connections with biblical passages that spoke of the servant of the Lord, who would be a light to the nations and open the eyes of the blind (Isa. 42:6; 49:6). Some understood this unnamed servant to be Israel, but others expected him to be God's messianic ruler, and readers familiar with this tradition would see in Jesus' actions a confirmation of his identity as the Messiah (cf. Luke 1:69, 79; 2:32).

Jesus next speaks about a shepherd and sheepfold, but some of his listeners are impatient and want a more direct statement: "If you are the Messiah, tell us plainly" (John 10:24). The problem is that Jesus cannot give a simple answer because he does not fit their categories. If he says, "Yes, I am the Messiah," then they will assume that he is the kind of Messiah they expect — presumably a hero who will defeat the Romans and reestablish Jewish independence. Yet if he says, "No, I am not the Messiah," then he is not being truthful, since he is the one whom God has sent.

So Jesus presents a third option, giving them an image rather than a direct answer. A shepherd was a traditional metaphor for a ruler, and the image was used for the heir to David's throne, the messianic king who would provide for the people of God (*Pss. Sol.* 17:40). To say, "I am the good shepherd" means, in part, that Jesus is the Messiah whom God has sent to provide abundant life for others (John 10:10, 14). The way Jesus does this, however, is by laying down his life for the sheep (10:11). He redefines messiahship in terms of his crucifixion. God has indeed given him power and authority *(exousia)*, and the way he will use it is by laying down his life in love (10:18).

The clash between competing views of messiahship continues as Jesus approaches Jerusalem at the end of his ministry. Perceiving Jesus in nationalistic terms, the crowd goes out of the city to meet him along the road, which was the way to welcome generals and kings. They also wave palm branches, the symbols used to celebrate national victories.[14] Finally, they acclaim Jesus in the words of Psalm 118:26, "Hosanna! Blessed is the one who comes in the name of the Lord." They then give this their own spin by adding "the king of Israel" (John 12:13). Given the nationalistic overtones, the Jewish authorities had good reason to think that people expected Jesus to foment a revolt against Rome (11:48).

Surprisingly, Jesus claims the mantle of kingship by finding a donkey to ride (12:14). The Gospel underscores the royal dimension by noting that the disciples later interpret this in light of the Scriptures, which speak of God's king riding a donkey (12:15-16; Zech. 9:9). The narrative moves the notion of kingship from a national to a global perspective. When Jesus approaches the city, the Pharisees complain that "the world" has gone after Jesus (John 12:19). Readers soon learn that this is "oh so true," because a group of Greeks now ask to see him (12:20). Their presence expands the horizon beyond the circles of Jewish and Samaritan believers that the Gospel has described, foreshadowing the time after the resurrection when Jesus will draw people from many different backgrounds to himself through the work of his disciples (12:32). As the messianic king, Jesus fulfills the promises God made to Israel, but he does so for all people. The sign above his cross, which will call him King of the Jews, will be written in Hebrew, Latin, and Greek, so that it is clear that Jesus' kingship serves people everywhere (19:20).

The crowd is right in perceiving Jesus as a warrior king, but they are wrong in the way they understand the battle. Jesus has come to cast out "the ruler of this world," who is not the Roman emperor but Satan (12:31). Jesus will dethrone the evil one when he is "lifted up," an expression that connotes both physical elevation on a cross and exaltation in glory (12:32). His crucifixion will be a victory in which Jesus wields divine love as a weapon against demonic hatred, divine truth against the world's falsehood, and the power of life against the forces of death (see pp. 117-20).

The crowd catches the allusion to Jesus' coming death but objects, "We have heard from the law that the Messiah remains forever. How can you say that the Son of Man must be lifted up?" (12:34). They seem to recall Psalm 89:36, which speaks of David's heir or "seed" remaining forever. The problem, from their perspective, is that death and remaining forever seem mutually exclusive. If Jesus dies, how can he be the Messiah? His death will terminate his reign. From John's perspective, however, the Messiah remains forever not by avoiding death but by overcoming it. The abiding reign of the crucified Messiah comes through resurrection.

The theme of Jesus' kingship culminates in the passion narrative. At his trial, his opponents charge that he has "made himself" a king (19:12), and Pilate has Jesus put to death. Readers have seen that Jesus does not "make himself" a king and does not allow others to do so (6:15). Rather, his kingship is from God above. When Pilate puts the sign above the cross proclaiming that Jesus is king, readers can see that this is true. Jesus has been given authority by God, and he uses his authority by laying down his life for the sake of others. This is how Jesus builds the kingdom of God, according to John.

Son of God

Questions about Jesus' identity finally lead to his role as the Son of God. In some contexts this title simply means Messiah. For Nathanael, the Son of God is the King of Israel because the heir to David's throne is God's adopted "son," a person claimed by God for a unique role as ruler of the people (1:49; 2 Sam. 7:14; Ps. 2:7). Yet throughout the Gospel Jesus refers to God as his Father and to himself as the Son in ways that go beyond traditional kingship. Jesus says that he comes from God, is doing the work of God, and is one with God. This is either solemn truth or outrageous blasphemy.

The issue is this: Is Jesus a human being trying to become God? Or has he come from God to manifest God's power and presence in a human life? The direction of the action makes all the difference. If Jesus is a human being scrambling upward, trying to put himself in the place of God, then he is the consummate rebel against God. But if he has come down from God in order to do the work of God, then he is the definitive revealer of God, the one in whom people encounter God. Jesus' opponents argue that he is trying to "make himself" into the Son of God and that he deserves death (John 19:7). The Gospel, however, seeks to show the opposite: he has come from God to make God known — and those who believe this receive life (20:31). We have already considered what it means for God to be Father (see pp. 47-51). Here we focus on what it means for Jesus to be his Son.

The related expression, "Son of Man," also identifies Jesus as the person in whom God is revealed. The expression often means "human being," and in some contexts in the other gospels Jesus seems to use it to mean "I myself." Elsewhere, a figure who is like a son of man is said to come on the clouds and receive dominion over many peoples (Dan. 7:13-14; cf. Matt. 24:30).[15] In John, however, the expression has its own distinctive qualities. For example, Jesus tells Nathanael that he will see the angels of God ascending and descending on the Son of Man. This recalls that Jacob once dreamed of angels going up and down a ladder to heaven. Now, in Jesus the Son of Man, God's glory will be revealed in a new way (Gen. 28:12; John 1:51). Later, Jesus says that the Son of Man comes from heaven and gives eternal life (John 3:13; 6:27, 53, 62). The Son of Man can even be worshiped as the one in whom God meets people (9:35-38). Yet understanding who the Son of Man is means recognizing that he is glorified in his betrayal and death (12:23-24; 13:31-32). God is revealed in the Son of Man who is lifted up in crucifixion (3:14; 8:28; 12:32-34).[16]

Word of God — Only Son of God

The opening lines of John's Gospel set a perspective from which the question of Jesus' relation to God can be viewed. The prologue does this through imagery rather than argument. An argument works by making several points in logical sequence, each with the appropriate supporting material. In contrast, the imagery of the prologue offers a way of seeing that can lead to understanding. The author recognizes that people see things quite differently, depending on where they are standing. A given vantage points allows people to see some things but not others. As long as they remain in that spot, it will be difficult for them to see things any differently. So the prologue takes readers to an elevated vantage point, where they can see things that those confined to the flat plain below cannot see. The author invites them to "Stand here for a moment. Try looking at things from this perspective. You'll see what I mean."

The prologue tells of the Word of God becoming flesh in Jesus (1:1, 14). We have seen that a word or *logos* is a form of communication. Although the term can have a wider range of meaning, it is commonly used for a spoken word or message (e.g., 2:22; 4:37; 5:24). Here the context recalls the opening of Genesis, where God spoke and the world came into being. By the Word, God communicates with the world. We have also seen that a word can be differentiated and yet identified with the one who speaks it. People normally speak of someone's identity by saying that the person "is," or else they refer to a relationship by saying that a person "is with" someone else. But in John's head-spinning introduction both are true: "the Word was with God, and the Word was God" (1:1). A person who speaks a word has an existence outside that word. Yet those who hear a person's word hear the person. When a person's word effects something, the person effects something. Similarly, the Word can be differentiated from God, yet when the Word brings things into being, it is God bringing them into being. When the world is addressed by the Word, it is addressed by God (see pp. 26-30).

Seeing Jesus as the Word assumes that he can be differentiated from God. Throughout the Gospel he refers to God as his Father and to himself as the Son. He says that he has come not to do his own will but the will of the One who sent him (6:38). When he prays, he prays to his Father and not to himself. The difference between Jesus and God is clear. Yet the prologue says that Jesus not only speaks but embodies God's Word. This sets the direction for the story. In Jesus, God addresses the world. God speaks to people by what Jesus says, what Jesus does, and who Jesus is. Each aspect of Jesus' ministry is communication. Through Jesus' words, God speaks. Through Jesus' signs, God's power and glory come to the realm of the senses. Even Jesus' death and resurrection are forms of address. Through them God communicates love and life to the world.

The hallmark of God's Word is the ability to give life (1:3-4). This was true at creation, when God spoke and gave life to the world. Readers are therefore to look for this in the Word made flesh. We have noted that life is a relational term. It has a physical dimension — the beating of the heart and breathing of the lungs — and in its theological sense it means relating to God in faith (see pp. 30-32). Jesus the Word gives life physically when he heals the sick, opens the eyes of the blind, feeds people with bread, and raises the dead. He also promises that those who come to know and believe in him enter the relationship with God that is true life. He meets people as the bread of life, the light of life, and the giver of the water that brings eternal life (4:14; 6:35; 8:12). He is the shepherd who brings abundant life; he is the way, the truth, and the life (10:10-11; 14:6). In his death and resurrection he communicates the divine love that gives life (3:14-16; 11:25). Where the incarnate Word gives life, God is present and active.

The vantage point shifts when the prologue says, "the Word became flesh and dwelt among us," and "we beheld his glory" (1:14). The language recalls Israel's sojourn in the wilderness, when God came to meet them in the tent or dwelling *(skēnē)* that was his sanctuary. The Scriptures tell of God's glory filling this tent or dwelling. In these contexts the glory or *doxa* is the majestic radiance that signifies God's presence and power (Exod. 40:34). The prologue invites readers to see Jesus this way. In him God's Word dwelt or made his tent (*eskēnōsen,* John 1:14). In his flesh one encounters God's glory. According to the Scriptures, God's power and presence were revealed in a particular physical place. Readers are now asked to see how God's glory is revealed in a particular person — Jesus.

At this juncture the prologue calls God "Father" and Jesus his "only Son" *(monogenēs).* Although some take the prologue to mean that God gloried in his Son as an earthly father might glory or take pride in his son (NRSV), this is unlikely. The echoes of Israel's history, which continue to the end of this section, show that God's own glory is in view (NRSV[fn]). For the only Son to reveal God's glory is to make God known (1:18).[17] The Gospel will later say that the Son shared the heavenly glory of his Father before the creation (17:5, 24). Glory is now what he brings into the world through works of power, like turning water into wine and raising the dead (2:11; 11:40). In this way Jesus reveals the glory of God (17:4). This continues through his passion and resurrection, for even in death Jesus conveys the glory of God — and how he does this is considered below (see pp. 120-23). Readers find that God's glory is not only revealed by Jesus but in him and through him.

Finally, God's only Son is "full of grace and truth" (1:14). The language again echoes Israel's sojourn in the desert, where Moses wanted to see God's glory but was not permitted to see God's face (Exod. 33:17-23). Instead, what Moses heard was that God was full of steadfast love and faithfulness, or "full of grace and truth" as John puts it (Exod. 34:6). This expression identifies who God is, and the Gospel says it also characterizes Jesus. The grace and truth of God, which were announced to Moses, "came" *(egeneto)* through Jesus Christ (John 1:17). Where this grace and truth come to people, God comes to them. This is what occurs in Jesus, according to John.

Exercising the Power of God

The question of what it means to call Jesus the Son of God is central to the disputes that flare up during his ministry. Jesus heals a paralyzed man on the Sabbath, which his opponents consider a violation of God's command to rest on the Sabbath. Healing was a form of work that was forbidden on the Sabbath unless someone's life was in danger. But this was not the case with long-term paralysis. Jesus could have waited a day to heal the man. Therefore, Jesus seems to flout the law of God by his actions (5:16). Jesus' response intensifies the dispute. He says, "My Father is still working and I am working" (5:17). Now it is no longer a case of Sabbath violation but one of open rebellion against God. They think that by calling God his Father, Jesus is trying to make himself equal with God (5:18). In what follows Jesus must show that the opposite is true. He is not a man trying to move upward to seize the place of God. Instead, he insists that he has come down from God and works in complete obedience to God. But how can he show this?

Jesus argues that the Son can work on the Sabbath because the Father does so (5:17). Initially this approach seems counterintuitive. After all, the law says that God created heaven and earth in six days and then *rested* on the seventh day. Therefore, people are to *rest* on the Sabbath because God rested on the Sabbath (Exod. 20:8-11). Nevertheless, it was understood that God does not halt all activity one day each week. The Father continues to give life on the Sabbath, just as he does every other day of the week.[18] Where there is life, there God is active. Jesus' opponents would agree. For them the issue is not the premise that God works on the Sabbath. It is the inference that Jesus can do what God does.

Next, Jesus makes the case that he is not defying God's will but carrying it out. The "Son can do nothing on his own, but only what he sees the Father doing; for whatever the Father does, the Son does likewise" (John 5:19). We noted earlier that here God is depicted as a craftsman, whose son watches him at work and thereby learns to do the same (see p. 37). God's "trade" centers on the giving of life. It was understood that God breathed life into people when the world was created and would bring the dead to life at the end of the age. Building on this premise Jesus says that his actions conform to those of God, for "as the Father raises the dead and gives them life, so also the Son gives life to whomever he wishes" (5:21). Jesus' actions bear out his claim. As God gives life to the dead, Jesus gives life to a boy on the threshold of death (4:49-50). As it is God's intent that the dead should rise, Jesus commands a paralytic to rise to his feet (5:8, 21). Jesus argues that his actions do not violate God's purposes but actually carry them out.

Then Jesus says that God the Father, who is the judge of all the earth, has now "*given* all judgment to the Son" (5:22). The direction of the action is crucial. If Jesus the Son judges, he is not usurping his Father's prerogatives. Rather, he is faithfully shouldering the responsibility the Father has given him. This means that God's judgment occurs as people respond positively or negatively to Jesus. Those who hear and believe him are no longer under judgment but pass from death to life (5:24). Conversely, those who do not believe reject the Son and the Father who sent him, and therefore remain under judgment. Jesus adds that what is true now will be true in the future, for the dead will one day hear the voice of the Son of God and come out, some to the resurrection of life and others to the resurrection of judgment (5:25-29; see pp. 176-79). The Father's power to give life and judge is exercised by the Son.

This unity in action in turn reflects an underlying unity of life. The Father "has life in himself" (5:26a). His life is not derived from any other source. Life originates in him. He can give life to others because he has it "in himself." The Father also gives life to the Son, which is not unusual, since giving life to their children is what fathers do. But the Father grants that the Son may have life "in himself," as the Father himself has it (5:26b). The direction of the action is clear: the Father gives life to the Son, the Son does not try to take it from the Father. And the Son is not a second source of life alongside the Father. Rather, the Son shares fully in the Father's life and has this life on the same terms that the Father does. This full participation in the Father's life is what enables the Son to give life to others. He can do what the Father does because he has life as the Father has it.

These points do not convince Jesus' opponents. Their challenge to this way of seeing him continues into Jesus' trial, and their perspectives deserve attention. Repeating the charge made earlier, they insist that Jesus is trying to "make" himself the Son of God. In their eyes he is a human being wrongfully elevating himself to divine status (19:7). Moreover, Jesus may claim the right to judge, but they insist that in their judgment he should be put to death. They assume the Roman governor will concur and will pronounce the sentence (18:30-32). Finally, they recognize that Jesus is purported to give life, but they expect the crucifixion to show that this is illusory. He will die like anyone else.

John's narrative offers responses to these issues. For the evangelist, Jesus the Son dies in obedience to his Father, not in rebellion against him. We have seen that on one level the crucifixion occurs because of human opposition to Jesus. The actions of his adversaries lead to his death (see pp. 70-74). But on another level, God commanded Jesus to lay down and then to take up his life. When speaking of the good shepherd who lays down his life for the sheep, Jesus says, "No one takes it from me, but I lay it down of my own accord. I have power to lay it down, and I have power to take it up again. I have received this command from my Father" (10:18; see pp. 44-46). This comment reverses the way one sees the passion narrative. If God has commanded Jesus to lay down his life, then Jesus obeys God by going to his death. His crucifixion is not the result of rebellion against God but of complete obedience to God. The evangelist assumes that Jesus did not have to lay down his life. Like the hired hand in the shepherd passage, he could have run away to preserve himself from danger (10:13-15). But he does not do so. Jesus lays down his life as his Father wishes. If Jesus' opponents see the cross as the outcome of Jesus' opposition to God, the evangelist regards it as the expression of the Son's complete unity with the Father's will.

As the Son of God, Jesus continues the work of judging throughout the passion. This occurs in part through role reversals during his interrogation. As the authorities try to question Jesus about his teaching and purported kingship, he questions them about their reasons for doing so (18:19-21, 34). When a soldier strikes him, he calls the soldier to account (18:23). But the principal judgment occurs when Jesus is brought to the judgment seat for sentencing. There his Jewish opponents insist that their only king is Caesar rather than God, and Pilate the Roman governor suppresses the truth and hands over an innocent prisoner for execution (see pp. 70-74). Readers of the Gospel can see what the actors within it cannot. As people reject Jesus, they place themselves under judgment. As the Son of God, Jesus silently serves as judge even as others condemn him to death.[19]

And what about giving life? That too is the work of God's Son, and he continues doing this through his crucifixion. The Gospel has shown that life in its theological sense means relating to God, and this occurs when people are brought to faith. The gift of love is the way that God evokes faith, and the most radical expression of love is to lay down one's life for someone else (15:13). *In Jesus' death for others he communicates God's love for the world, and when this love calls forth faith, it brings people into the relationship that is true life* (3:14-16; see pp. 44-46). The crucifixion does not negate the Son's claim to give life. It is integral to the way he carries out this God-given responsibility, and through the resurrection that follows, he gives this life a future (see pp. 179-82).

Embodying the Presence of God

The Gospel also points readers to a deeper sense of union between the Father and the Son. The prologue began by identifying the Son of God with the Word of God. If the Word was not only with God but was God, then the Word made flesh embodies God's presence (1:1, 14). John assumes that there is only one true God (5:44; 17:3). God's identity was revealed to Moses at the burning bush when he said, "I Am who I Am. . . . Say to the people of Israel, I Am has sent me to you" (Exod. 3:14). In some Old Testament passages the expression "I Am" was translated into Greek as *egō eimi*. For example, God said, "Behold, behold that I Am and that there is no god beside me" (Deut. 32:39). God the Creator declared, "I Am and there is no other" (Isa. 45:18). In John's Gospel Jesus uses the "I Am" or *egō eimi* for himself. For the evangelist, this does not make Jesus a second god. Rather, the idea is that the one true God meets people in Jesus.[20]

The responses people make when Jesus utters the "I Am" reflect the sense of an encounter with God. When the soldiers come to arrest Jesus in the garden, he asks whom they are looking for. They say, "Jesus of Nazareth," and he replies, *"Egō eimi."* Although the words are often translated "I am he" or "It is I," the heavily armed troops draw back and fall to the ground as one might do in the presence of God (John 18:5-6). In other contexts Jesus emphasizes the connection to God by using the "I Am" expression where it makes no grammatical sense and stands apart as absolute. During debates in the temple he tells his detractors, "you will die in your sins unless you believe that I Am"; and when "you have lifted up the Son of Man, then you will realize that I Am" (8:24, 28). Finally, he pushes the connection to the breaking point by saying, "Very truly I tell you, before Abraham was, I Am" (8:58). Here the link to God is all too clear — and his listeners attempt to stone him for blasphemy.

The bystanders in the temple work with well-defined categories: God is not a human being and a human being is not God. What Jesus says is understood to violate the categories, and this provokes the negative response. But in this same context Jesus works to redefine the categories.[21] He links the "I Am" to the image of light, saying, "I Am the light of the world" (8:12). This metaphor provides another way of seeing. It brings together several different and seemingly contradictory facets of Jesus' identity in a single image. The effect is like that of a musical chord, where several notes are struck at the same time, creating a unified multidimensional sound.

The debates themselves disclose the various dimensions encompassed by the image. Some bystanders wonder whether Jesus can be considered a *teacher*. The light imagery fits this aspect of his identity. It was said that God's law was a light for the nations and that those who instructed people in God's ways brought light to the world (7:14-24; Isa. 51:4). Others question whether Jesus might be the *Messiah*. It was understood that the Messiah too was to be a light for the nations, bringing the light of justice, peace, and salvation (John 7:25-44; Isa. 9:1-7; 42:6; 49:6). Finally there is the conflict over his *relationship to God* and his right to use the "I Am" for himself. And God was widely identified with light. The prophets said, "Arise, shine, for your light has come, and the glory of the Lord has risen upon you" (Isa. 60:1). They promised that "the Lord will be your everlasting light" and salvation (Isa. 60:19-20; Ps. 27:1).[22] Given existing categories, Jesus' use of the "I Am" sounds outrageous, yet "light" creates a new category that encompasses multiple dimensions of Jesus' identity in a single image. A teacher is light, the Messiah is light, and God is light. In the light of Jesus the teacher and Messiah, people encounter the light of God's presence.

The debate does not end there. The question of Jesus' unity with God is raised again in the discourse about the good shepherd, where Jesus says "I and the Father are one" (John 10:30). And readers learn that this is what it means for him to be the Son of God (10:36). The hearers' reaction is immediate and intense. They prepare to stone Jesus as a man who is trying to take God's place (10:33). The context underscores the problem of comprehending Jesus' identity within existing categories. This exchange takes place during the Festival of Dedication or Hanukkah. The story of the festival included a hero and a villain. The villain was Antiochus IV, a Syrian ruler who suppressed Jewish practices and turned the Jerusalem temple into a shrine to Zeus (1 Macc. 1:41-61; 2 Macc. 6:1-2). He used the title "Epiphanes," which connoted a "manifestation" of the divine. His actions were seen as blasphemous attempts to become equal to God (2 Macc. 9:12, 28). The hero in the story was Judah Maccabee, a Jewish military leader who recaptured the temple and rededicated it to the worship of God (1 Macc. 4:52-59). In this context, these are the alternatives: military hero versus blasphemer. So which is Jesus?

Jesus' response again redefines the categories. He introduces a metaphor that creates another way of seeing. He says, "I Am the good shepherd," and again fuses several contradictory facets of his identity in a single image (John 10:11). On one level, Jesus is a *human being*, and a shepherd is a common image for a human leader. As a shepherd protects and provides for the flock, a good leader is to protect and provide the people (Ezek. 34:2). This is what Jesus does for his followers. On another level, the shepherd was an image for the *Messiah*, who was to be a unique ruler for the people of God. It was said that God would establish over his people one shepherd, the heir to David's throne, who would feed and care for them (Ezek. 34:23).[23] And we noted above that John understands Jesus to be the promised Messiah (see pp. 91-96). On a third level, the consummate good shepherd is *God*, who said, "I myself will search for my sheep" and give them good pasture; "I myself will be the shepherd of my sheep" (Ezek. 34:11, 15; cf. Ps. 23:1-2). In Jesus' shepherding, God himself is shepherding.

From their vantage point, Jesus' opponents see Jesus as a human being and insist that a human being cannot be God. But John says, "Try looking at him as a shepherd and ask what that means." Jesus claims to have come in order that people might have eternal life, and his works of healing bear witness that this is his ultimate purpose (John 10:28, 37). So does he give eternal life as a human being or as God? Or at this point do the usual categories break down?

To say "I and the Father are one" is a simple statement that expresses a complex relationship. There is a double subject: I and the Father. The verb is plural: we are. But the descriptive term is singular: one. The Son is differentiated from the Father and yet identified with the Father. Jesus does not say "I am the Father," but he does say "the Father is in me and I am in the Father" (10:38).[24] Within the differences between the Father and Son is a unity that is expressed but not fully defined. Where Jesus works, God works. The Son has life as the Father has life. To encounter the Son is to encounter the Father who sent him.

The depth of Jesus' unity with God was not recognized during his ministry. The Fourth Evangelist seems quite clear about this. Even at the last supper Jesus' own followers are unable to discern the depth of the connection. As Thomas asks him questions, Jesus replies, "If you know me, you will know my Father also. From now on you do know him and have seen him" (14:7). The response is incredulity. To know Jesus is to know God and to see Jesus is to see God? This is difficult to fathom, so Philip says, "Lord, show us the Father, and we will be satisfied" (14:8). Jesus repeats, "Whoever has seen me has seen the Father," for "I am in the Father and the Father is in me" (14:9-10). The words Jesus speaks point to the Father's presence within him, and Jesus' actions show that "the Father who dwells in me does his works" (14:10-11). Where Jesus acts, his Father is active. The Father and Son can be differentiated, yet Jesus can say that "I am in the Father and the Father is in me" (14:11). One is present in the other.

Thomas's question at the last supper initiated this exchange about Jesus' unity with the Father. But the appearance of the crucified and risen Jesus to Thomas will show that the implications can only be grasped after the resurrection, not before it. Only when the risen Jesus shows Thomas the marks of the crucifixion can Thomas respond, "My Lord and my God" (20:28). Here, for the first time since the prologue, Jesus is identified as "God." The words about Jesus' relation to God, which Thomas heard at the supper, shape the context in which he encounters the risen Christ. This encounter, in turn, discloses the meaning of the words, as we will see (pp. 126-27).

But here we must ask, what does it mean to call Jesus "God"? The Gospel assumes that there is only one true God, and in the crucified and risen Jesus one meets him (5:44; 17:3). Jesus is not a second god. Rather, it is the one true God who is present and active in Jesus. In the theological world of John's Gospel, the term "God" is broad enough to encompass both the Father and the Son. When Thomas sees Jesus he does not see the physical form of God. The prologue acknowledges that no one has ever seen God in a physical sense, and this remains true throughout the Gospel (1:18a). Yet the Son, who is also called "God," has made God the Father known (1:18b). Where the Son speaks, the Father speaks. Where the Son acts, the Father acts. Knowing who Jesus is means knowing who God is. Through his death, Jesus gives himself completely in love for others, and this love gives them life. Through his resurrection Jesus shows that this life has a future. To see the love and the life that the crucified and risen Jesus gives is to see who God is. Therefore, when shown the wounds of the living Christ, Thomas can say, "Here I see God."

CHAPTER 5

Crucifixion and Resurrection

The crucifixion is a stark and disturbing element in the story of Jesus. If Jesus was from God and was doing the work of God, then why was he put to death? If God had sent him and he spoke the truth about God, then why were his opponents able to execute him? The death of the Messiah is troubling enough, but the brutality of the process intensifies the issue. One of the disciples in Jesus' inner circle turned against him, making arrangements for his arrest. After being seized, Jesus was interrogated by the Jewish and Roman authorities (18:1-40). His captors subjected him to scourging and ridicule, clothing him with a purple robe and a crown of thorns to show contempt for his purported kingship (19:1-3). On the way to the place of execution Jesus carried his own cross, creating a degrading spectacle that warned the public about the consequences of defying the law (19:17). Crucifixion was supremely painful, as nails were driven through the wrists and ankles, so that when placed on the cross the body would weigh down on the wounds (19:18). Some forms of execution allowed the victim to retain a measure of dignity, but crucifixion did not. To crucify someone was to hang him on the "tree of shame."[1]

The meaning of the crucifixion was sharply disputed. The Jewish leaders thought it right for Jesus to be put to death because he seemed to flout the law of Moses, and his actions created such a sensation among the people that they feared he would foment a disastrous revolt against the Roman order. Executing him was a way to end the threat he posed to social stability (10:33; 11:48-50; 19:7, 12). Pilate the Roman governor was told that Jesus had made himself into a king, and crucifying a pretender to the throne was politically expedient, since it showed Pilate's loyalty to the emperor and let the public know that opposition to Roman rule would not be tolerated (19:12-22). For people on the street, the crucifixion discredited the idea that Jesus could be the Messiah. If the Messiah was to rule with strength and honor, the cross meant defeat and disgrace. If the Scriptures said the Messiah would bring in God's everlasting kingdom, the hope that Jesus might do so was shattered when he was "lifted up" to die by crucifixion (12:32-34). In a context of conflicting viewpoints, the writer of John's Gospel faced the challenge of showing that it was precisely by dying that Jesus would reveal the power of God, and that the cross was the proper place to proclaim the Messiah's reign.

The resurrection created its own set of issues. Rather than resolving the problem of Jesus' death by bringing the story to a happy ending, the message of the resurrection made things more difficult. After all, why would anyone believe it? There were other more plausible ways of coming to terms with a tragic death. Many people already believed that there would be a resurrection at the end of the age. Those who mourned the loss of family members or friends could take comfort in the hope that they would return to life on "the last day," when the present world of sorrow would end and the blessed age to come would dawn (11:24). Others thought of death as a transition point, when the person's body died, freeing the soul to ascend to life in heaven. According to John's Gospel, Jesus had spoken about leaving the world and returning to his Father (16:28). Therefore, one might assume that death brought an end to Jesus' bodily suffering and allowed his soul to depart to heavenly rest. It would be difficult to object to this point of view. Yet the Gospel moves against the stream by saying that Jesus rose, bodily, from the dead.

Allusions to the cross and resurrection span the whole of Jesus' public ministry, from the moment John the Baptist introduces him as the Lamb of God until Jesus approaches Jerusalem and tells the crowds welcoming him with palm branches that he will be lifted up in death (1:29; 12:32-33). Reading John's account of Jesus' death and resurrection in the context of the Gospel as a whole discloses multiple dimensions of meaning.[2]

The Significance of Jesus' Crucifixion

Many of the forces that brought about Jesus' crucifixion have already been considered theologically in previous chapters. On one level we have seen that Jesus' death was the product of human sin and unbelief. His adversaries did not accept his claims and put their unbelief into action by having him put to death (pp. 70-72). On a second level Jesus' death was brought about by demonic evil. Satan carried out his hostile designs through human agents, using deception and hatred to kill the Son of God (pp. 76-78). On a third level the perspective changes dramatically as readers learn that Jesus' death carried out the will of God. In the face of human sin and demonic evil, God commands Jesus to lay down and take up his life in order to convey God's love to the world. It is not God's will that Jesus should die, as if the cross were an end in itself. Rather, God's will is that the world that is alienated from him should believe and have life. Love is communicated through crucifixion in order to evoke the faith that brings life (pp. 41-47). On a fourth level Jesus' death is the result of his obedience to God. Although his opponents charged that Jesus should be executed for rebellion against God, the Gospel discloses that he went to his death in obedience to God's command. He laid down his life as God directed him, in order that God's purposes might be fulfilled (10:17-18).[3]

In what follows, we shift from the theological factors behind the crucifixion to ask about the *results* of the crucifixion. What did Jesus' death do for people? Everyone in the Gospel agrees that Jesus died. Friend and foe alike acknowledge the reality of his death. At the end of the day, the soldiers who carried out the crucifixion broke the legs of those who were crucified with Jesus, and when they came to Jesus they saw that he was "already dead" (19:33). The issue is not whether Jesus died but what his death means, and if readers are to understand it as something more than a senseless tragedy, the Gospel must reveal this. Here we will consider Jesus' death as an expression of love in human terms, as a sacrifice for sin, as a victory over evil, and as a revelation of divine glory.[4]

Love in Human Terms

Beginning at the simplest level, John's Gospel indicates that Jesus' death conveys love in human terms. During the last supper Jesus said, "No one has greater love than this, to lay down one's life for one's friends" (15:13). In a basic sense this saying is a commentary on the crucifixion, indicating that Jesus will go to his death willingly out of love for his friends. The idea is that if people show love by what they give for others, the most complete form of love is revealed through the most complete form of giving, the giving up of one's own life for other people. Readers would not need to belong to the circle of Jesus' followers to understand this. Plato, Aristotle, Seneca, and Paul agreed that true love and friendship might mean that one person would willingly die for another.[5] Drawing on this familiar idea, John's Gospel turns it into a lens that brings the meaning of the crucifixion into focus. Jesus defines love by his words so that readers will see that he conveys love by his death.

John's account of Jesus washing the disciples' feet reinforces the point. The passage begins by saying that Jesus, having "loved his own who were in the world, he loved them to the end" (13:1). By introducing the scene with an explicit statement about Jesus' love, the Gospel enables readers to see the footwashing as a tangible expression of that love — and most early readers would have needed help seeing the footwashing in this way. If Jesus' statement about laying down one's life for one's friends suggests the lofty tones of virtue and heroism, his act of washing feet smacks of scandal and self-abnegation. People normally washed their own feet or had them washed by a slave. Free people did not wash the feet of others. A host would offer guests a basin of water, but people then washed their own feet or else the washing was done by a slave.[6] Therefore, when Jesus the master washes the feet of the disciples, he does the work of a slave; and Peter emphatically objects to his behavior, saying, "You will never wash my feet" (13:8). There were of course rare instances when a free person would assume the role of a slave and wash another person's feet as an expression of complete devotion, but these were extremes — which is why the action suits Jesus' purposes so well. He washes feet to show extreme love, to convey scandalous devotion, and to foreshadow his consummate act of self-giving on the cross.

The love expressed through the footwashing anticipates the love given through the crucifixion. The Gospel links the footwashing to the crucifixion by framing the episode with references to the impending betrayal (13:2, 18-30), and by saying that Jesus "laid down" his garments, echoing what was said earlier about laying down his life (10:17-18; 13:4). The introduction to the footwashing said that Jesus loved his own "to the end," which in Greek is *eis telos* (13:1), and this expression anticipates his final word from the cross: *tetelestai*, "it is accomplished," "the *telos* has been reached." Connecting the footwashing to the crucifixion enables readers to see that the love Jesus shows in a preliminary way by washing feet, he gives in a definitive way by laying down his life.

Presenting the crucifixion as love in human terms recognizes that if love is to be given to human beings, it must be given in forms that can be grasped by human beings. Jesus comes from heaven above, but cannot reveal the things of God in heavenly speech. Human beings belong to the earth, and in his teaching Jesus refers to the things of the earth — like bread, light, and water — to convey what comes from above. In the same way, Jesus washes feet like a slave and speaks of laying down one's life for a friend, drawing on patterns of earthly life to communicate with earthly people, that they might grasp the love he gives through his service in life and finally through his death.

Love is also conveyed in human terms so that it can be lived in human terms. Jesus' death is both the source and the norm for Christian discipleship, according to John. After showing love by washing his disciples' feet, Jesus directs them to wash one another's feet, saying, "as I have loved you, you also should love one another" (13:34). Again, when explaining that the highest form of love is to lay down one's life for others, he relates this to the new commandment, that the disciples are to love one another as Jesus loved them (15:12-13). Since Jesus' love is the source and norm for Christian discipleship, he gives his love in tangible worldly forms so that his disciples might give their love in tangible worldly forms. Jesus' love is conveyed in human terms so that it may be lived in human terms.[7]

Sacrifice for Sin

Readers discover a different theological perspective when they consider the death of Jesus through the words of John the Baptist, "Behold the Lamb of God, who takes away the sin of the world" (1:29). Here we move from the realm of love and service to the sphere of sin and sacrifice.[8] Rather than relating the crucifixion to the circle of Jesus' friends, the passage relates it to the world and its sin. This perspective on the death of Christ presupposes a more radical sense of human alienation from God. Jesus is called the Lamb of God at the moment he first enters public view in chapter 1, and no one follows Jesus until John the Baptist says again, "Behold the Lamb of God," prompting two of John's own disciples to follow Jesus (1:29, 36). To discern the theological implications we must consider each part of John's statement in turn.

First is the expression "the Lamb of God." Introducing Jesus as the

Lamb at the beginning of the Gospel anticipates his death at Passover at the end of the Gospel. According to John's account, Jesus ate his last meal with the disciples on the night before Passover, rather than on Passover evening as in the other gospels (13:1). On the morning before Jesus' execution, the Jewish authorities avoided entering the praetorium in order to keep themselves pure for the Passover meal that evening (18:28). Jesus was taken out to be crucified on the day of preparation for the Passover at about noon, when the sacrifice of the Passover lambs began in the temple (19:14). The slaughter of the lambs was to be completed before sundown, and John relates that the soldiers saw that Jesus was dead before evening fell (19:31). The soldiers broke the legs of the two men who hung beside Jesus, but they did not break Jesus' legs since he was already dead. The Gospel relates this to the Scripture passage that says, "His bones shall not be broken" (19:36), citing the biblical stipulation that the bones of a Passover lamb were not to be broken.[9]

The link between the crucifixion and the Passover sacrifice seems clear, but its meaning is not simple. A Passover lamb was not generally regarded as a sacrifice for sin, but was more closely associated with deliverance from death. According to Exodus 12, the people of Israel observed the first Passover in Egypt by putting lamb's blood on their doorposts and lintels, not to atone for sin, but to prevent the destroyer from entering their homes and slaying their firstborn. The annual Passover sacrifice of the lambs commemorated this deliverance. To account for the connection between the Lamb of God and sin, some suggest that the Gospel combines Passover imagery with that of the suffering servant of Isaiah 53, who is compared to a lamb that is led to the slaughter and who is said to bear the sins of many.[10] By drawing on these and other backgrounds the Gospel develops a new type of imagery, in which Jesus the Passover Lamb of God delivers people from death precisely by delivering them from sin.

This brings us to the second element in John the Baptist's testimony: "the sin of the world." Sin, in John's Gospel, is a problem in one's relationship with God, which by extension affects one's relationships with other people. Sin is the alienation from God that is expressed in a refusal to believe in Jesus, the one whom God has sent. The particular sins that people commit manifest this underlying antipathy toward God and Jesus, so that sin encompasses both unbelief and the actions that proceed from it (15:18-25). The sin of the world is fundamentally the world's alienation from God and the one whom God sent.

We have seen that human sin leads to the death of the Lamb, according to John (see pp. 70-72). Those who do not believe that Jesus is from God regard him as a blasphemer and a threat to the social order. Conflict intensifies throughout Jesus' ministry. As unbelief takes its course, it leads to his arrest and condemnation by representatives of "the world," both Jews and Gentiles. This means that in a very basic sense, Jesus' death is the product of human sin. The Lamb suffers the consequences of sin because he is put to death by those who do not believe. Yet the paradox is that Jesus' death is not only the result of human sin — it is God's means of overcoming sin.

This brings us to the third element of John the Baptist's testimony, which is that the Lamb of God "takes away" sin. The Gospel regularly uses this verb (*airein* in Greek) to mean taking away or removing something.[11] If sin is the unbelief that separates people from God, then the Lamb of God removes sin by removing unbelief. In Johannine theology, sin is taken away when faith is evoked. Sin is the opposite of faith, and both are relational notions. If sin is a deadly alienation from God, then faith is a life-giving relationship with God. The death of Christ takes sin away when it creates faith in the face of unbelief.[12] For this to occur, the death of Christ must call forth human faith in God by conveying God's love to humankind.

The dynamics of divine sacrificial love are reflected in John 3, which anticipates that as Moses lifted up the serpent on the pole, so must the Son of Man be lifted up on the cross, so that whoever believes in him may have eternal life (3:14-15). The passage goes on to say that it was because God so loved the world that he gave his only Son — and in light of the previous verses God's giving of the Son includes giving him up to die (3:16). It was because God so loved the world that he gave his only Son up to death, so that whoever believes in him might not perish but have eternal life. If on one level the crucifixion conveys Jesus' love for those who followed him, on another level it conveys God's love for the world that hated him.

John's profound sense of the depth of the world's sin is what gives this text its edge. The "world" in John's Gospel is not characterized by radiant sunsets and gentle breezes, by the colors of spring flowers or the golden hues of fall — it requires no sacrifice to love a world like that. But in John's Gospel God loves the world that hates him; he gives his Son for the world that rejects him. He offers his love to a world estranged from him in order to overcome its hostility and bring the world back into relationship with its Maker. The proper theological term for this is "atonement," for if atonement means reconciling parties that have been separated, then the sacrificial love of God, conveyed through the death of Jesus, brings about atonement in a Johannine sense when it overcomes the hostility of unbelief by bringing about faith.

This understanding of atonement differs from the idea that Jesus' death is the sacrifice that pays the penalty for human sin.[13] The notion that Jesus' self-sacrifice removes the penalty for sin revolves around the two poles of justice and mercy or law and grace. The idea is that when someone transgresses a law, justice requires that the person be punished. In cases of severe wrongdoing, justice might require that a person surrender his or her own life. As an act of mercy, however, a transgressor might be allowed to offer something in exchange for his or her life. By sacrificing something, the demands of the law are met, but in a way that allows the person to live. When this paradigm is transferred to the realm of theology, human beings are regarded as sinners who are justly condemned by God. Because God is just he expects the penalty for sin to be paid, but because God is merciful he allows the penalty for sin to be paid by his own Son Jesus, who dies in the place of sinners. The result is that Jesus' self-sacrifice honors the need for divine justice, while making room for divine mercy.

John's Gospel, however, operates with a different theological framework. The Gospel does not focus on the legal penalty for sin but on the matter of sin itself. It does not say that the Lamb takes away "guilt" but that he takes away sin — he removes unbelief. The Gospel does not relate Jesus' death to the need for divine justice but to the need for human faith. When the Gospel speaks of the wrath of God, it says that wrath threatens those who do not "believe" (3:36). When Jesus tells his opponents that they will die in their sins, he adds that they will die in their sins unless they "believe" (8:24). When the Advocate, the Spirit, comes to convict the world of sin after Jesus' return to the Father, readers are told that the sin is that the world does not "believe" (16:8-9). According to the Gospel of John, people fall under divine judgment because of unbelief, and they are delivered from divine judgment by being brought to faith (3:17). *When the love of God, conveyed through the death of Jesus, overcomes the sin of unbelief by evoking faith, it delivers people from the judgment of God by bringing them into true relationship with God.* This is atonement in the Johannine sense.

Proponents of a substitutionary interpretation of Jesus' sacrifice sometimes point out that the Gospel says that the good shepherd lays down his life "for" *(hyper)* the sheep (10:11, 15).[14] Nevertheless, there is no suggestion that the good shepherd lays down his life to deliver the flock from divine judgment. The specific threat against the flock comes from thieves and bandits, not from God's wrath. The point is that the shepherd conveys his devotion by laying down his life for the flock, in contrast to the hired hand who cares nothing for the sheep (10:13-14). Later, Caiaphas remarks that one man must die "for" the people (11:50). From Caiaphas's perspective, Jesus' death will save people from the consequences of a popular uprising. The evangelist then adds that Jesus' death will gather his followers into one (11:51-52). But again, there is no suggestion that dying "for" the people equals paying the legal penalty for sin. The Fourth Gospel has a different understanding of sacrifice.

The crucifixion of the Lamb "takes away sin" by taking away unbelief. To say this does not create an understanding of the atonement that is purely "subjective." The love that the Lamb conveys must come to people from outside themselves, from God. Change comes when the love communicated through the Lamb's self-sacrifice acts on people from without. Can this be reduced to what some call the "moral influence" approach to atonement, in which the Lamb's selfless example moves people to amend their lives? Hardly. According to the moral influence theory, "everyone becomes more righteous — by which we mean a greater lover of the Lord — after the Passion of Christ than before," since it inspires "greater love" and "deeper affection" in people.[15] The underlying assumption is that to some degree people are already righteous and lovers of God, and that this tendency is encouraged by Christ's example. But this is not the outlook of the Fourth Gospel, which has a more radical notion of human estrangement from God. Given the Gospel's understanding of sin, something more than good influence is necessary for change to occur.

The death of Christ must *overcome* sin by evoking faith. When we looked at Jesus' death as love in human terms, we noted that he spoke of laying down his life for his friends (15:13). But when speaking of the Lamb, the Gospel envisions a world that is alienated from God by sin. Sacrificing one's life for a friend may express a relationship of love that already exists, but sacrificing one's life for a sinful world is done to create a relationship of love where one does not exist. Jesus' death may provide an example of love for people to follow, but a sinful world needs more than an example or it will not follow. The Lamb is sacrificed to create a relationship of faith in the face of the alienation created by sin. If a label is needed for this way of construing the death of Christ, it is *kerygmatic*. God addresses a hostile world with his radical Word of love in the crucified Lamb of God. When the crucified Word creates faith, it brings people to the relationship that

God intends. And when the crucified Word evokes such faith, God can say, "Now I am satisfied."[16]

Victory over Evil

Another theological perspective opens up when we hear Jesus say, "Now is the judgment of this world, now will the ruler of this world be cast out; and I, when I am lifted up from the earth, will draw all people to myself"; and the narrator explains that Jesus said this to show by what death he was to die (12:31-33). Rather than speaking of love and friendship or sin and sacrifice, this passage interprets the crucifixion in terms of conflict and victory in a world dominated by a hostile power.[17] Here the basic problem is not so much human sin as it is the oppressive power of evil. People are not only sinful and in need of atonement, they are oppressed by evil and in need of liberation. Jesus' opponent, according to this passage, is the ruler of this world, whom the Gospel also calls Satan, the devil, and the evil one (13:2, 27; 17:15). John never fully describes Satan, but by telling of Jesus' clashes with opponents he reminds readers that evil works through human actions such as hatred and deceit (7:7; 8:44). Therefore, as the battle with evil reaches its climax in the passion, Jesus must meet hatred with divine love and deceit with divine truth.

Judas is the devil's ally in the passion story. Judas is initially linked to evil in John 6, but the plot thickens in John 13 where readers learn that the devil himself has determined that Judas will betray Jesus (13:2-3). Jesus' strategy in the conflict with evil is to show unwavering love (13:1). He assumes his battle dress by laying down his garments, girding himself with a towel, and taking up a basin to wash feet. The text makes clear that Jesus does not act out of weakness, but out of the strength of one who has come from God, who is going to God, and who has been given authority by God to manifest his power in an act of devoted love (13:1, 3). John says that God put all things in Jesus' hands, and Jesus now uses his hands to wash the disciples' feet, apparently including the feet of Judas. Therefore, if Judas remains unclean, as the text says he does, it is not because Jesus excludes him from his cleansing love, but because Judas is resistant to what Jesus offers (13:11).

The Gospel indicates that Jesus possesses superior battlefield intelligence and knows that Judas will hand Jesus over to his enemies. Yet when asked to identify the betrayer, Jesus dips bread into the supper dish and gives it to Judas — a gesture commonly understood to show favor. This gracious act on Jesus' part provokes intense demonic resistance in Judas, for when he receives the bread, Satan enters him (13:27). The action and response disclose the nature of the conflict, for what evil resists is the graciousness that Jesus extends. The Gospel says that Jesus chooses Judas, washes Judas, and gives Judas food (6:70-71; 13:1-11, 26), so that Satan's entry into Judas marks opposition to the graciousness Jesus shows. This opposition does not mean that evil is the superior force, however, for Judas does not depart from the table until Jesus allows him to do so, saying, "Do quickly what you are going to do" (13:27). Judas leaves the table only at Jesus' bidding, and in scenes to come Jesus will turn the destructive designs of evil toward the accomplishment of God's saving ends.

Jesus tells the disciples who remain with him, "I will no longer talk much with you, for the ruler of this world is coming. He has no power over me; but I do as the Father has commanded me, so that the world may know that I love the Father. Rise, let us be on our way" (14:30-31). When Jesus finally leaves the supper and arrives in the garden, he is met by Judas and a group of Roman soldiers and Jewish police, who serve as agents of the ruler of this world. Jesus seizes the initiative by asking whom they are seeking. When they reply "Jesus of Nazareth," he says "I Am," using words that recall the name of God; and Judas and the soldiers draw back and fall to the ground. The episode bears out that the ruler of this world has no power over Jesus (18:5-6).

Many a scriptwriter would end the scene here, with Judas and the soldiers lying helplessly on the ground and Jesus standing coolly erect after his effortless victory, but John does not do so. At the end of the episode the soldiers arrest Jesus, bind him, and take him away. So why subdue the opposition only to be taken captive? Jesus subdues the opposition long enough to secure the release of his disciples: If "you are looking for me, let these men go" (18:8). John tells the story to show the extent to which Jesus cares for his own. Divine power is used for human deliverance. Jesus subdues the opposition so that others might be set free. But he himself is bound and taken away by his captors because the battle is not yet over: he must infiltrate more deeply into his opponents' territory where judgment will take place.

John's Gospel understands that people are judged by their positive or negative responses to Jesus. A saying earlier in the Gospel sets the tone: "Those who believe in him are not condemned; but those who do not be-

lieve are condemned already" (3:18). Jesus engages in this conflict by rejecting the weaponry of the world and meeting his opponents armed only
with truth (18:36-37). In some of the Gospel's most ironic scenes, Jesus' accusers make charges that bring Jesus closer to death while bringing the accusers themselves under judgment.

We have seen that the Jewish leaders charge that Jesus is guilty on two
counts: rebellion against Rome and rebellion against God. Arguing that Jesus is a rebel against Rome, they insist that he is making himself into a
king. Ironically, however, they are the ones who demand the release of
Barabbas the insurrectionist and thereby show that they are guilty of opposing Roman rule (18:40; 19:12). They also insist that Jesus is a rebel
against God, who tries to usurp God's prerogatives by making himself out
to be the Son of God. The trial, however, enables readers to see that the reverse is true, for Jesus' accusers finally declare that their only king is Caesar
— and Caesar was the man who was put in the place of God (19:7, 15).[18] Pilate the Gentile fares no better. Pilate claims to have the power to do whatever he wants with Jesus, and he declares three times that Jesus is innocent,
which is true. But if Pilate knows the truth, he proves incapable of doing
the truth, for in the end he knowingly hands over an innocent man to be
crucified (18:38; 19:4, 6, 10, 16). In one sense this episode is a defeat, for the
claims made against Jesus lead to his death, but in another sense it is a victory for truth, since the world's pretensions to power and right are exposed
to the readers. In passing judgment on Jesus the world reveals the truth
about itself (see pp. 70-72).

"Now is the judgment of this world; now will the ruler of this world be
cast out" (12:31). John's Gospel describes no mythic fall of Satan, but it inti-
mates that the ruler of this world is cast out as the crucified Jesus is lifted
up as the world's true sovereign. Jesus is given his royal robe and crown of
thorns during the scourging that prepares him for death; Pilate acclaims
him a king before handing him over to his executioners; and Jesus is en-
throned by means of crucifixion. The sign above the cross reads, "Jesus of
Nazareth, the King of the Jews." It says this in Hebrew, in Latin, and in
Greek for all the world to see. On the cross one sees the proper ruler of this
world, the king whose love and truth cast out the power of hatred and deceit. His kingdom is not "from" the world since his power comes from
above rather than below (18:36; cf. 6:15); yet Jesus does reign for the world
and rightly bears the title "Savior of the world" (4:42).[19]

The theme of conflict and victory enables John's story of the crucifixion to confront readers with two forms of dominion. One is that of the crucified Jesus, whose resolute love, witness to the truth, and obedience to God bring him to his throne on Golgotha. The other is that of the sinister ruler of this world, who entwines his allies in a web of hostility and deception as he seeks to bring about the death of the Son of God. From this perspective, readers find that there is no place for neutrality. In the cosmic battle between God and evil, the question is: Which claimant to the throne will obtain the readers' loyalty? The fourth evangelist is a participant in the conflict, exposing the pretensions of evil in order to capture the readers for the crucified and risen king.

Love remains central to John's understanding of the crucifixion, but when viewed in the context of conflicting powers, it assumes a new vitality. Love is a weapon in a conflict, and it serves along with truth to dethrone the forces that oppose it. Those who follow Jesus are called to love as he loved, and if Jesus wielded love in the face of evil, then his disciples' love may also take militant forms. The expression of love is complex rather than simple. Jesus loved by washing feet and contending with Satan. For those who follow, love means service to others and witness to truth; it entails giving of oneself and opposing evil. For the writer of the Fourth Gospel, authentic love encompasses all of this.

Revelation of Divine Glory

Shifting our perspective one last time, we can consider the crucifixion in terms of glory. Jesus' final prayer before his arrest sounds the theme: "Father, the hour has come; glorify your Son so that the Son may glorify you. . . . I glorified you on earth by finishing the work that you gave me to do. So now, Father, glorify me in your own presence with the glory that I had in your presence before the world existed" (17:2, 4-5). The theme of glory takes us into yet another theological world, one that deals with the human need to know God.[20] The word "glory" *(doxa)* sometimes connotes honor (5:41), but in John's Gospel glory also has to do with the way God is revealed to human beings.

This perspective recognizes that people were created to know God, and the prayer in John 17 therefore states that eternal life means knowing the one true God and Jesus Christ, whom God has sent (17:3). To know God is to be in relationship with God, yet the Gospel also recognizes that people have no immediate knowledge of God. "No one has ever seen God," the Gospel says (1:18). God's presence is hidden until God chooses to reveal it. The theme of glory has to do with the way revelation takes place. To discern what this might be we must consider Jesus' saying in light of the wider gospel story.

First, Jesus said that he glorified God on earth by accomplishing the work that God gave him to do. Jesus' earthly ministry was done to glorify God, and in a basic sense this means he honored God through his faithful obedience to God's commands. During his public ministry Jesus claimed to teach what God wanted him to teach, and to perform the healings and other works that God wanted him to perform. Such faithfulness honors God (8:49). In another sense, however, Jesus glorified God by revealing God's power. Biblical writers sometimes use the term *doxa* or "glory" for the way the power of God is brought within the realm of human experience. According to John's Gospel, Jesus made divine power visible by the miraculous signs he performed. At the beginning of his ministry Jesus manifested his glory by turning water into wine at Cana (2:11); and at the end of his ministry he revealed the glory of God by calling the dead man Lazarus back to life (11:40). John's account of Jesus' career encompasses these and other miraculous acts, which reveal divine glory by revealing divine power.

A second element in Jesus' prayer concerns the glory he will resume in heaven once his ministry on earth is over. This heavenly glory is something that the Son of God enjoyed before the world existed. To share in such glory is to share in divine honor, divine majesty, and divine power. It was out of love that the Father gave the Son such glory before the foundation of the world, so that sharing in God's glory means sharing in God's love. By means of his passion Jesus will return to the Father and enter a heavenly glory that his followers on earth cannot fully perceive, but can hope to see in the future. Therefore, Jesus concludes his prayer by asking that those whom God has given him may one day be with him in God's presence, to see the fullness of the glory that God gave to him in love (17:24).

The prayer traces a movement from glory on earth to glory in heaven, and given only the lines we have considered thus far it would be easy to bypass the cross without comment. Yet other passages connect glory to the crucifixion itself. When Jesus enters Jerusalem at the end of his ministry, he says, "The hour has come for the Son of Man to be glorified," and he compares himself to a seed that must fall into the earth and die (12:23-24). When Judas receives the piece of bread and departs to carry out the betrayal, Jesus says, "Now the Son of Man has been glorified, and God has been glorified in him" (13:31). The saying does not limit glorification to what happens after the crucifixion, but links glorification to the process of betrayal that culminates in the crucifixion.[21] And this brings us back to the prayer in John 17, where Jesus says that he has glorified God on earth by finishing the works that God gave him to do. The Greek word for "finish" is *teleioō*, a form of the word Jesus will utter at the time of his death when he says *tetelestai*, "it is finished." If Jesus glorifies God on earth by accomplishing God's works, then he glorifies God by the crucifixion that completes these works. The question is how he does this.

Given the way Jesus manifested divine glory by miraculous acts of power during his ministry, we might expect a battery of miracles to occur during his crucifixion. In Matthew, Mark, and Luke, for example, the story of the crucifixion is vividly framed with displays of divine power. The eerie pall of darkness that the other gospels place over the crucifixion is a visible sign of supernatural force, and the dramatic tearing of the temple curtain reveals the hand of God. God's glory seems palpable in Matthew's account of the earth quaking and the saints rising on Good Friday (Matt. 27:45-54; Mark 15:33-38; Luke 23:44-45). The irony is that these traditional signs of divine power *are missing* from John's Gospel. John gives his readers no portents in heaven or on earth. If readers are to see glory in the crucifixion, they must see it in another way.

Put briefly, if the signs reveal God's glory by displaying divine power, the crucifixion reveals God's glory by conveying divine love.[22] The crucifixion completes Jesus' work of glorifying God on earth, for by laying down his life he gives himself completely so that the world may know of Jesus' love for God and God's love for the world (John 3:16; 14:31). By his resurrection and ascension Jesus returns to the heavenly glory that God prepared for him in love, and Jesus prays that his followers will one day join him in the Father's presence to share in this glory and love (17:5, 24-26). To the eye of faith, however, the glory of the exalted Lord is already present in the crucified body of Jesus.[23] If glory defines what the crucifixion is, the crucifixion defines what glory is. The crucifixion manifests the scope of divine power by disclosing the depth of divine love.

A similar perspective is reflected in statements about Jesus being "lifted up" *(hypsoō)*. The term can indicate either physical elevation or exaltation in the sense of honor, and when used for Jesus, both meanings are included. The contexts that speak of Jesus being "lifted up" make clear that it refers to his crucifixion, not to his ascension to heavenly glory. In so doing, these passages link the honor or glory of Jesus to the cross. We have seen that in 3:14-15 Jesus is said to be lifted up on the cross as Moses lifted up the serpent on the pole, and yet this underscores that the crucified Jesus also gives life (see pp. 44-46). Later, Jesus speaks about being "lifted up" by his adversaries, which occurs through his crucifixion (8:28). At the end of his public ministry he says, "I, when I am lifted up from the earth, will draw all people to myself," and the narrator explains that "he said this to indicate the kind of death he was to die" (12:32-33). Jesus' exaltation on the cross defines the character of his glory.

The centrality of love holds together the human and divine, the sacrificial and militant dimensions of Jesus' death. Love also creates the consummate paradox in John's understanding of the crucifixion: the death of Jesus can be a source of life. It is by dying that Jesus reveals the love of God, and when this love evokes faith, it brings people into the relationship with God that is true life (3:16).

The Significance of Jesus' Resurrection

John understands Jesus' death as the consummate expression of divine love, but recognizes that this is only apparent in retrospect, from the vantage point of the resurrection. In Johannine theology, the action of the risen Jesus is what brings people to the faith through which his life and death can be understood. The resurrection is essential for authentic faith because faith is a relationship with a living being. According to John, the crucifixion communicates the divine love that is the basis for a relationship with Jesus, and the resurrection means that this relationship is more than remembering one who has died. Faith is active trust in a Jesus who is unseen yet alive. Finally, the resurrection of Jesus defines hope for the future. The followers of Jesus face the prospect of a death that is as real as the death of Jesus himself. The message of resurrection is that the relationship with Jesus that begins now, in faith, has a future through the believer's own resurrection.[24]

Resurrection and Faith

Jesus' followers understood that his death was real and complete. Those who placed him in the tomb may have honored him by putting a hundred pounds of spices on the corpse, but this only underscores death's reality. Spices are placed on a body that is expected to decay, not on a person who is expected to return to life (19:38-42). At the beginning of this chapter we noted that there were ways in which people were able to deal with the death of someone close to them: One might hope that the person would rise in the future, when this age of sorrow ended; or one might treat death as the point where the person's soul was released from bodily suffering so that it could depart to a better life elsewhere. The message that Jesus had risen was not the obvious way for his followers to deal with his death.

The conclusion of the Gospel focuses on people who know that Jesus has died. They do not come to resurrection faith because they are unwilling to accept the fact that Jesus is dead and cling to the hope that he might still be alive. For them, Jesus' death is a given. They are certain that his adversaries killed him and that his corpse was placed in a tomb. The question is how anyone can believe that he has risen. This is the problem that John must address in his resurrection account.

The action begins with Mary Magdalene, who goes to the tomb and discovers that the stone has been removed from the entrance. John's narrative underscores the reality of Jesus' death, for Mary's response is immediate and commonsensical. She assumes that Jesus is still dead and that someone has taken the body: "They have taken the Lord out of the tomb and we do not know where they have laid him" (20:2). Her perception is shaped by ordinary experience. Thieves sometimes disturbed tombs when searching for any valuables that had been placed there with the body.[25] Alternatively, violating a tomb could be a hate crime, a malicious action designed to intimidate the family and friends of the deceased. Whatever the case, Mary is convinced that Jesus is dead and that the open tomb can readily be explained by the practice of grave robbery. Any faith in resurrection must *overcome* this fundamental conviction.

In the next scene, Peter and the Beloved Disciple continue the theme as they come to the burial place of Jesus (20:3-10). Readers are told that the Beloved Disciple sees the grave cloths lying in the tomb and that Peter sees the head cloth rolled up in a place by itself. The presence of the cloths, some neatly rolled up, makes the idea of grave robbery implausible, since intruders would either steal the wrapped body or else ransack the tomb while leaving both the body and cloths behind. And the Gospel says that the Beloved Disciple sees these things and believes. This seems to be a climactic moment, and to some extent it is. Although the evangelist does not say *what* the Beloved Disciple believes, it seems probable that he believes that Jesus has been released from death. This disciple is consistently faithful elsewhere, and is presumably the first to believe when he sees the empty tomb and the grave cloths. But what is surprising is that the narrator notes that his faith does not yet include understanding or prompt the disciple to say anything.[26] Moreover, there is no indication that Peter believes. In his case, seeing does *not* mean believing.

In John's Gospel, the faith that leads to telling others that Jesus is alive must come from something more than a vacant tomb. To be sure, it is important for John that the tomb is empty. No one can say "Jesus is risen" if the body still lies in the grave. Yet it is clear that seeing the open tomb and the discarded grave cloths does not guarantee faith or lead to proclamation of the resurrection. Theologically, the empty tomb is a presupposition for resurrection faith, but it is not the basis of resurrection faith. Such faith requires an encounter with the risen Jesus himself.

The story continues as Mary Magdalene remains unwavering in her conviction that the body has been stolen, even when she looks into the tomb and sees two angels in white, sitting where the body of Jesus had been (20:12). Readers might expect Mary to be startled by these supernatural beings, but she is not. When the angels ask why she is weeping, she speaks to them as she spoke to the disciples. She voices her conviction that the body has been taken, then turns away without giving the angels a chance to say anything that might make her change her mind (20:13).

The pattern persists even when Mary sees the risen Jesus. We might expect seeing to bring resurrection faith, but Mary does not recognize Jesus. Again, seeing is not believing. Mary's logic is impeccable. She naturally assumes that the man in the garden must be the gardener. So she speaks to him as she spoke to the disciples and the angels, expressing her conviction that the body was stolen: "Sir, if you have carried him away, tell me where you have laid him and I will take him away" (20:15). Readers may wonder why Mary is unable to recognize the risen Jesus, but speculating about this detracts from the flow of the narrative. The Gospel does not explain why Mary cannot recognize the risen Jesus. Rather, each successive scene builds suspense and makes one wonder what it will take for her to realize that he is not dead but alive.

Mary recognizes Jesus when he calls her by name. "Jesus said to her, 'Mary!' She turned and said to him in Hebrew, 'Rabbouni!' (which means Teacher)" (20:16). This is the pivotal moment. Being called by name is what moves Mary from the conviction that Jesus is dead to the realization that he is alive. This encounter is unique in many respects, yet her experience anticipates the way people of future generations will come to faith. The Gospel speaks to those who have not seen the risen Jesus (20:29), and Mary's story shows that seeing the tomb, seeing the angels, and even seeing Jesus himself do not guarantee faith. Like Mary, others will be called to faith by the risen Jesus. This is reflected in Jesus' comments about the good shepherd, who "calls his own sheep by name" and leads them out, and they recognize his voice (10:3-4, 16, 27).[27] Jesus calls Mary by name outside the empty tomb, but he will also call others to recognize him, sending them as he sent Mary to tell others what has happened.

The call to resurrection faith occurs, for people of later generations, when the message *about* the risen Jesus is made effective *by* the risen Jesus. According to John, faith is not based on inferences drawn from an empty tomb. If there is to be resurrection faith, it must arise from an encounter with the risen Jesus himself. This is the dimension of Johannine theology that informs the story of Thomas.

After Jesus appears to Mary, he comes to his disciples as a group, but Thomas is not with them. When they later tell him they have seen the Lord, he declares, "Unless I see the mark of the nails in his hands, and put my finger in the mark of the nails and my hand in his side, I will not believe" (20:25). Thomas is often said to doubt, but his words actually state his refusal to believe until certain conditions are met: If he sees and touches, then he will believe.[28] In the wider context his insistence on seeing seems ironic, since he had apparently seen Jesus call Lazarus out of the tomb, which was the dress rehearsal for Easter. The first time Thomas is mentioned in the Gospel is when Jesus announces that he is going to awaken Lazarus, even though his adversaries are seeking to kill him, and Thomas declares, "Let us also go, that we may die with him" (11:16). Assuming that Thomas actually goes, he presumably sees the dead man emerge from the tomb. Nevertheless, seeing Lazarus's resurrection does not create in Thomas any readiness to think that Jesus will rise from the dead.

Thomas is subsequently told two things, and these sayings will create the context in which the risen Jesus will work. The first saying comes at the last supper, when Thomas objects that he does not know where Jesus is going, and Jesus replies, "If you know me, you will know my Father also. From now on you do know him and have seen him" (14:7). Here Thomas is told that truly seeing Jesus means seeing God. The second saying comes after the resurrection, when the other disciples tell Thomas, "We have seen the Lord," and he responds with a refusal to believe (20:25). The words that Thomas heard from Jesus and about Jesus have not brought about a discernible faith, but they create the context in which the risen Jesus will encounter him. When Jesus meets Thomas after the resurrection, Thomas says, "My Lord and my God" (20:28). By calling Jesus "my Lord," Thomas makes his own what he heard from the disciples, who said they had seen "the Lord." By calling Jesus "my God," Thomas makes his own what he heard at the last supper, that seeing Jesus means seeing God.

Readers of John's Gospel are like Thomas in that they are not among those who initially saw the risen Christ. They are also like Thomas in that they have received testimony about Jesus — the Gospel itself conveys such witness. John's account of the resurrection shows that seeing does not guarantee believing — one can see the empty tomb, the grave cloths, the angels, and even the risen Jesus without coming to faith. By extension, readers learn that faith is not the result of accumulating more and more information about the situation at the tomb. John has shown that no matter how clear something appears to be, it is susceptible to alternative interpretations. The reports *about* the risen Jesus evoke faith when they are made effective *by* the risen Jesus. It is true that Thomas eventually saw the risen Jesus with his own eyes, and this will not be the case for the readers, at least until "the last day" (6:39). Yet the Gospel assumes that resurrection faith continues to be generated because the risen Christ continues to be active, encountering people through the witness of his disciples and the work of the Holy Spirit.

Relationship in the Present

This brings us to the second dimension of the resurrection, which concerns the way people continue to relate to the risen Jesus. Faith, according to John's Gospel, is a relationship with a living being. To believe in the risen Jesus is to be in relationship with the risen Jesus. The problem is that Jesus does not remain visibly present with his followers. The issue is evident in Jesus' words to Mary Magdalene outside the tomb: "Do not hold on to me, because I have not yet ascended to the Father" (20:17). When Jesus calls Mary by name, she responds by calling him her teacher, but now she finds that she cannot hold on to him in this way. Jesus' resurrection alters his relationship with his followers; it is not a resumption of things as they were before his death.

Jesus also speaks of ascending to the Father, which raises the prospect of being separated from him. During his public ministry, Jesus tells his opponents that he is going away, and they will seek him but will not find him (7:33; 8:14, 21). Later, he tells the disciples that he is leaving the world and going to the Father, and they find this disturbing, since it seems to mean that they too will be separated from him (14:28; 16:5-6, 28). For Jesus himself, the prospect of returning to his Father is positive. In the prayer before his arrest, Jesus speaks of returning to the glory that he had with God before the foundation of the world, a glory that manifests God's abiding love for him (17:5, 24). Jesus also prays that one day his followers will be with him in glory, though this remains a future hope. For the present, Jesus' return to the Father is troubling. So if the risen Jesus is no longer in the world, but his followers are in the world, is relationship still possible (17:11)?

According to John's Gospel, the answer is "yes." Jesus' words to Mary Magdalene identify his return to the Father as the beginning of a new type of relationship rather than an end to relationship. After telling her not to hold on to him, he directs her to "go to my brothers and say to them, 'I am ascending to my Father and your Father, to my God and your God'" (20:17). Jesus is not simply going away, he is going to the Father; and the Father is not absent from the world. John's Gospel clearly distinguishes God from the world, often using spatial imagery: God is identified with heaven above and people with the world below. Yet the Gospel also assumes that the Father continues to be at work, seeking people to worship him, giving bread to the world, and drawing people to Jesus (4:23; 5:17; 6:32, 44). If the Father is engaged with the world, the same will be true of Jesus, who is with the Father.

Jesus also emphasizes the relationship by referring to God as the Father of his followers. Throughout his ministry Jesus speaks of God as "my Father," but in the message to the disciples he says that God is also "your Father." The intimate bond of kinship that Jesus shares with his Father is extended to others, as we have seen (pp. 47-52). To see Jesus through the eyes of faith is to see the Father, and to believe in Jesus is to believe in the one who sent him (5:23; 12:44; 14:9-10). Because of this bond, Jesus now calls his disciples his "brothers" for the first time. Earlier in the Gospel, Jesus' "brothers" were those who were his biological kin, even though they did not believe in him (2:12; 7:3-5). After the resurrection, the term is used for all those brothers and sisters who are related to Jesus by faith.

John's Gospel identifies two ways in which people continue to be brought into the family of faith after the resurrection. The first is through *the Holy Spirit,* which is sent by the risen Christ. At the last supper Jesus said, "I tell you the truth: it is to your advantage that I go away, for if I do not go away, the Advocate will not come to you; but if I go, I will send him to you" (16:7). John's Gospel includes no description of Jesus visibly ascending into heaven. Instead, the disciples will know that he has returned to the Father because the Advocate, the Spirit, will come to them. Given the references to Jesus going away and leaving the world, one would expect the Spirit to arrive in Jesus' absence, but this is not the case. In John's Gospel, the risen Jesus comes and stands among the disciples, and then breathes on them, saying "Receive the Holy Spirit" (20:22). By giving the Spirit, Jesus shows that his return to the Father is complete, yet the Spirit comes from a Jesus who is present rather than absent (see pp. 147-52).

The Spirit given by the risen Christ enables people to know God as their Father. Previous passages depicted the process of coming to faith as being born or begotten of God. The prologue observes that all people are born physically through the natural processes associated with blood and human desire, but to be born or begotten of God means believing in the Word of God, who is the source of life. Through this birth into faith, people become children of God (1:12-13). Later, the Spirit is identified as the means by which God brings people to the new birth that is faith (3:3-8), and after speaking about "my Father and your Father," the risen Jesus gives the Spirit that makes this relationship with God possible (20:22). By breathing the Spirit into people, the risen Jesus acts in concert with God, his Father, who breathed the breath or spirit of life into the first human being at the creation (Gen. 2:7).

Second, the risen Jesus continues bringing people into the community of faith through *the work of his disciples.* This is depicted in the story of the great catch of fish in John 21. Peter says, "I am going fishing," and some of the other disciples go with him. Embarking on the fishing trip evidently seems promising, but it eventually proves to be fruitless, for they fish all night and catch nothing. Then, in the morning, the risen Jesus stands on the shore and directs them to cast their net into the water on the right side of the boat. At this point the main action centers on the verb "draw" *(helkō)*. When the disciples put their nets into the water, they are not able to "draw" it because of the great quantity of fish (21:6). Later, Jesus tells them to bring some of the fish to him, and Peter "drew" the net to the land" (21:11). On their own, the disciples' work proves fruitless, but through the risen Christ, their efforts are fruitful.[29]

The significance of the "drawing" becomes clear when it is read in connection with earlier passages. After feeding a crowd beside the sea, Jesus says, no one can come to me unless the Father who sent me *draws* him or her (6:44). The statement recognizes that coming to Jesus is a human impossibility. People have no inherent capacity to generate their own faith. Nevertheless, Jesus promises that people can and will be "drawn" to him by the power of God. This is taken a step further at the end of Jesus' public ministry, when Jesus identifies himself as the one who does the drawing. He says that when lifted up from the earth he will "draw" people to himself (12:32). This, in turn, begs the question as to *how* the crucified and risen Jesus will draw people, and the story of the great catch shows that he accomplishes this "drawing" through his disciples. Without Jesus the disciples are no more able to produce a catch of fish than people can produce faith in themselves or anyone else. But through the risen Jesus, the disciples do gather in many and bring them to Jesus. The way the risen Jesus continues to work through the Spirit and the witness of his followers is a major theme in the Gospel, which will be considered further in the next chapter (see pp. 151-60).

Hope for the Future

This brings us to a final question: What is the significance of Jesus' resurrection for those who face the prospect of their own deaths? John's Gospel repeatedly affirms that Jesus' resurrection means that people find life by relating to him in the present, through faith. But the Gospel also is candid in recognizing that people of faith will die. Threats ranging from terminal illness to violent death confront all people, including Jesus' followers (11:3; 16:2; 21:19, 23). The Gospel relates Jesus' resurrection to the deaths of others most directly in the story of Lazarus, who dies of an illness when Jesus seems to be absent. After a delay, Jesus arrives on the scene while Lazarus is still in the tomb. He tells the man's sister Martha, "I am the resurrection and the life. Those who believe in me, though they die, will live, and everyone who lives and believes in me will never die" (11:25-26). We will consider this passage in more detail later, but here will ask how Jesus' experience shows readers what resurrection means.

Jesus can say, "I Am the resurrection" because he goes the way of death and resurrection, and comes to embody the resurrection hope. Resurrection presupposes a wholistic understanding of what it means to be a person.[30] The Gospel assumes that people are embodied selves who live embodied lives. Since Jesus is fully human, this is also true of him. Those who live as embodied selves then die as embodied selves. Death affects the whole person, not simply a part of the person. This is basic to what resurrection means. It is not only the body that dies; the person dies. Therefore, resurrection involves giving life to the whole person, whether to Jesus or to others.

Resurrection's wholistic sense of death and life differs from the common idea that a person can be neatly divided into a body (*sōma* in Greek) and a soul (*psychē* in Greek). According to this dualistic approach, the soul is encased in the body during a person's lifetime, and death is what releases the soul from the body. The mourners place the dead body in the tomb, where it decays, while the soul ascends to enjoy spiritual life in heaven. Some statements of Jesus could conceivably be interpreted in this dualistic way. He said, "I came from the Father and have come into the world; again, I am leaving the world and am going to the Father" (16:28). One might conclude that this movement in and out of the world meant that Jesus was a soul who momentarily clothed himself with a body, only to shed his body at death so that his soul could ascend to its celestial home. But the wider context of the Gospel subverts this dualism.

Each term, "body" and "soul," refers to Jesus as a whole person, and each is used for his death and his resurrection. When Jesus drove the merchants out of the temple, he said, "Destroy this temple and in three days I will raise it up"; and the evangelist explains that Jesus spoke about the temple of his "body" (*sōma*, 2:21). The Gospel assumes that Jesus died and was raised as an embodied person. Death and resurrection involve the whole. Later, Jesus uses *psychē* as an expression for his "life" or "self," rather than for an inner "soul." He says, "I lay down my life *(psychē)* in order to take it up again. . . . I have power to lay it down, and I have power to take it up again" (10:17-18). The *psychē* is what Jesus lays down in death and what he takes up in resurrection. Again, death and resurrection involve the whole person of Jesus — body and soul.

Having said this, the Gospel also assumes that resurrection means the transformation of the whole person. It is not the same as bringing a corpse back to life. Resurrection of the body means transformation of the body into another kind existence. It is not a restoration of the body to its previous condition of mortality. The Gospel uses "flesh" *(sarx)* for what is limited and perishable. Therefore, when the Word becomes flesh, he becomes a person who will die (1:14). Similarly, Jesus gives his flesh for the life of the world through his crucifixion (6:51). Nevertheless, the Gospel does not say that Jesus' "flesh" is resurrected, since Jesus is not brought back to mortal life. "Body" *(sōma)* and "life" or "self" *(psychē)* are more flexible terms, which are used for Jesus as a whole person, who undergoes death and is resurrected to a life that is no longer subject to death.

The Gospel includes suggestive contrasts between the resurrection of Jesus and the raising of Lazarus, which brings the dead man back to life for a limited time. Jesus calls Lazarus out of the tomb, and he emerges still wrapped hand and foot in the grave cloths, so that he must be unbound and let go (11:44). In contrast, Jesus leaves his own grave cloths behind in the tomb.[31] The implication is that by his resurrection he is loosed from death and will not die again, as Lazarus will. Jesus' followers look for his body in the tomb, but he is not there. An embodied Jesus meets Mary Magdalene outside the tomb and shows the marks of the crucifixion to the disciples, yet the embodied Jesus is not subject to the limitations of the flesh, since he comes to the disciples wherever they are, even behind closed doors. Resurrection brings a new mode of embodied life, not a resumption of mortal life as it was.

A theology of resurrection means saying with absolute honesty that death is real. Yet it also means believing that death is not final. Neither Jesus nor his followers are exempted from the experience of dying. For both, resurrection means undergoing death and then overcoming it through the gift of life. By his crucifixion Jesus laid down his whole life, not merely a part of his life. In death he gave himself completely, not partially, for the sake of others. The completeness of Jesus' death paradoxically conveys the completeness of divine love that brings life to others, and it is through resurrection that this relationship of love continues into the present and the future (see pp. 179-82).

CHAPTER 6

The Spirit

John has often been called the "spiritual" gospel because of its soaring introduction and discourses on things above. But it might better be called "spiritual" because of its intriguing perspective on the work of God's Spirit. In the opening chapter the Spirit descends and reveals the identity of Jesus to John the Baptist (1:33). Later, during a nighttime conversation with Nicodemus, Jesus says one must enter God's kingdom through water and the Spirit (3:5). He tells the Samaritan woman that true worship takes place in Spirit and truth (4:23). Worshipers in the temple hear of the Spirit's living water, which meets the human thirst for God (7:37-39). At the last supper Jesus discloses to the disciples that the Spirit will be their Advocate, abiding among them and leading them to all truth (14:16-17; 16:13). And in a climactic scene Jesus breathes the Spirit into his disciples as he sends them into the world (20:22).

The Spirit's importance seems clear, but exactly how the Spirit works has long been a matter of debate. Some associate new birth in the Spirit with a specific kind of religious experience, such as a conviction of sin, a sense of grace, and the awakening of committed faith. Many identify worship in the Spirit with spontaneity and excitement. In some circles the Spirit is also expected to move people to speak in ecstatic tongues and prophesy. Others connect the Spirit primarily to the sacramental worship of the church, offering prayers for new birth and the blessing of the Spirit in formal baptismal liturgies (see pp. 17-21). Given the different viewpoints, many prefer to say little about the Spirit, or perhaps regard it as a vague unnamed power that gives people a quiet sense of the transcendent.

133

John's Gospel does not explore the usual questions of spiritual gifts, such as speaking in tongues. When Jesus breathes the Spirit into the disciples at the conclusion of the Gospel, he empowers them to forgive and retain sins, but nothing is said about ecstatic speech (20:22-23). Instead, John's Gospel relates the Spirit to several fundamental issues. One is that human beings are created for life with God, but are separated from God, and their need for relationship must be met from God's side. This occurs when the Spirit evokes faith. Second, Jesus came to bring life to the world, but those living after his ministry ended are not able to see or hear him. The Spirit discloses the presence of the risen Christ and his Father in the ongoing life of the community. Third, the disciples of Jesus are sent to bear witness in a world of conflicting truth claims. According to John, the Spirit empowers the community to discern the significance of Jesus and to bear witness to him as they continue living in a contentious world.

Interpreters sometimes distinguish passages in the first half of the Gospel, which tell of the Spirit giving life, from those in the second half, where the Spirit is called the Advocate and the focus shifts to the Spirit's abiding presence, teaching, and witness. Yet the various Spirit passages are interconnected and create a web of meaning. The expression "Holy Spirit" occurs in each major section (1:33; 14:26; 20:22), and the call for worship in Spirit and truth is later followed by the promise of the Spirit of truth (4:23; 14:17; 15:26; 16:13). In the beginning the Spirit enables John the Baptist to discern and bear witness to Jesus' identity, much as the Advocate is later said to do for later disciples (1:29-34; 14:26; 15:26; 16:13). At the last supper Jesus promises to send the Advocate along with peace and joy, and this promise is realized when he gives the disciples the Spirit, peace, and joy after the resurrection (14:25-27; 16:12-22; 20:19-23). We will consider the Spirit within John's Gospel as a whole.[1]

The Spirit Makes Jesus Known

The Spirit's first action is to make Jesus' identity known, and this is a hallmark of the Spirit's work later in the Gospel as well. As the story begins, a delegation from Jerusalem approaches John the Baptist and asks whether he might be the Messiah, Elijah, or the prophet. John replies that he fulfills none of these roles, and that the one whom God is sending already stands among them, although they do not know him. People cannot tell whom

God has sent simply by looking (1:26-27). Later, John points to Jesus and says, "Here is the Lamb of God" (1:29), but he adds that without the Spirit he would not have been able to recognize Jesus (1:29-31). The point is significant. No one — not even John the Baptist — has any inherent way of knowing the one whom God sends to take away the world's sin. Apart from God's action, Jesus' identity remains hidden.

The process of revelation begins when God speaks. God tells John the Baptist what to look for. John says, "I myself did not know him, but the one who sent me to baptize with water *said* to me, 'He on whom you see the Spirit descend and remain is the one who baptizes with the Holy Spirit'" (1:33). *The word John receives establishes the context in which the Spirit will work.* Having told John what to look for, God follows through by sending the Spirit. When John sees the Spirit descend, this experience confirms what he has already heard.

To some extent John's experience is exceptional, since God speaks to him directly, which will not be the case for others. (God speaks with a voice from heaven in 12:28, but the bystanders cannot fathom what it means.) Yet the pattern anticipates the situation of people living after the end of Jesus' ministry. They too will receive a word from God, but for them it will be communicated through Jesus and passed on in the community of faith. And this word creates the context in which the Spirit will work.

The connection between the Spirit and the word in this depiction of John the Baptist anticipates the role of the Spirit for subsequent generations in at least two ways: First, the Spirit will continue to bear out the truth of the gospel message for people in later generations. Simply hearing the words does not make the message compelling. Rather, people come to know that the word is true through the action of God's Spirit. Second, the message of Jesus helps people discern where the Spirit is at work. Spiritual experience is ambiguous. It is difficult to know when something is the work of God's Spirit and when the experience is produced by other factors. The Fourth Evangelist shows that the Spirit makes Jesus known. When people come to know who Jesus is, this is where the work of God's Spirit is evident.

Returning to the story of John the Baptist, we find that the Spirit's descent prompts him to bear witness that Jesus is the Lamb of God and Son of God (1:29, 34). This again is extraordinary, since others will not understand Jesus in this way until after his death and resurrection. During Jesus' ministry his followers may call him Son of God, but they will not comprehend what this means until after Easter (1:49; 11:27). Moreover, introducing Jesus as the Lamb of God at the beginning of the Gospel foreshadows his crucifixion at the end. So one might wonder how John the Baptist could already know that Jesus' death will take away sin. Yet the question of greater theological interest is what John's experience might mean for readers living after Jesus' resurrection. Like John, they have no inherent knowledge of Christ. If John could not recognize or bear witness to Jesus apart from the Spirit, the same will be true for readers of later generations. If they are to know that Jesus has come from God, and if they are to bear witness that his death takes away sin, then they too will do so by God's Spirit. What was true for John, in this respect, will be true for them as well.

In the opening chapter of the Gospel, the Spirit comes to reveal who Jesus is, not to give Jesus the spiritual power he previously lacked.[2] Prior to this scene, readers have already learned that Jesus is the Word of God made flesh. If the Word was with God and if the Word was God from the beginning, then the Spirit does not need to elevate Jesus to a higher spiritual plane. This means that Jesus is different from other figures in Israel's history, who were moved by the Spirit in order to lead the people or prophesy. For example, Moses, King David, Elijah, and other prophets began as ordinary human beings who were later empowered by God's Spirit (Num. 11:17; 1 Sam. 16:13-14; 2 Kings 2:9-15). But this is not the case with Jesus. According to John 1, Jesus is already God's Word and God's Son, and the Spirit makes this known.

John also testifies that the Spirit remains or abides *(menō)* on Jesus (John 1:32-33). This anticipates the promise that the Spirit will remain or abide *(menō)* with the community of faith after Jesus' death and resurrection (14:17). By abiding, the Spirit will make the presence of the risen Christ known to them (see pp. 149-51). John also says that Jesus will baptize with the Holy Spirit, which is a comprehensive way to speak of what the Spirit will do after Jesus' resurrection (1:33).[3] Through the gift of the Spirit, Jesus will bring about the new birth that is faith and call people to true worship of the Father (3:5; 4:14, 23; 7:37-39). By sending or baptizing with the Spirit, Jesus will move his followers to discern the truth about what he has done and empower them to bear witness to the world (14:16-17, 26; 15:26-27; 16:7-15; 20:22).

Source of Faith and Life

The Gospel recognizes that people are created for life with God, yet are separated from him. God has life in himself, but human beings do not, since they are creatures, who have limitations (3:6; 5:26). God is from above and people are from below, and those who belong to the earth have a fundamental inability to know and relate to God. In John's Gospel, true life is relationship with the God who created all things. According to John, the Spirit is the means by which God evokes the faith that brings such life.

New Birth into Faith and Life

The Spirit's role in bringing about faith is pictured as new birth in Jesus' conversation with a Jewish leader named Nicodemus (3:1-21). The scene begins when Nicodemus says that Jesus must be a teacher from God, given the signs Jesus has performed. But Jesus abruptly shifts the plane of conversation by declaring that no one can see the kingdom of God without being born anew. This startling change in topic might make sense if one assumes that Nicodemus has unspoken questions about the coming reign of God. But it is Jesus rather than Nicodemus who introduces the theme. What is more, Jesus soon shifts from speaking about the kingdom to speaking about "life," which then becomes the focus of this passage.

Note how the imagery unfolds during the conversation. At first Jesus contrasts the realm of the flesh, which is outside the kingdom, with the activity of the Spirit, which provides access to the kingdom. The transition between these realms is called new birth (3:3-8). In the middle Jesus distinguishes what is earthly from what is heavenly and contrasts perishing with eternal life. Here the transition into life is identified with faith (3:9-18). In the end Jesus contrasts the darkness of sin and evil with the light of God that illumines the world. Now the transition between spheres is depicted as "coming to the light" (3:19-21). Together the kingdom, eternal life, and the gift of light identify what God offers to the world. Similarly new birth, faith, and coming to the light are different ways to speak about relating to God. New birth is a peculiar image for entering a kingdom, but it is a vivid way to speak about entering life, which is what the kingdom signifies.[4]

Being brought to faith is described by the Greek word *gennaō* (3:3, 5). This can indicate either being born from a mother, which is how

Nicodemus takes it, or being begotten by a father, which fits a Gospel in which God is known as the Father. The metaphor catches Nicodemus off guard, and he can only sputter that no one can physically reenter the mother's womb and go through the birth process a second time. Readers are better positioned to understand the imagery, since it was used for faith in the Gospel's opening lines. There it was said that all people are born physically through the natural processes associated with blood, the will of the flesh, and the will of a man. But to be born or begotten of God means believing in the Word of God, who is the source of life. Through this birth into faith, people become children of God (1:12-13). All people come into being through God's Word and are related to him as his creatures (1:4). Yet some reject the Word while others receive and trust him (1:10-11). Faith is life-giving in a way that unbelief is not. Therefore, to believe in God's Word is to be in a life-giving relationship with God. This is what it means to be God's child in the Johannine sense.

The source of birth into faith is also described by the Greek word *anōthen,* which has a double meaning (3:3, 7). The word can have a temporal sense, indicating that birth must occur "again" or "a second time," which is the way Nicodemus interprets it. Yet in John's Gospel the word more often has the spatial sense, "from above" (3:31; 19:11, 23). This is the way Jesus develops the idea, emphasizing that this birth occurs through the Spirit that comes from God above. Translating the word as "anew" helps preserve the ambiguity, since both meanings are at play. The primary sense is that birth comes "from above," by the power of God's Spirit. On a secondary level, Jesus does speak of another, second birth, which goes beyond physical birth. But the primary meaning slips right by Nicodemus.[5]

So Jesus underscores God's action, saying that one must be born "of water and the Spirit" (3:5). The significance of the water is not explained. Some assume it refers to physical birth from the water in the womb, while others link it to baptism (see pp. 140-41). But the emphasis is on the Spirit, which is the power from above that brings new birth. Jesus contrasts what is born or begotten of the flesh with what is born or begotten of the Spirit. To be clear, flesh is not inherently evil — after all, God's Word becomes flesh — but it is limited. Flesh can generate relationships in its own sphere, but not human relationships with God, which are of another order. Such relationships occur only when God initiates contact with people in a life-giving way.

In a bewildering shift, Jesus now uses the word *pneuma* or "spirit" with a different meaning. He says that what is born or begotten of God's Spirit can also be called "spirit" (lowercase, 3:6). Confusing though this is, it extends the work of God's Spirit into the human realm. In this context the lowercase "spirit" is a relational term. As God meets people through his Spirit, the encounter calls forth a new spirit of faith. This spirit of faith is what enables people to relate to God who meets them.

Then altering the sense one more time, Jesus makes an analogy to wind, since the Greek term *pneuma* can mean both spirit and wind. He says that the Spirit "blows where it chooses, and you hear the sound of it, but you do not know where it comes from or where it goes. So it is with everyone who is born of the Spirit" (3:8). The point is that people cannot see the Spirit any more than they can see the wind. They can see the effects of the wind as it shakes the trees and rustles the grass, yet they do not know the wind's ultimate origin or destination. Similarly, the world can see the effects of God's Spirit, as it moves people to faith, but it does not recognize the Spirit's heavenly origin or ultimate direction. The same is true of the world's perception of those who are born anew. The world may hear the sound of their witness, but it cannot discern the heavenly origin or destination of their faith.[6]

Here Nicodemus — and perhaps the readers — wonder, "How can these things be?" (3:9). So Jesus drops the metaphor of new birth and speaks about faith. He contrasts perishing with having eternal life. And instead of saying more about the Spirit, he says that as Moses lifted up the serpent in the wilderness, so must the Son of Man be lifted up (3:10-15). We noted earlier that Moses lifted up a bronze serpent on a pole in order that those who turn to it might be healed of illness and live (Num. 21:4-9). By analogy, Jesus is lifted up on the cross, so that those who turn to him in faith find life, for his death reveals God's love for the world (see pp. 44-46).

The work of the Spirit, which is central in the first part of the conversation, is linked to the work of Christ, which is the focus of the second part. If it is necessary *(dei)* for people to be born anew by the Spirit, it is also necessary *(dei)* for the Son of Man to be lifted up so that people might believe and have life (John 3:7, 14). The conversation with Nicodemus does not spell out how God's gift of the Spirit is related to his gift of the Son, but placing them together shows that neither can be taken without the other. In the wider context of the Gospel we find that the Spirit works through the message of Christ, and the message of Christ is effective because the Spirit makes it so.[7]

Spirit and Baptism

Jesus' cryptic comment about birth "of water and the Spirit" has long been debated, and many of the questions have to do with baptism (3:5).[8] Different responses have been developed, most of them drawing on the whole New Testament and aspects of Christian tradition (see pp. 18-21). Here we will interpret the verse within the literary context of John's Gospel.

Jesus addresses his comment about water and Spirit to Nicodemus, who is a Pharisee and ruler of the Jews (3:1). Earlier scenes in the Gospel show why he does this. As the Gospel opens, a delegation of Pharisees or Jews ask John the Baptist about his use of water for baptism (1:19, 24-25). John testifies that he baptizes with water in order to reveal the identity of Jesus, who baptizes with the Holy Spirit (1:31-33). The use of water establishes the context in which the Spirit makes Jesus known. In the next chapter, readers are reminded that Jews use water for rites of purification (2:6-7). So when Jesus meets a Pharisee and ruler of the Jews it is not surprising that he takes up the question of water again, since the use of water for baptism and ritual washing has been a consistent theme.[9] Jesus assumes that Nicodemus is interested in the water used for cleansing, but he now emphasizes the limits of what water can do by using the metaphor of new birth. No amount of washing brings new birth. For that to occur, a power of another order must be involved. Jesus assumes that washing with water is a given practice. What he emphasizes is that God's Spirit must be involved, along with the washing (3:6-8).[10]

Water's connection to baptism is developed in the scene that follows, where Jesus and his disciples are said to perform many baptisms in the region of Judea (3:22-36). The literary pattern is that the water motif is briefly mentioned in 3:5, then elaborated later in the chapter. This same thing occurs with the motif of darkness, which is noted in passing in 3:2 and more fully developed in 3:19-21. Other themes also tie the scenes in this chapter together. If new birth comes "from above," so does Jesus (*anōthen*, 3:3, 7, 31). If new birth comes through the Spirit, Jesus is the bearer of the Spirit (3:5, 34).[11] Earthly and heavenly things (3:12, 31), people rejecting testimony to what has been seen and heard (3:11, 32), belief and eternal life (3:16-18, 36) — all these themes bind the two halves of the chapter to each other.[12]

The evangelist says that Jesus and his disciples baptize in Judea while John the Baptist baptizes at Aenon, where there is a good deal of water (3:22-26). The passage assumes that ritual washings are practiced by the followers of Jesus, by John the Baptist, and by other Jews. To judge by appearances, all these groups do similar things with water. Readers may have learned earlier that Jesus would baptize with the Spirit (1:33), but that does not mean he omits the water. The Gospel assumes that water baptism continues to be practiced by Jesus and his followers — and this creates the problem. If every group uses water, then what sets the baptism offered by Jesus' followers apart from the washings available elsewhere?

John the Baptist's disciples bluntly state the issue. They complain that people are going to Jesus and his followers for baptism, although they should be coming to John, since John was baptizing before Jesus came onto the scene. Yet John replies that people rightly go to Jesus because it has been granted from heaven (3:27). Jesus comes "from above" (3:31), and those going to his followers for baptism find there the life that comes from above. John compares this to a wedding, where Jesus is the bridegroom and those coming to him for baptism are like the bride. The implication is that those who come to Jesus and his followers for baptism are joined to Jesus, much as the bride and groom are joined together at a wedding (3:26-30). A new relationship results.

This scene is set during Jesus' ministry, but it anticipates that his followers will continue to baptize with water after his return to the Father. A parenthetical comment even notes that Jesus himself does not do the baptizing. It is done by his disciples, as will certainly be the case after his resurrection (4:2). During his ministry, people are joined to Jesus, the bearer of the Spirit, by baptism (3:26-30). By analogy, those baptized by Jesus' followers after his resurrection continue to be joined to him because the Spirit he bears remains active within the Christian community.

The Spirit brings new birth, according to John's Gospel. Water alone does not. The Gospel does not fully explain the relationship of water and Spirit, but gives both a role in engendering the faith that is new birth. If baptism with water brings new birth, it does so as a context in which God's Spirit works. At the same time, the Gospel recognizes that the Spirit's activity is not limited to baptism. When people come to Jesus and his disciples for baptism, this shows that God has already been at work. People come because it has already been granted "from heaven" (3:26-27). In this case baptism is the fruit of God's activity, the result of a faith awakened through witness borne to Jesus (3:28-34). Taken together, the scenes in John 3 recognize that God can work before baptism and through baptism, binding people to Jesus.

Being Born Again and Christian Experience

Another issue that is often debated by modern readers concerns the Spirit's work in new birth. According to John's Gospel, God's Spirit evokes faith; and many have debated whether the experience of faith follows a set pattern. Jesus told Nicodemus about his need to be born anew or "born again," and this has often been taken to mean that people must have a conversion experience. Many assume that being born again involves a clear movement from unbelief to belief at a specific moment in a person's life. Since physical birth happens at a definite time and place, one might infer that the same is true of new birth in the Spirit. After all, Jesus makes sharp contrasts between belief and unbelief, life and perishing, salvation and judgment (3:16-18). He says that people either remain in the darkness or come to the light; their deeds are either evil or done in God (3:19-21). The imagery seems to allow no middle ground.

So does the Gospel assume that the transition from unbelief to belief is always clear and identifiable?[13] When looking at the characters John portrays, we find that the evangelist can press for clarity in one's faith commitment, and he also recognizes that the dynamics of faith take many different forms. Nicodemus himself is an intriguing test case. Nicodemus is initially linked to darkness. He comes to Jesus by night, fails to understand Jesus' teaching, and Jesus reproves him for his unbelief. Case closed (3:2, 9-12). Or is it? Nicodemus does "come" to Jesus, even though it is night, and Jesus says that those who come to him belong to the light, not to the darkness (3:2, 20). Nicodemus comes to the light, though he does not actually see the light.

Nicodemus appears again in the middle of the Gospel, as some of the authorities condemn Jesus as a lawbreaker and want him arrested. Here Nicodemus makes no bold confession of faith but simply asks an innocent question: "Our law does not judge people without first giving them a hearing and finding out what they are doing, does it?" (7:51). His question undercuts the authorities' credibility (at least in the eyes of the readers), since it shows that they are the ones who disregard the law by neglecting to give Jesus a fair hearing. It is not clear that Nicodemus is a believer at this point, but it makes one wonder.

Tensions persist to the end of the story, where Nicodemus attends to the body of Jesus after the crucifixion (19:39).[14] The evangelist recalls that Nicodemus formerly came "by night," implying that he now steps into the light, since he apparently claims the body of Jesus before evening, while it is day. Moreover, Nicodemus brings a hundred pounds of spices in order to give Jesus a burial fit for a king. The gift of so much spice presumably honors Jesus, but it also shows that Nicodemus is not expecting King Jesus to rise from the dead any time soon. The resurrection will make the piles of spices unnecessary. So Nicodemus comes in the daylight to the crucified Jesus, yet the Gospel does not actually say that he believes. Is he one of the secret believers who are chided by the Gospel writer for refusing to make a public confession (12:42)? Or do Nicodemus's actions speak louder than words? The tensions in the story encourage open commitment to Jesus while recognizing that it is not always easy to determine when a person comes to genuine faith.

One might object that Nicodemus does not adequately illustrate the movement from darkness into light, and that the man born blind is a better example. Indeed, Jesus heals the man, giving him his physical sight, and the man gradually comes to see the identity of Jesus, the light of the world. Yet it is surprisingly difficult to determine the precise moment that the man comes to faith. Perhaps it is at the beginning of the story, when the man silently obeys Jesus' command to go and wash in the pool of Siloam (9:7). The man's obedience is certainly positive, yet when asked what happened, he simply acknowledges that the man called Jesus healed him (9:11). In the middle of the story the man ventures further, declaring that Jesus must be a prophet and someone who has come from God (9:17, 33). Yet only at the end does he actually say, "Lord, I believe" while bowing down in worship (9:38). Does that mean he is truly a believer only at the end, or has faith emerged along the way?

The Gospel's sharp distinctions between unbelief and belief press for clarity in commitment to Jesus. But its portrayals of various people show an appreciation for the many forms that the journey can take. We will consider more of these faith stories later, and find that they exhibit similar variety (see pp. 163-74). Here we simply note that if the movement into faith can take different forms during Jesus' ministry, the same is presumably true of the faith evoked by the Spirit after his resurrection.

Living Water That Brings Life

If "new birth" identifies the Spirit's role in bringing people to faith, the image of "living water" shows the Spirit continuing to sustain faith. The Gospel describes the human need for God as "thirst" (see pp. 61-63), and the Spirit is how God meets that need. The theme is developed in Jesus' conversation with the Samaritan woman as she comes to draw water from a well (4:6-7). The conversation opens with playful verbal repartee and cryptic sayings that draw readers into the story. Jesus initially asks the woman for water, but then abruptly reverses roles and announces that he can give her "living water" (4:10).

"Living water" ordinarily means flowing water, like that in a stream or spring, rather than the stagnant water stored in a cistern (Gen. 26:19; Jer. 2:13). Taken this way, Jesus' offer is absurd, of course, as the woman immediately senses. It is ludicrous to expect a drink from a man who does not even have a bucket. But Jesus uses "living water" as a metaphor for the gift of God. He contrasts it with ordinary well water, which quenches thirst for a short time. The living water is a divine gift, which leads to life eternal: "Everyone who drinks of this water will be thirsty again. Whoever drinks of the water that I will give him will never be thirsty, but the water that I will give will become in him a spring of water welling up to eternal life" (John 4:13-14).

Interpreters discern two aspects of meaning in this metaphor. If living water is a gift that Jesus offers *during* his ministry, then it is his words, which reveal the truth about himself, about the woman, and about God. Therefore, when she is given the truth, the woman can leave her water jar behind and go to bring others to Jesus (4:17-18, 25-29). But if the living water is what Jesus promises to give in the hour that "is coming," *after* his death and resurrection, then it is an image for the Spirit (4:21). If Jesus can "declare all things" to the Samaritan woman during his ministry, the Spirit will remind later generations of "all things" that he has said and "declare" what is to come (4:25; 14:26; 16:13). Later, the Gospel explicitly identifies living water with the Spirit, and this becomes the primary meaning (7:39). Both aspects flow together after Jesus' resurrection, however, for the Spirit will make the words of Jesus effective in the community of faith (14:26).[15]

If "living water" is primarily the Spirit that Jesus gives, then the Spirit creates a "spring" of water within a person, welling up to eternal life (4:14). This means that the Spirit evokes faith. Throughout the Gospel, faith is said to bring eternal life since it brings relationship with God. The link between faith and eternal life appears repeatedly in the surrounding chapters, enabling readers to see that the flowing spring the Spirit creates is the faith that brings life (e.g., 3:15, 16, 36; 5:24; 6:47). Recall that when Jesus tells

Nicodemus that what is born of God's Spirit is spirit, he indicates that God's Spirit generates a new spirit of faith in a person (3:6). Using the water imagery, he communicates the same idea to the Samaritan woman. The living water of the Spirit generates the life-giving spring that is faith. This is what meets the human thirst for God (6:35).

The Spirit's relationship to Jesus and believers is taken up again when Jesus speaks in the temple during the feast of Booths. The festival traditionally included prayers for water, and Jesus uses the image of living water when addressing the worshipers (7:37-38):

> If anyone thirsts, let him come to me,
> and let the one who believes in me drink.
> As the Scripture said,
> "Out of his heart shall flow rivers of living water."

Then the evangelist explains that Jesus refers to the Spirit that will be given after his glorification (7:39). The translation of the passage given here assumes that the first two lines are parallel: The thirsty person is to come to Jesus, and the believer is to drink from him. The last two lines state the reason: The Spirit's living water will flow from Jesus. Such a parallel structure is typical of the Gospel's style (e.g., 6:35). Some translations differ, proposing that the living water flows from the believer's heart, much as the Samaritan woman was told that the water would become a spring within the person (4:14). Yet this is unlikely. In John's Gospel the believer does not become a source of living water for others. The water or Spirit is given by Jesus. More importantly, this passage anticipates the passion, when the water flows from the pierced side of the crucified Christ (19:34).[16]

When read in parallel, the first two lines repeatedly direct people to Jesus. All are to come to him and drink the water he provides. What is peculiar is that the first line calls the *thirsty* person to come, and the second line invites the *believer* to drink. This suggests that thirsty people and believers are in some way alike, which nuances and deepens the Gospel's understanding of faith. Elsewhere it seems more clear-cut: Apart from faith people thirst, and those who believe no longer thirst (4:14; 6:35). But this passage recognizes that thirsting and believing actually coexist. Neither coming to Jesus nor drinking the Spirit's living water is a one-time occurrence. Even believers have an underlying thirst for God. That is why they are to keep drinking of the living water. The sense is that people keep thirsting and keep coming; they continue to believe and continue to drink.[17] This is the rhythm of belief.

Jesus' promise of living water looks ahead to his crucifixion. There those who thirst are shown the Messiah, who gives life to others at the expense of his own. After recounting Jesus' journey to the place of execution, the evangelist tells of him being hung on the cross alongside two others. Later in the day, the narrator says that everything is "finished"; but before dying, Jesus says, "I thirst" (19:28). The one who has invited the thirsty to come and drink is now thirsty himself. His gift is not costless but costly. He meets the thirst of others as he suffers thirst himself. Then after drinking sour wine, Jesus bows his head and dies, or literally "hands over the spirit" (19:30). It is clear that Jesus does not actually give the Spirit until after his resurrection, when he breathes it into his disciples (20:22). But some suggest that "handing over the spirit" at the time of death foreshadows his post-Easter gift. According to John, the Spirit comes from the Jesus who was both crucified and raised.[18]

Late on the afternoon of Good Friday, the soldiers come to remove the body of Jesus from the cross. One of them pierces Jesus' side with a spear to ensure that he is dead, and blood and water flow from the wound (19:34). The blood streaming from Jesus' body emphasizes that here we have a genuinely human death. The water is more evocative. Some suggest that it is a clear liquid that is naturally part of the body, while others see it as a miraculous occurrence.[19] But whatever the character of the water, its theological significance comes from Jesus' promise that living water would flow from him. This underscores the central paradox of the Gospel. Piercing Jesus' side shows that he is truly dead; yet the water flowing from the wound reveals that even in death Jesus is a source of life for others. Here is where the human thirst for God is met.

Two dimensions of meaning come together at the cross. One is that Jesus' death conveys the love of God that gives life. The gift of love is central to John's understanding of the crucifixion, as we have seen. By giving up his life for others, Jesus communicates God's love for the world (pp. 41-46, 109-23). The other dimension is that God gives life by bringing people to faith, and this occurs through the Spirit. If the crucifixion communicates God's love in a singular way, the Spirit enables the Gospel's witness to the crucifixion to grasp people in an ongoing way. The crucifixion and the gift of the Spirit serve the same end, which is that people might believe and have life.

The Advocate's Abiding Presence

John's Gospel tells of God accomplishing his purposes through Jesus' life, death, and resurrection. But the importance that the Gospel ascribes to Jesus also creates a problem for the readers. People of Jesus' time may have seen him heal the sick, feed the crowds, and appear to the disciples after his resurrection, but this is not the experience of those who read the text. They have "not seen" Jesus in this way (20:29). An ever-increasing temporal gap separates them from the ministry of Jesus, and the passing of time makes the issue of relating to Jesus more pressing. According to John, however, the risen Jesus is not absent from the world but is present among his followers. And the Spirit makes his presence known.

The Spirit as Advocate

The Spirit is a recurring and potentially volatile topic during Jesus' last supper with his disciples. He tells them, "I will ask the Father, and he will give you another Advocate, to be with you forever," namely, "the Spirit of truth" (14:16-17). Throughout John 14–16 the Spirit is identified by the suggestive term *paraklētos* or Advocate. The Greek word refers to someone who is called to one's side as a source of help. The verb on which the noun is based can mean to encourage, to exhort, to make a strong appeal for something, and to comfort. A *paraklētos* may be someone who speaks on behalf of a person in need, intercedes in a conflicted situation, encourages the dispirited, or consoles the grieving. The term Advocate is a suitable translation, since it is based on Latin roots with a comparable range of meanings. Other translations include Comforter, Counselor, and Helper.[20]

Where does the Spirit or Advocate come from? Jesus initially says that the Father will send the Spirit at Jesus' request (14:16). But later he says that the Father will send the Spirit in Jesus' name and that Jesus will send the Spirit from the Father (14:26; 15:26; 16:7). The bewildering shifts in language connect the Spirit to Jesus and the Father in every conceivable way — which seems to be the point. Both Father and Son are involved in the Spirit's mission to the world, just as both are involved in Jesus' mission to the world (4:34).

Jesus calls the Spirit "another" Advocate, which assumes that Jesus himself is already an Advocate (14:16). Giving Jesus and the Spirit the same distinctive title means they share some of the same functions. The Spirit will keep doing the work that Jesus began on earth after Jesus' return to the Father. Note that Jesus and the Spirit have a common origin: both come from the Father and are sent into the world. Neither of them speaks on his own: Jesus communicates what he has received from his Father, and the Spirit declares what he has received from Jesus (7:17; 16:13). If Jesus glorifies God, the Spirit glorifies Jesus (16:14; 17:1). Both of them teach, bear witness to the truth, and expose the sin of the world (3:20; 7:14; 14:26; 15:26; 16:8; 18:37). And in both cases, the reaction is the same: the world refuses to recognize and receive Jesus or the Spirit (1:11; 14:17).[21]

Yet calling the Spirit "another Advocate" does not mean he is "another Jesus." The Spirit continues Jesus' work without taking Jesus' place.[22] As the Word made flesh, Jesus reveals God through the life he lives and the death he dies. But the Spirit does not become incarnate and is not crucified for the sin of the world. The Spirit will disclose the truth about Jesus' life, death, and resurrection, but will not replicate those events. After Jesus' return to the Father, the Spirit remains with the disciples; but this does not mean the Spirit replaces Jesus. Rather, the Spirit discloses the presence of the risen Jesus and his Father to the community of faith.

The Advocate is also called "the Spirit of truth," a title that binds the Spirit to Jesus and his Father (14:17; 15:26; 16:13). According to John's Gospel, God is true, his word is truth, and Jesus bore witness to the truth he received from God (7:18; 8:26, 40; 17:17). By embodying God's Word, Jesus also embodies God's truth and can say, "I am the way, and the truth, and the life" (14:6). To say that the Spirit is "of truth" means that the Spirit conveys God's truth as revealed in Christ. It is how the Spirit engages with the world. In John's Gospel, truth is not a timeless ideal that is reached by contemplation. It is a power that counters the enslaving dominion of falsehood. Truth is communicated in order to free people from bondage to sin (8:32), to awaken authentic worship of God (4:23-24), and to shape actions that are truly life-giving (3:21).

Similar qualities are suggested by the expression "Holy Spirit" (14:26; cf. 1:33; 20:22). This connects the Spirit to the Father who is holy and to Jesus the Holy One of God (6:69; 17:11). In contemporary usage, holiness can have the negative connotations associated with moralistic piety. In its basic sense, however, what is holy is "set apart" from what is common and is dedicated to God's purposes. According to John, being holy or set apart is not an end in itself but a prerequisite for engaging the world. Those who are fully identified with the world are not in a position to speak the truth to it. They have no means to confront it. But Jesus was sanctified or set apart in order to be sent into the world with a truth that is different from what the world offers (10:36). He can speak to the world precisely because he is not held captive to the world. Jesus in turn sets his followers apart by entrusting them with the truth. And this is the reason for his action: He sets them apart from the world in order to send them into the world as his witnesses (17:17-19). As they are sent they are given the Holy Spirit, who will empower them to confront the world's sin and to extend the offer of release (20:22-23). This is a form of engagement, which brings change, as we will see below.

Jesus also says that the world cannot receive the Spirit of truth because it neither sees nor recognizes it (14:17). Here he refers to "the world" as the realm where people are alienated from God. "The world" consists of those who are hostile to Jesus and his followers (15:18). Saying that the world cannot receive the Spirit does not mean that an unbeliever cannot become a believer. Rather, it means that "the world" estranged from God cannot receive the Spirit while remaining unchanged. For the world to receive the Spirit means that it is no longer "the world" in the Johannine sense. It loses its identity as "the world," for it is no longer alienated from God.[23]

Abiding Presence

Jesus' promise of the Spirit or Advocate is given under the shadow of his coming death. His disciples are disturbed by his enigmatic remarks concerning his return to the Father, since he is embarking on a route that goes by way of Golgotha. Jesus tells the disciples that he will be with them only a little longer. They will look for him, but where he is going, they cannot come (13:33). Readers can see the problem even more clearly. They know from the prologue that Jesus not only speaks but embodies God's Word. He makes God known by what he says, what he does, and who he is. Therefore, crucifixion means more than the loss of a beloved rabbi. Jesus' death brings an end to the incarnation. So if God encounters people through the Word made flesh, what happens when Jesus' ministry is over?[24]

Jesus indicates that the Spirit will make his presence known within the community of faith during the period between his resurrection and future return.[25] He assures the disciples that his death is not the end of his relationship with them. How so? One dimension involves his resurrection. He says, "In a little while the world will no longer see me, but you will see me; because I live, you also will live" (14:19). This looks to the moment when the risen Jesus will come to his disciples at the end of the Gospel. John's account of the resurrection tells of Jesus coming to meet them in their gathered community. The world will not see him, but the disciples will recognize that Jesus is alive, not dead, and they will rejoice (20:20).

The problem is that these appearances will not continue indefinitely. Readers of the Gospel will not see the risen Jesus as the first disciples do. For the readers, the resurrection appearances belong to the past, to a time and place that is out of reach (20:29). For them, the resurrection is a memory that others have passed on to them; and the vitality of memory fades with time. Yet the Gospel counters this by saying that through the Spirit believers will continue to encounter the risen Christ. For John, the risen Jesus is a living presence, and the Spirit discloses this within the community of faith in the period after Easter.

The second dimension of the Spirit's work has to do with Jesus' promise to return in the future. At the last supper he tells the disciples, "In my Father's house there are many dwelling places. If it were not so, would I have told you that I go to prepare a place for you? And if I go to prepare a place for you, I will come again and will take you to myself, so that where I am, there you may be also" (14:2-3). This passage is considered in more detail below (see pp. 182-84). Here we simply note that it speaks in traditional terms about Jesus' departure to God and his future return to the disciples. It emphasizes that Jesus' relationship with his followers has a future dimension. He promises to prepare a "dwelling place" *(monē)* for them, so that one day they can dwell in his Father's house. This evocative Greek word is related to the verb *menō* or "abide." The sense is that Jesus goes to prepare a place where the disciples will "abide" with him and the Father at some point in the future.

Here the problem is that the future can seem even more remote than the past. The Gospel tells readers of a Jesus who rose in years gone by and it promises that he will return in the time to come. But when this will be is left unclear. The readers live in the present, in a conflicted world where they do not seem to fit. At present they might be described as "orphans" who have no place to belong (14:18). The imagery captures the feeling of having no true home and the sense that one is alone in the world. The promise of finding a home someday may be comforting to those who feel "orphaned" now. But the hope of a home "someday" can seem fragile for those who feel truly alone.

Here the Gospel's understanding of the Spirit takes a surprising turn. As Jesus goes to prepare a dwelling place *(monē)* for the disciples to abide in the future, the Spirit discloses that Jesus and his Father come to make their dwelling place among believers right now. He says, "Those who love me will keep my word, and my Father will love them, and we will come to them and make our home *(monē)* with them" (14:23). This reverses the dominant flow of the action. The future comes into the present. As Jesus goes away to prepare an abiding place for believers with the Father, he and his Father come to make their abiding place with believers; and their presence is revealed through the Spirit that abides or dwells among Jesus' followers (*menō*, 14:17). In short, the Spirit brings the realities of the past and the future into the present for believers. *The Jesus who rose in the past continues to be present; the Jesus who will come again is already present; and the Spirit now makes the presence of Jesus and his Father known within the community of faith.*

Jesus' words intimate that this work of the Spirit is both personal and communal. He says that the Spirit will abide and be *en hymin,* a Greek expression that includes both dimensions (14:17). On the one hand, this means that the Spirit will be "in you," since the Spirit evokes faith in each member of the community. This fits the promises made earlier, where Jesus said that each person who is thirsty can receive the Spirit's living water and that the Spirit will generate the "spring" that is faith, welling up in every believer (4:14; 7:37-39). On the other hand, the Greek word "you" is plural and can mean that the Spirit is present "among you," that is, among the members of the community together. The Spirit connects believers to each other as well as to Jesus.

Teacher and Witness

Jesus' promise of the Spirit is given in the face of worldly conflict. Jesus encounters sharp opposition from others, who judge him to be a sinner, a blasphemer, and a threat to society. At the last supper he tells his followers that they too will experience hostility from those who do not share their convictions (15:18-25). Yet he also promises that the Spirit will keep disclosing the significance of what Jesus has said and done, and will expose the truth about the world's estrangement from God and Jesus. As the disciples bear witness, the Spirit also will witness in order that others might come to believe.

Teaching, Reminding, and Leading to Truth

Questions about Jesus are raised by his followers as well as his foes. His disciples typically trip over his metaphors, ironic statements, and cryptic allusions to things to come. They are loyal, but often uncomprehending. Even at the last supper the questions continue: Where is Jesus going, and why can they not follow him (13:36; 14:5)? Where is Jesus' Father, and why will Jesus show himself to the disciples and not to the world (14:8, 22; 16:17)? The disciples will eventually understand some things more clearly, yet new questions will intrude as the world challenges their beliefs. Therefore, Jesus tells them that "the Advocate, the Holy Spirit," will "teach you all things and remind you of all things that I have said to you" (14:26).

The two words "teach" and "remind" describe the way the Spirit gives believers new insight into the story of Jesus. First, "reminding" maintains the connection with the past, with what Jesus said and did during his ministry. The Spirit calls to mind things that Jesus has already made known. It brings people back to the message they have already received. Second, teaching opens up new insights into the legacy of Jesus. To teach "all things" *(panta)* is to bring fresh insight to "all things *(panta)* that I have said to you" (14:26). If reminding anchors the life of the community in what it has already received from Jesus, teaching ensures that the message continues to speak to the changing contexts in which Jesus' disciples live.

What does it mean to remember Jesus with new insight? The Gospel narrative provides some glimpses into the process. John recalls that during his ministry Jesus drove the merchants out of the temple and overturned the tables of the moneychangers. When bystanders demanded a sign, he replied, "Destroy this temple and in three days I will raise it up" (2:19). Then the evangelist explains that Jesus spoke figuratively of the destruction and resurrection of the "temple of his body" (2:21). This meaning was not grasped at the time, and it was only after the resurrection that the disciples "remembered" and discerned what this meant (2:22). They also "remembered" the Scripture that said, "Zeal for your house will consume me," and recognized that Jesus acted out of passionate commitment to God (2:17; Ps. 69:9).

Similarly, at the end of his ministry Jesus came to Jerusalem, where he found a young donkey and sat on it as the crowd waved palm branches. The evangelist says this fulfilled the Scripture, which said that Zion's king would come, sitting on a donkey's colt (John 12:12-15; Zech. 9:9). Then he adds, "His disciples did not understand these things at first; but when Jesus was glorified, then they remembered that these things had been written of him and had been done to him" (John 12:16). Again, the Gospel reflects the process of remembering with new insight.

The act of remembering anchors the Christian community's reflections in the works and words of Jesus. The evangelist assumes that there are certain "givens" in the story, like those noted above: the incident in the temple, the approach to Jerusalem, the crucifixion, and the resurrection. The Spirit will "remind" people of what Jesus said and did by keeping the tradition alive. This provides a basis for reflection. And teaching is what brings insight into the story of Jesus. By teaching, the Spirit moves people beyond the repetition of the tradition toward a more vital sense of what it means.

As the disciples continue discerning the significance of Jesus, they must also come to terms with the world in which they live. At the last supper Jesus tells them, "If the world hates you, be aware that it hated me before it hated you," for if "they persecuted me, they will persecute you" (15:18, 20). For believers, the unbelief of the world may not be easy to understand or accept. If opposition becomes strong enough, it may seem simplest to abandon one's commitments and to let the world have its way. By disclosing the world's true character, the Spirit gives believers the perspective they need to resist, so that they can maintain the integrity of their convictions.

Jesus speaks of the confrontational side of the Spirit by saying that it will "prove the world wrong about sin and righteousness and judgment" (16:8). Proving something wrong *(elenchō)* means bringing it into the open so that it can be seen for what it is (3:20).[26] The idea is that the Spirit will enable believers to see the truth about the world even if the world cannot see the truth about itself. This is the pattern reflected in the Gospel. The people portrayed in the story belong to the world, and they charge that Jesus is guilty of sin *(elenchō,* 8:46). Yet the Gospel shows readers that those who condemn Jesus for telling the truth are actually held captive by untruth. Readers can see this; the characters in the story cannot. Similarly, the Spirit continues to show believers the truth about the world, even though the world cannot see the truth about itself.

The Gospel gives three examples of this: First, the Spirit will prove the world wrong "about sin, because they do not believe" in Jesus (16:9). Sin is unbelief, and this unbelief motivates the world's actions. In the Gospel, the Jewish authorities accuse Jesus of rebellion against God and Rome, yet the evangelist enables readers to see that they are actually guilty of these charges (see pp. 70-72). Similarly, Pilate knows that Jesus is innocent, and yet abandons truth and has Jesus put to death. His sin, too, is brought to light for the readers (see p. 72). The Spirit continues this process of disclosure. After Jesus' return to the Father, the world will continue its unbelief. But in this conflicted situation, the Spirit will enable the faithful to see that the unbelief should be resisted, since it manifests the world's sin and alienation from God.

Second, the Spirit will prove the world wrong "about righteousness" because Jesus goes to the Father and his disciples will see him no longer (16:10). According to the Gospel, God is righteous, and to pursue righteousness is to act according to God's will (5:30; 17:25). In the eyes of the world, Jesus was crucified because he was an unrighteous opponent of God; and his adversaries can argue that no one sees Jesus now because he is dead and gone. Yet the Gospel insists that this is to judge by appearances rather than with right judgment (7:24). The evangelist says that God commanded Jesus to lay down his life and to take it up again (10:17-18). By willingly going to the cross, Jesus obeys God. If his disciples no longer see him, it is because Jesus has completed his work and returned to the Father. The Spirit enables believers to see that the world has judged Jesus wrongly, and that by laying down his life Jesus acted in righteousness. Therefore, people can continue to believe in him.

Third, the Spirit will prove the world wrong "about judgment, because the ruler of this world has been judged" (16:11). The purported ruler of this world is Satan, who is judged in the course of Jesus' trial and crucifixion (12:31-33). Satan operates through deception, hatred, and death, and these are the devices that Jesus' opponents use against him. After the resurrection, the Spirit — like the Gospel — enables people to see that the crucifixion was not a victory for Satan but the point at which Jesus overcomes him by the power of truth, love, and life, as we have seen (pp. 117-20). To believe that evil reigns supreme is a call to despair. To remain faithful, people must resist the illusion that evil has triumphed. This message is already disclosed in the Gospel. In the period after Jesus' resurrection, the Spirit enables believers to continue confessing that the claims of the evil one are empty and that in the crucified and risen Messiah they see the world's true sovereign.

Then Jesus makes one of his most provocative comments about the Spirit. He says, "I still have many things to say to you, but you cannot bear them now. When the Spirit of truth comes, he will lead you in the way to all truth" (16:12-13). His comment raises a number of issues: What is this "truth" to which the Spirit leads people? How does the Spirit's truth relate to what Jesus has already revealed? Is every new idea the work of God's Spirit?

"Truth," in John's Gospel, is what characterizes God. To know the truth is to know the God who is true (5:32; 7:28; 8:26). God sent Jesus to bear witness to the truth (18:37). Jesus does this by words and actions that make God's grace and truth known (1:14, 17). Jesus finally embodies God's truth, for he says, "I Am the way, and the truth, and the life" (14:6). Therefore, to know the truth is to know the God revealed in Jesus. This gives a focus to the Spirit's work.

The Spirit's action is described by the verb *hodēgeō*, which is based on the words "way" *(hodos)* and "lead" *(agein)*. For the Spirit to "lead in the way" to all truth means that the Spirit brings people to Jesus, who is the way and the truth (14:6). Before the Spirit leads people in the way, Jesus must go "the way" of the cross and resurrection. What this means will not be understood at the time, but afterward the Spirit will lead the community to the truth of what Jesus' death and resurrection mean and what these actions convey about God. This is the crucial point. If Jesus has already revealed and embodied God's truth, then the Spirit enables believers to discern what this truth means for them.

The Spirit's truth cannot be separated from the truth that Jesus has already made known. Earlier Jesus said that people would know the truth by continuing in his word (8:31-32). In that context knowing the truth meant continuing to hold onto the message Jesus had given them. Jesus did not speak of knowing the truth through later revelation. Rather, people come to know the truth through the word they have already received. Now he promises that after the resurrection, the Spirit will lead people to truth by enabling them to understand Jesus' words and actions.

The Gospel assumes that the risen Christ will continue to speak through the Spirit. Jesus says, the Spirit "will not speak on his own, but will speak whatever he hears" (16:13b). This statement uses the future tense, which anticipates that after Easter the living Christ will remain active. Yet the Gospel is reticent about *how* the Spirit will convey the words of the risen Jesus. Some suggest that the passage expects the Spirit to speak through specially designated Christian prophets (Acts 13:1; Rom. 12:6; 1 Cor. 12:28),[27] yet in these discourses the Spirit's activity seems more broadly connected with discernment within the community as a whole. Rather than dealing with the means of communication, the passage emphasizes the continuity between the Spirit and the risen Jesus. The Spirit does not speak independently, but conveys the word of Jesus. Therefore, as believers try to discern what the Spirit brings from the risen Jesus, they can assume that it will be congruent with what they have already received from Jesus in the Gospel.

Some wonder, however, whether the Spirit might reveal something more, like secrets concerning the future. After all, Jesus says the Spirit will "declare to you the things that are to come" (John 16:13). One might think this refers to the Spirit inspiring people to predict coming events.[28] But this is not the focus of the passage. Note that the Spirit is said to "declare" *(anangellō)* things. This verb is occasionally used for telling about the future, but in John it has to do with making known what something means, whether the nature of true worship, the identity of Jesus, or his resurrection from the dead (4:25; 5:15; cf. *angellō*, 20:18). Also note that Jesus is speaking about the Spirit at the last supper, shortly before his arrest. In this context "the things that are to come" *(ta erchomena)* are primarily the events of his passion and resurrection. The Gospel uses this same expression when Jesus leaves the supper and goes to the garden. He is prepared for his arrest because he knows "the things to come" *(ta erchomena,* 18:4). The primary meaning of this passage is that the Spirit will declare the meaning of the death and resurrection, which are coming, by showing how they reveal Jesus' love and obedience in the face of the world's sin.[29]

In a secondary sense the Spirit may also declare the meaning of the world's opposition to the Christian community. This too is among the things that are "coming" after Jesus' return to the Father (16:2, 4). How this occurs is again reflected in the Gospel. Recall that the Spirit is understood to convey the words of the risen Jesus (16:13-14). The Gospel itself seems to include passages that do the same thing. Note that in 3:1-10 the earthly Jesus speaks to Nicodemus, but in 3:11-21 the perspective changes so that it sounds as if Jesus has already ascended into heaven and speaks from that vantage point (3:13). Jesus also uses plural forms of speech as if picturing a community of people bearing witness to what they have seen and heard despite the unbelief of others. It seems as if Jesus is speaking about the situation of believers in conflict with the world after his resurrection and return to the Father. This passage gives readers some idea of the kind of testimony the Spirit is to bring from the risen Jesus. It is not prediction of specific events but a perspective on the situation of the Christian community in its conflict with the unbelieving world.[30]

Finally, Jesus says that the Spirit "will glorify me, because it will take what is mine and declare it to you" (16:13-14). The Spirit glorifies Jesus by making him known among the faithful. Jesus glorified his Father by revealing God's power through his actions and by conveying God's love through his death (see pp. 120-23). The Spirit now glorifies Jesus by enabling the faithful to see who he was and is.

Witness of the Spirit and the Community

The Spirit empowers the community of faith that Jesus sends into the world. At the beginning of the Gospel, the Spirit's descent made it possible for John the Baptist to discern who Jesus was and to bear witness to others (1:29-34). This continues among Jesus' followers after his resurrection. At the last supper Jesus says, "When the Advocate comes . . . he will bear witness concerning me; and you also continue bearing witness, because you are with me from the beginning" (15:26-27). Witnessing means voicing one's convictions in contexts where the truth is not obvious. In a formal sense witness might be given in a courtroom, where the arguments proffered by the prosecution and defense collide. But witness also occurs wherever people must testify to what they believe, despite claims to the contrary. Jesus tells the disciples that the world will hate and persecute them. Such opposition does not call for withdrawal but for witness, for truthtelling.

Jesus joins the witness of the Spirit to that of his disciples. He assumes that the disciples who were with him from the beginning of his ministry preserve the tradition of his words and actions. This means their witness is linked to what Jesus said and did on earth. Jesus also says that the Spirit will bear witness concerning him, since the Spirit will be given to the community after his return to the Father. The vitality of the disciples' witness comes from the interplay of their work with that of the Spirit. The words they speak have no inherent power to evoke faith in their hearers, but their witness can become effective through the activity of the Spirit. At the same time, the Spirit does not work in a vacuum but uses the testimony of human beings to accomplish its purposes.

Jesus gives the Spirit to his disciples after his resurrection in a scene that recalls the promises he made during the last supper. Before his death Jesus said, "Peace I leave with you, my peace I give to you" (14:26-27). Later he said that the Spirit would come, that the disciples would see him again, and that their sorrow would turn into joy (16:13, 22). The Gospel ties these themes together in a climactic scene where Jesus comes to the disciples after his resurrection and says, "Peace be with you"; the disciples then see him, they rejoice, and he breathes the Spirit into them (20:19-23). The action is reminiscent of God breathing the breath or spirit of life into human beings at the time of creation (Gen. 2:7).

Jesus gives the disciples the Spirit along with this commission: "As the Father sent me, so I send you" (John 20:21), and "If you forgive the sins of any, they are forgiven them; if you retain the sins of any, they are retained" (20:23). The passage makes Jesus' sending of the disciples analogous to the Father's sending of Jesus. The way the disciples forgive and retain sins is therefore an extension of what Jesus has done. This passage has been related in various ways to the practices of contemporary churches. Some assume that the disciples represent the clergy, who are charged with forgiving and retaining sins. In the context of the Gospel, however, the disciples represent all of Jesus' followers. The other commands given to these disciples — such as "love one another" — pertain to all Christians. Similarly, the Spirit is promised to the community as a whole, not just to one group within it (14:16-17).[31]

First, we must ask what it means to forgive sins.[32] Surprisingly, John does not picture Jesus forgiving sins during the course of his ministry as the other gospels do (e.g., Mark 2:1-12). Instead, attention centers on the crucifixion, which removes sin. Jesus is the Lamb of God who takes away the sin of the world (John 1:29). His crucifixion is designed to bring change, to alter a situation defined by sin. In this gospel sin is unbelief and the actions that come from it (see pp. 65-70). Sin is taken away when unbelief is removed and people are restored to relationship with God. The crucified Lamb removes sin by conveying the divine love that evokes faith (see pp. 112-17).

Jesus' commission to the disciples uses the word *aphiēmi,* which is usually translated "forgive," though it literally means "release." The word indicates change. It does not mean acceptance of sins but release from them. Forgiveness does not endorse the situation defined by sin but alters it — just as the Lamb "takes away" sin. Here the word "sins" is used in the plural for the many ways in which unbelief is put into action. "Sins" remain the antithesis of faith, since they show alienation from God and ultimately lead to death, the ultimate separation from God (8:24). Jesus envisions a situation in which people are trapped by their sins. The underlying sin, or estrangement from God, is expressed in the many sins that affect relationships with other people. As sin affects one relationship after another it defines the situation in which people find themselves. Sins and their consequences hem people in, so that they cannot move forward without some act of release. This is what forgiveness provides. It is the act of release that allows people to move forward. Otherwise the sins that have defined life up to the present will continue to define the future.

The disciples bring release from sins by communicating the love of God that Jesus has conveyed. Divine love intrudes into the human situation through the crucified Lamb. Therefore, before sending the disciples into the world, Jesus shows them the marks of crucifixion (20:20), and by giving them the Spirit, he empowers them to extend the benefits of his death to others. *When the message of what God has done in Jesus brings faith, sins no longer define the situation. There is release.*

Second, we must consider what it means to retain sins. To retain (*krateō*) is to "hold fast," which is the opposite of "release." Holding fast means holding people to account. If there is no accountability, there is no need for forgiveness. If people are not held responsible, then forgiveness can be taken to mean simply accepting sin. Rather than altering the situation, forgiveness allows sin to continue unchallenged. Jesus held people to account by bringing their sin to light and warning them of its consequences. If true life comes from faith, now and in the future, then the alienation from God that is sin brings death now and in the future (8:21, 24). When Jesus spoke of the blindness of unbelief, his adversaries insisted that they could already see the truth. So Jesus held them to account for their animosity and said "your sin remains" (9:41). To "retain" sins in a Johannine sense involves exposing sin, identifying sin, and holding people to account for sin.

Retaining sins is not an end in itself. The goal is not to perpetuate alienation from God and other people but to bring change. Retaining can startle people into seeing the truth about themselves so that they recognize the need for change and hear the call to faith and life. Jesus holds his opponents to account by saying, "I told you that you would die in your sins, for you will die in your sins *unless* you believe that I Am" (8:24). The word "unless" is crucial since it marks the transition between the word of judgment against sin and the invitation to faith. Jesus confronts his listeners with the reality of sin and its consequences in order to shake them from their complacency so that they recognize the need for faith and the life that comes from it. Retaining sins is a confrontational action that reaches its goal when the hearers recognize their accountability and are moved to change by embracing the release that comes through faith.

The Spirit continues to confront the world's sin after Jesus' resurrection, as we have seen (16:8-11). The disciples, who receive the Spirit, are also called to challenge the patterns of sin at work in the world. Forgiveness or release from sins is mentioned first in Jesus' commission to the disciples, since this is the goal of their work. The Father sent Jesus to bring release from sin (1:29; 3:17), and Jesus sends his followers to bring this message to the world. Yet retaining sins by holding people to account is the essential corollary to this, since forgiveness without accountability lets sin continue unchallenged. Jesus identified sin in order to overcome it, and this also shapes the mission of his disciples. The Spirit "blows where it chooses" (3:8), but its handiwork can be seen where faith is evoked, where sin is brought to light, and where people come to know the risen Jesus and his Father, who abide within the community of faith.

CHAPTER 7

Faith, Present and Future

Faith is the reason that John's Gospel was written. Its purpose is that "you may believe that Jesus is the Messiah, the Son of God, and that through believing you may have life in his name" (20:31). The Gospel assumes that people were created for life with God, are separated from God, and receive life when they are restored to relationship with God through Jesus. This relationship that gives life is faith — and this makes the question of faith inescapable. If people are created for life, they will seek whatever they think will bring it. The issue is not *whether* people will seek life — that is a given. The issue is *where* their pursuit of life will take them and where their faith will be centered.

For John, true faith is possible because God calls people into relationship through his Word. It is not that people are such competent seekers. No one has ever seen God; he remains hidden from human eyes and the need for relationship with the unseen God must be met from God's side (1:18). So the Gospel tells of God's Word coming to people in the flesh, and it identifies belief as the positive result of this encounter. The complicating factor is that people in the past may have seen Jesus the incarnate Word, but readers of the Gospel have not. The evangelist writes for those living years after Jesus' ministry has ended — and the challenge he faces is formidable. He calls readers to believe in a God whom they have not seen by believing in a Jesus whom they have not seen (20:29)! If faith is possible at all in such a situation, people must have some way of continuing to encounter Jesus and his Father. This happens, according to John, through the ongoing work of God's Spirit, who bears witness to Je-

sus and makes the presence of Jesus and his Father real for later generations of believers.

One would think that faith would be portrayed in harmonious tones,
since peace and joy are gifts that the risen Christ and the Spirit bring to believers (14:26-27; 20:19-22). And there is indeed a graceful side to the theme
of faith. Yet in John's Gospel the claims of faith are at odds with those of
the world. John portrays a context in which deception opposes truth, hatred works against love, and death seeks dominion over life. Therefore,
those who come to know the God who gives life in Jesus find themselves
contending with powers that reject God and diminish life (15:18-25). This
conflict creates a dissonance that presses for resolution. The Gospel says
one thing; the world says another. This dissonance is real and yet John insists that it is not final. Believers do have life with God now, in faith. And
the Gospel provides glimpses of a future in which people will no longer
find life in the presence of conflict but in the presence of Jesus and his Father (17:24). To explore the implications of faith for the present and future
is our focus here.

Faith and the Present

Faith, on a basic level, is trust. It is a positive form of relationship. Significantly, John regularly uses the verb *pisteuō*, which is to trust or believe,
rather than the noun, *pistis* or faith. This makes trusting or believing a
form of activity, a way of relating. It centers on Jesus, for those who believe
in him also believe in the God to whom he bears witness (12:44; 14:1). People are to believe "in" Jesus (2:11; 3:16; 4:39) and "in his name" (1:12). Sometimes they are called to believe Jesus' words, for in believing what he says
they trust Jesus himself (5:47; 11:26). When used on its own, "believe"
points to a bond with Jesus (4:53; 6:47; 9:38; 20:29).[1] The people portrayed
in the Gospel show readers the dynamics of faith. They give a human face
to questions of belief and unbelief. We have already seen how characters
exemplify separation from God (see pp. 53-80). Now we consider how they
show what it means to believe.

Hearing, Seeing, and Believing

A question throughout the Gospel is how believing is related to hearing and seeing.[2] The issue is most directly connected to Jesus' signs and resurrection appearances. For John, a sign or *sēmeion* is a miraculous act that conveys the power of God in a manner accessible to the senses. In his account of Jesus' public ministry, John recounts seven signs: turning water into wine, healing the royal official's son, curing the invalid at Bethzatha, feeding the five thousand, walking on the sea, healing the blind man, and raising Lazarus from the dead. An eighth miracle, the great catch of fish, takes place in the final chapter. Jesus' resurrection appearances are similar to the signs, since they too are extraordinary actions, which make the risen Christ visible to the disciples.[3]

The Gospel sometimes speaks of signs in positive terms. The disciples believe when they see the water turned to wine (2:11), the royal official responds in faith when his son is healed (4:53), and some people believe after Jesus raises Lazarus from the dead (11:45). Therefore, Jesus can say that his works give people reason to believe (10:38; 14:11), and the Gospel recounts the signs for this same purpose (20:30-31). But signs also foster unreliable faith and unbelief. Jesus does not trust those whose faith depends on the signs (2:23-25). His public ministry concludes on a sharply negative note: "Although he had performed so many signs in their presence, they did not believe in him" (12:37). In the end, the Gospel pronounces a blessing on those who have not seen and yet believe (20:29). Therefore, some interpreters conclude that the Gospel disparages belief based on signs. Others take the opposite view, emphasizing that signs are supposed to evoke faith. Still others propose that signs bring people to an initial immature faith, which can later grow into a more mature faith that no longer needs signs.[4]

We can clarify the issue at two points: First, John writes about the signs Jesus performed during his ministry in a manner that addresses the needs of readers living at a later time. The disciples who initially followed Jesus may have seen his signs and resurrection appearances, but the readers of the Gospel have not (20:30-31). Therefore, we must ask how the experiences of the characters in the Gospel relate to the situation of those who read it. Theologically, John's understanding of faith is not limited to those who meet Jesus during his ministry but includes the faith that is possible for the readers.

Second, we will find that signs in themselves are not the issue. People do not merely see signs, they interpret them. Their responses are not governed by seeing alone. The question is what they see *in* the sign, that is, what they think the sign means. Everyone sees the signs from some point of view. So we must ask what shapes that point of view. For example, some of the characters have a worldview that is shaped by a certain approach to Jewish law. According to their tradition, no work is to be done on the Sabbath. Therefore, if Jesus heals on the Sabbath, they see this as a sign of his sinfulness, since he is breaking God's law (5:16; 9:16). Others have a worldview in which everything must be understood in political terms. Therefore, if Jesus feeds the crowd, this is a sign that he is aspiring to political office (6:14-15). If he raises the dead, this is a sign that he is trying to attract followers in order to mount a revolt against Rome (11:47). If people are able to see the signs in a more positive way, it means that their perspective has been shaped by something else.

Characters in the Gospel respond to the signs with genuine faith if they have already been brought to faith by what they have heard from or about Jesus. The path of discipleship begins when people are called to follow or when they hear something that prompts them to trust Jesus. This trust creates a perspective from which people can see the signs in a manner helpful for faith. For them, the sign is not the beginning of a relationship with Jesus but something that occurs within an existing relationship. They begin following because of something they hear, and this in turn shapes what they see. The Gospel also shows that Jesus' signs bear out the truth of his words. He not only says that he is the bread of life but feeds the five thousand with barley loaves (6:11, 35). He calls himself the light of the world, then brings light to the eyes of a man who was born blind (8:12; 9:4-7). When he says that he is the resurrection and the life, he calls Lazarus out of the tomb (11:25-26, 44).

During Jesus' ministry the words people hear from or about Jesus enable them to make sense of the signs they see. For readers living after Jesus' resurrection, this means that they have what is essential: they have received the words from and about Jesus. These words evoke faith and shape the perspective from which people see what faith means in their own situation. The words do what is essential, even for those who have not seen the signs themselves.

John's account of the first disciples establishes the pattern. These people come to faith through an initial experience of hearing. As the narrative begins, John the Baptist declares that Jesus is "the Lamb of God," and two people who hear this follow Jesus. The Baptist's words evoke a curiosity, a willingness to follow. When Jesus turns and asks them what they are looking for, they respond with a question, "Rabbi . . . where are you staying?" (1:38). Jesus could have given them an answer: "I am staying at so-and-so's house. Go three blocks down, take a left, and it will be the second house on the right." But he does not do so. Instead, he offers an invitation: "Come and see" (1:39). This statement creates a new situation for the seekers. Their question will not be answered in advance. They will only learn more by following Jesus. When they do, they "see" where he is staying, and through the encounter they come to recognize that he is the Messiah (1:39-41).

The pattern is repeated when one of these disciples tells his brother Peter, "We have found the Messiah," and he brings Peter to Jesus (1:41-42). Then Jesus calls Philip, who goes to his friend Nathanael with the astonishing claim, "We have found him about whom Moses in the law and also the prophets wrote, Jesus son of Joseph from Nazareth" (1:45). Thoroughly unimpressed, Nathanael replies, "Can anything good come out of Nazareth?" At this point Philip might have tried to marshal a collection of Scripture passages to answer Nathanael's objection, but he does not do so. Instead, he repeats the invitation, "Come and see" (1:46).

Now Nathanael is in a new situation. He could demand that his question about Jesus be answered at the outset, or he could go to Jesus with his question unanswered — which is what he does. In the encounter, Jesus speaks to Nathanael, telling him that he saw him under the fig tree before Philip called him (see p. 92), and Nathanael acclaims Jesus as Son of God and King of Israel (1:47-49). He believes because of what Jesus "said" to him without seeing any miracles (1:50). Then Jesus says that having come to faith, Nathanael and others like him "will see" greater things. They "will see" the glory of God revealed in the Son of Man (1:51).

The sign Jesus performs in the next scene confirms the truth of his words. The disciples, who already believe, accompany him to a wedding at Cana. There he turns the water in six stone jars into wine. The evangelist says that by doing this he "revealed his glory" and "his disciples believed in him" (2:11). The disciples who see the glory in the sign have already come to believe based on what they have heard. Their faith does not originate with the sign. They have already identified Jesus as the Messiah foretold in the law and the prophets, and have called him Son of God and King of Israel. What they see at Cana confirms what they have heard. And what they have heard gives them the perspective they need to see the glory in the sign.

The story of the royal official gives greater sharpness to the Gospel's portrayal of faith. The man has a son who is dying of a fever. This creates a crisis in which the man must act. He travels halfway across Galilee to find Jesus — not because he has seen Jesus do any miracles, but because he has heard about Jesus (4:47). The man goes with a clear sense of expectation about the proper course of action. He wants Jesus to accompany him back to his home in order to heal the dying boy. But Jesus' response runs counter to anything the man might have anticipated. He says, "Unless you see signs and wonders, you will not believe" (4:48). Undeterred, the man persists in asking that Jesus come with him before the child dies. Then Jesus says, "Go; your son will live" (4:50).

Jesus' statement poses a different kind of crisis. The man has expected Jesus to come to his home to heal the boy, but Jesus has only given him the promise that the boy will live. At this point the man must either continue asking Jesus to work on his terms, or else he must trust the word Jesus has spoken — and he will not know for some time whether Jesus' word is true. Here readers do well to linger, so they can fully sense the weight of the moment. The man has come to Jesus in a situation of life and death and has not received the response he expected. Instead, he is called to venture forward on the basis of Jesus' promise of life without any more tangible form of assurance. Everything hinges on the integrity of Jesus' promise. If the promise is true, then the man has the gift of life that he seeks; if it is not true then his journey to Jesus will end fruitlessly in death. And only the future will disclose whether Jesus' promise of life is true or false.

This is the moment where faith is specifically mentioned in the episode. Here readers see what it entails. The man "believed the word that Jesus spoke" (4:50a). He jettisons his expectation that Jesus will come along with him, and he sets out for home (4:50b). This belief or trust is what sets the man on a course of action. Readers learn that *to believe is to return home without visible proof that the boy is alive.* This, for John, is the character of faith — for the readers as well as for the Galilean official.[5]

Faith continues at the end of the story when the man is still on his way and his servants meet him with the news that his son is living. Even here the official has not actually seen the sign for himself. What he has is the report of the servants. Yet this seems to be sufficient. Jesus said the boy would live and the servants now say the same. Their words bear out the truth of Jesus' words. This sign is not the basis of the man's faith. Instead, it confirms the faith that began with what he heard from Jesus (4:51-53). The readers of John's Gospel are encouraged by the end of the episode, though their own situation is actually most like that of the royal official in the middle of the story. Like the official they have received a promise of life from Jesus — the Gospel itself communicates the word of life to them. And they are also like the official in that they will not know whether the promise of life is true prior to believing it. The only way to find out is to trust it and move forward. That is what the official did. The question is whether the readers will do the same.

The story of the man born blind in John 9 continues this pattern. At the beginning the blind beggar sits in silence as Jesus' disciples ponder theoretical questions about the cause of his blindness. But Jesus alters the situation when he puts mud on the man's eyes and says, "Go, wash in the pool of Siloam" (9:7). The pool is located elsewhere in Jerusalem. The man cannot see. All he has is the directive to go and wash — and Jesus does not even explain *why* he should grope his way across town to the pool instead of wiping the mud off his eyes at the place where he was sitting. Yet Jesus' words evoke a willingness to trust. The man goes as Jesus tells him to do, even though he has not yet experienced healing.

After washing, the man discovers that he can see. His initial trust in Jesus seems well placed. The man sees — *but he does not see Jesus.* His healing takes place at a time and place that Jesus is not visibly present. What is apparent to the man's eyes is conflict, not Jesus himself. It starts when the man's neighbors question whether he is the one who used to sit and beg; then it intensifies as he is questioned by the authorities, who debate whether Jesus is a lawbreaker for healing on the Sabbath. The man's parents refuse to say more than the minimum, leaving the man to fend for himself in court. As the legal battle grinds on, the authorities finally end the debate and cut the man off from his community, sending him back to the street (9:24-34). Conflict and dislocation — this is what discipleship looks like for the man who is healed. Significantly, he sees Jesus for the first time only at the end of the story. That is when Jesus finds him and asks whether he believes in the Son of Man (9:35). The beggar must ask who the Son of Man is because he has never before seen his healer (9:36). Then Jesus makes himself known, and the beggar says, "I believe" (9:37-38).

Readers who believe are like the man born blind in that they are to respond to words from and about Jesus, even though they have not seen him.[6] Their situation is most like that of the beggar in the middle of the story. They too have heard the word of Jesus, and those who believe it have the light of life. They also find that faith means believing in a Jesus whom they have *not seen* in the face of conflicts that they *do see*. To bear witness to the light sets them at odds with the world. Yet the story of the beggar also extends the hope that those who have responded to Jesus' words will one day see him for themselves, and that the faith affirmed in conflict has a future in the presence of God (see pp. 176-79).

John's account of Lazarus's death continues to press the issue of faith. Here again it is not a question of believing without seeing. It is believing *in spite of* what one sees. Lazarus's sisters send word of his illness to Jesus, who is some distance away, but Jesus delays in coming and Lazarus dies (11:1-16). In ordinary human terms Jesus' actions are inexplicable. It is clear that Jesus loves Martha, Mary, and Lazarus, and yet he does not go to heal his friend. People show love by coming right away in a crisis, but what the women see is that Jesus delays, and the meaning of that is far from clear. Moreover, when Jesus arrives in Bethany, Lazarus has been in the tomb for four days. What the sisters have seen is death, and that is the visible reality to which the Gospel must speak.

Note that Lazarus's illness and death take place when Jesus is not visibly present with him, which fits the situation of the readers. They too experience death without Jesus being visibly present.[7] The sisters who are with Lazarus during the crisis send word to Jesus who is elsewhere, yet their message is met with silence. This again fits the context of those in later generations, who appeal to a seemingly absent Jesus for help and receive only silence in return. The issues that are raised in the story correspond to those faced by its readers.

When Jesus comes to Bethany, Martha says, "Lord, if you had been here, my brother would not have died" (11:21). It is difficult to know whether this is a lament over Lazarus's death, a reproach for Jesus' failure to come sooner, or both. Regardless of the tone, however, Martha shows continuing trust in Jesus and is convinced that God will give him whatever he asks (11:22).[8] One might imagine that Martha harbors the hope that Jesus might still do a miracle and bring her brother back to life. That would compensate for his inexplicable delay. But this is not the character of Martha's response. There is no suggestion that she thinks Jesus will do a miracle. When Jesus promises that Lazarus will rise again, she assumes it will occur in the future, on the last day, not later that same afternoon (11:23-24). She is not looking for a surprising post-mortem healing.

Then Jesus says, "I Am the resurrection and the life. Those who believe in me, even though they die, will live, and everyone who lives and believes in me will never die. Do you believe this?" Readers must pause at this point to sense the full weight of the question. Lazarus remains dead. The grieving woman's brother is still in a closed tomb. Jesus' question would sound quite different if he had kept it until the end of the story, when the stone was removed and Lazarus came back to life. It would be one thing to ask, "Do you believe?" as Lazarus comes out of the tomb alive and stands before his grieving sister. It is quite another thing to ask the question while the body still lies in the grave. Yet it is here, in the middle of the story, that the question of faith is most pressing. *If there is to be faith, it must come despite the visible presence of death.* And what Jesus offers Martha is simply a word: "I Am the resurrection and the life."

Martha tells Jesus, "Yes, Lord, I believe that you are the Messiah, the Son of God, the one coming into the world" (11:27). Martha says this in the middle of the story, and she must do so in spite of what she sees. Lazarus is clearly dead, and Martha assumes that he will remain dead for the foreseeable future. She does not even want the stone removed from the tomb's entrance (11:39). Martha's faith will be confirmed by the sign, but it is not based on the sign. She confesses her faith in spite of Jesus' delay and her brother's death. Jesus says that faith will enable Martha to see God's glory in the sign (11:40), but the idea is not that she will initially come to faith in God by seeing her brother brought back to life. Instead, faith creates the perspective from which she can see God's power at work.

Martha's confession of faith in Jesus as the Messiah and Son of God is the same confession the evangelist wants readers to make (20:31). And like Martha, later generations will be called to believe in Jesus in the face of death. The raising of Lazarus and Jesus' own resurrection confirm the truth of Jesus' words, but the issue of faith remains. The readers find themselves in situations like those in the middle of the story, where death is the visible reality with which they must contend. Like Martha, the readers are given Jesus' word to trust, and those who believe it must do so despite what they see.

Jesus, the doer of the signs, eventually goes to his own death by crucifixion. At the end of the day people see that he truly has died (19:33). What his followers later see on Easter does not, in itself, change the conviction that he remains dead. We have noted how Mary Magdalene sees the open tomb, the angels, and even the risen Jesus himself, yet steadfastly believes that he is still dead and that his body has been stolen. Nothing she sees brings faith in the resurrection. Her perception only changes when the risen Jesus calls her by name. The words Mary hears alter the way she sees (20:16; see pp. 124-26). Similarly, Thomas's encounter with the risen Christ occurs in a context that has already been shaped by the words he received from and about Jesus. What he hears enables him to respond in faith to what he sees (see pp. 126-27).

John's Gospel is written for people who have not seen the risen Jesus or the signs he performed. In its pages readers find that genuine faith is evoked by the words people receive from or about Jesus. During Jesus' ministry, the faith generated through words is sometimes confirmed by signs. It also creates the perspective from which signs can be understood. It even persists without signs. For people in later generations, the words that can evoke faith are communicated through the witness of Jesus' followers, including that of the Fourth Evangelist. Through the Gospel the signs of Jesus come to readers in verbal form. The signs are made visible through the words of the Gospel. Readers need not look elsewhere for wonders to believe in. They find in John's text the words and works of Jesus that call them to faith.

Faith, Crucifixion, and Resurrection

Faith centers on a Jesus who was crucified as well as resurrected. The words and actions of his public ministry lead up to his death and are re-defined by it. The crucifixion is integral to the way God engages the world and conveys his love to it (see pp. 41-46). Therefore, genuine faith is shaped by the crucifixion, as well as by the ministry of Jesus that precedes it and by the resurrection that follows. The cruciform quality of faith is intimated at the beginning of the Gospel, where John the Baptist points to Jesus as the sacrificial Lamb of God, and two people begin following him (1:36). The seekers are drawn by the Lamb who will be crucified. To follow him is to learn what this means.

Allusions to the crucifixion occur throughout John's account of Jesus' ministry, and the way people respond discloses the character of their faith. Readers see that it is one thing to follow a wonder-worker, but coming to terms with a crucified wonder-worker is something else. Consider what happens after Jesus raises Lazarus from the dead. Many people are im-pressed by the sign and assume that it means Jesus is ready to take the throne of Israel. Because they interpret the sign this way, they treat Lazarus as a celebrity and welcome Jesus as a hero, putting palm branches on the road and giving him royal titles (12:13-18). Yet their belief that Jesus will fit into their current model of kingship collides with the message that he will be "lifted up" in crucifixion. He says, "I, when I am lifted up from the earth, will draw all people to myself," and thereby indicates "the kind of death he was to die" (12:32-33). The crowd responds with incredulity, since they assume that the Messiah will remain forever by avoiding death.

The announcement of the crucifixion marks the end of their way of believing. Their approach to faith, based on their interpretation of the signs, collapses at the prospect of him being lifted up. At the end of Jesus' public ministry, the evangelist's judgment is: "Although he had performed so many signs in their presence, they did not believe in him" (12:37). Yet if the cross marks the end of one kind of faith, it also signals the beginning of another. The crowd is repulsed by the idea that Jesus will die, yet Jesus also says that in being lifted up he will "draw" people to himself (12:32). In the theological world of the Gospel this can happen because the crucifixion conveys the divine love that draws people to faith. The cross is the visible sign of God's love for the world, and the drawing to faith continues through the work of Christ, who will remain forever — not by avoiding death but by overcoming it.

The cruciform quality of faith is suggestively depicted at the end of the passion narrative, where Nicodemus makes a final appearance. Throughout the Gospel he has seemed hopelessly out of step. When he meets Jesus he gets off on the wrong foot by focusing on the signs and claiming to know all about Jesus, yet he is quickly tripped up when Jesus speaks about being born anew and about the Son of Man being lifted up like the serpent on the pole (3:1-21). In his second appearance he asks a question about proper judicial process, then vanishes from view (7:51). So when he steps forward to claim the body of Jesus for burial, many question how much he really comprehends. The mound of spice he puts on Jesus' corpse shows that he is not expecting a resurrection any time soon (19:39-40). But rather than asking about Nicodemus's mindset, it might be better to ask how the scene relates to Jesus' promise. Before his death, Jesus said that when lifted up he would draw people to himself. From this perspective, his promise begins to bear fruit as Nicodemus is drawn out of the shadows to claim Jesus the crucified.[9]

Faith and Understanding

Readers often find that John's Gospel makes sharp contrasts between belief and unbelief. The Gospel calls people to faith, promising that those who drink the living water will not thirst, those who eat the living bread will not hunger, and those who receive the light will not walk in darkness (4:14; 6:35; 8:12). John distinguishes believing from not believing, life from death, being saved from being judged (3:16-18). He says that Jesus' followers are called out of the world, while his opponents remain part of the world. Those who attempt to have it both ways are criticized for keeping their faith a secret in order to advance their status in an unbelieving society (12:42-43).

The Gospel contrasts belief and unbelief in order to press for clarity of commitment to Jesus. Readers are not to linger in the gray areas, keeping the claims of God at a secure distance. Recognizing that life is complex, one might want to retreat into the comfort of ambiguity, where no commitment is required. Yet those who do so find the Gospel raising uncomfortable questions: Is there really no difference between life and death? Between truth and falsehood? Between belief and unbelief? The Gospel is unequivocal in its declaration of God's love for the world, and this light intrudes into the shadows with piercing intensity. God's love for the world is his commitment to the world, and it comes in the uncompromising form of crucifixion. That is the extent to which God will go, according to John. And the reason God does this is to draw people out of the shadows and into relationship with himself (3:16-21).

John poses clear alternatives when calling people to faith and life. Yet if taken alone, this can make his Gospel seem simplistic. One might conclude that people either know nothing of God or they know him completely, that they are either in the darkness or are fully enlightened. Here it is essential to recall how the Gospel portrays specific human beings. John insists that there is a difference between belief and unbelief, yet he recognizes that it is not always clear when someone has moved from one category to the other (see pp. 142-43). He also understands that faith is not static and that sin remains an issue even in the community of faith. People believe despite their unbelief, and relate to God despite the pull of sin.

For John, faith is the context in which understanding develops. At a basic level faith is trust. In the section on hearing, seeing, and believing, we have already noted how those who show an initial trust in Jesus do not have their questions answered at the outset. They come to understand him as they follow. The Gospel uses words for knowing *(ginōskō, oida)* alongside terms for believing (6:69; 10:38; 17:8). Theologically, knowing involves recognizing someone's identity or character. To know God is to be aware that he is the source of life (17:3). To know Jesus is to recognize that he has come from God, that he is the Holy One of God, and that he brings salvation (4:42; 6:69; 17:8). Accordingly, there is a cognitive dimension to faith. To believe that Jesus is the Messiah means recognizing that he is the one in whom God's promises are fulfilled (1:41, 45; 20:31). Similarly, believing that Jesus is the Son of God means that Jesus is the one in whom God is present and active (20:31).

The Gospel often makes sharp contrasts between knowing and not knowing. Jesus' followers are those who know that he has come from God, and that God has given him all that he has (17:7-8, 25). But Jesus' opponents do not know where he comes from (8:14, 19, 55). They put their lack of understanding into practice by opposing Jesus and those who follow him (15:21; 16:3). The difference between knowing and not knowing seems clear, yet the Gospel also has a deep realism about how this works. There is a persistent tension between knowing God and not knowing God, an abiding separation between the human and the divine. Faith can bridge it, but the separation does not fully go away. Again, the portrayals of specific characters illustrate this.

One of the Gospel's most complex characters is the Samaritan woman.[10] She meets Jesus beside a well, then flounders in her attempt to understand the living water. When she finally asks for this water, she seems to expect it to work like magic plumbing, eliminating the need to come to the well each day (4:15). She moves toward greater clarity when Jesus tells her about her personal life and she discerns that he must be a prophet (4:19). She comes close to genuine insight when she introduces the topic of the Messiah. Then after Jesus identifies himself, she tells her townspeople, "Come and see a man who told me everything I ever did" (4:29a). She sounds like a true believer. Yet her final words are a question that technically expects a negative answer: "He can't be the Messiah, can he?" (4:29). She invites people to "come and see," but she does so despite lingering uncertainty. What she has received from Jesus enables her to bear witness, but it has not fully eliminated her questions.

One might expect Jesus' disciples to be more perceptive. After all, they conclude that Jesus is the Messiah before the end of the first chapter. Yet they often prove to be as uncomprehending as the Samaritan woman. While in Samaria they go into a nearby village looking for food, much as the woman comes out of the village looking for water. When they bring lunch, their attention focuses squarely on material food. They tell Jesus, "Rabbi, eat something" (4:31). Jesus alludes to higher realities by saying that he has food that they do not know about. Undeterred, the disciples remain preoccupied with the meal, and wonder whether someone might have brought Jesus something to eat during their absence (4:33). Jesus explains that his food is to do the will of God, but the disciples make no further comment. In their case faith is not a triumphant march toward ever-new heights of understanding. They move from insight to confusion and back again. What is important is that their relationship with Jesus continues despite the uncertainty, since faith is the context in which understanding develops — and their questions continue to the end of Jesus' ministry (14:5, 8; 16:17).

The man born blind, whose story we have already considered, also illustrates the complex relationship of faith to understanding. Throughout the story the man speaks the truth, but what he knows is limited. The beggar says with certainty that the man called Jesus told him to go to Siloam and wash, but when asked where Jesus is, he confesses, "I do not know" (9:11-12). When the Pharisees denounce Jesus as a sinner, the beggar replies that he does not know whether Jesus is a sinner, only that he himself was once blind and now can see (9:25). In the final scene, when the man sees Jesus for the first time, he still shows the limits of his understanding, since he has to ask who the Son of Man is (9:36). Only then does he say, "I believe." The tension between knowing and not knowing, between light and darkness, is fully resolved only in the end, when the man sees Jesus face to face.

These portraits of human beings give readers a sense of realism about the dynamics of faith. To be human is to be created for life with God, to be separated from God, and to receive life with God by being brought to faith. To be human also means recognizing that separation from God is overcome by faith, but it does not fully go away. Belief is awakened in the face of unbelief, knowing comes in the face of not knowing, and light shines despite the darkness. John's Gospel was written for human beings who, like the man born blind, have never seen Jesus. Like the man, the readers are called into the light, and like him they can hope to be fully enlightened only when they too see Jesus face to face.[11]

Present Faith and Future Hope

Faith brings life with God in the present, but how John envisions the future is a matter of debate. Many interpreters emphasize the current aspects of salvation. They stress that judgment and deliverance occur now, as people respond negatively or positively to the Gospel. John includes no scenes of Christ returning on the clouds or a final apocalyptic battle, so that one might conclude that God's actions against sin, evil, and death are complete. This is "realized eschatology," which maintains that God's promises of life are fully realized in the present. Others point out that the Gospel speaks of a future coming of Jesus and of the resurrection and judgment that will occur on "the last day." This is usually called "futuristic" or "final eschatology." Neatly separating these categories, however, creates problems, as both perspectives play a role in the Gospel. Therefore, we will ask how the past and present relate to the future, according to John.[12]

A Rift in Time

The Fourth Evangelist describes a world that has been decisively changed by the coming of Jesus. The Word, who was with God and was God, became flesh in Jesus of Nazareth. In him the true light that enlightens everyone has come into the world, altering the context in which people live (1:9). Jesus manifested the truth by his words and actions (8:12; 12:46). He came as the Lamb of God who takes away sin and as the Son of God who liberates people from bondage (1:29; 8:36). When he was lifted up in crucifixion, the satanic ruler of the world was cast out. The sign above the cross announced to the world that the crucified Jesus was its true sovereign (12:31; 19:19-20).

The Gospel gives the vivid sense that future hopes have become present realities. Many expected the dead to be raised at the end of the age, when the kingdom of God arrived and the present world of sorrow came to an end (11:24), and now Jesus has risen from the dead, calling people to new life in him (5:25; 11:25-26). The Spirit has come like a stream of living water, bringing people the gift of eternal life and true worship of God (4:10, 14, 23-24). Through the message of Jesus and the work of the Spirit, a community of faith has been formed, gathering together those who have come to know God in Jesus.

Yet the time in which the Gospel's readers live is also marked by conflict. A rift has occurred. Some have come to see the light of God in Jesus,
but others have been blinded and reject him (9:39). Some find the light liberating and are drawn to it, while others retreat into the shadows, finding
the darkness comfortable and protective, and not wanting to be exposed
(3:19-21). With searing irony the Gospel can say that the Lamb who came
to take away sin has also provoked sin, because his words and actions elicit
unbelief. To reject Jesus is to reject the God who sent him and this, according to John, is sin (15:22-24).

Jesus may have dethroned the ruler of this world, but the powers of evil
continue to operate on the cosmic stage. Although Jesus ascended to glory
in his Father's presence, his followers remain in the world and need ongoing protection from the evil one (17:11, 15). The risen Jesus may give his followers life with God, but bodily illness, death, and grief remain an all-too-
familiar part of Christian experience (11:3, 14; 21:19, 23). Moreover, in calling people to faith, Jesus sets them apart from a world that does not accept
their convictions. "Because you do not belong to the world, but I have chosen you out of the world — therefore the world hates you" (15:19).

John's sense of time — his eschatology — is shaped by his recognition
that in the coming of Jesus the light has made a decisive difference between
the past and the present. But John also knows that the present is the scene
of conflicting claims. True life is a current reality, yet so is death; some people can now see, yet others have become blind. These truths grate against
each other like dissonant sounds pressing for resolution. The Gospel assumes that there is no going back, as if Jesus never came. There can only be
going forward to the point where the dissonance resolves into harmony.
But how does this take place, according to John? What vision of the future
does the Gospel offer?

Present and Future of Judgment

John understands that there are both present and future dimensions to faith
and unfaith. Beginning with the present, John makes a contrast between the
realm of life and light, where people are saved from divine judgment, and
the realm of perishing and darkness, where people remain under condemnation (3:16-21). God sent his Son into the world in order that people might
enter the realm of light by coming to faith. Accordingly, judgment occurs in

the present as people respond positively or negatively to Jesus. Those who receive the love that God extends in Jesus are not under judgment since they are no longer alienated from God. But those who reject the love of God place themselves under judgment since they refuse what God offers.

The Gospel also relates judgment to human actions: "This is the judgment, that the light has come into the world, and people loved darkness rather than light because their deeds were evil," whereas "those who do what is true come to the light, so that it may be clearly seen that their deeds have been done in God" (3:19, 21). The Gospel can speak of judgment in terms of faith and unfaith, and then relate judgment to human deeds because what people do expresses what they believe. John says that God loves the world and gave his Son for it (3:16). Those who really believe this will express love in the way they live (13:34), but those who do not believe this can be expected to show hatred toward God's light and to ally themselves with the forces of hatred (3:20; 15:18).

Significantly, John does not give readers a simple list of do's and don'ts, as if avoiding judgment means achieving a satisfactory average on a scorecard of personal virtues. The Gospel recognizes that what people do depends on which relationships really matter to them. If God is true, then those who trust him "do what is true." Their actions fit the relationship; their deeds are "done in God" (3:21). Similarly, if God gives the light of life in Jesus, then believing this means acting in ways that bring life (3:19; 8:12; 9:4). Conversely, if the relationships that really matter are with those who oppose God, then rejecting God's truth means practicing deception, and refusing God's life means diminishing life for oneself and others (8:41, 44).

The judgment that takes place now, as people respond positively or negatively to Jesus, has a future dimension. In 5:24-25, Jesus begins with the present, when he says, "anyone who hears my word and believes him who sent me has eternal life, and does not come under judgment, but has passed from death to life." This makes true life a current reality. He underscores this by saying, the "hour is coming *and is now here*" when those who are dead will hear the voice of the Son of God and live. Thus far Jesus speaks about the spiritually "dead," who come to life through faith.

Then Jesus extends the horizon into the future. The judgment that is now occurring has a future dimension. In 5:28-29 he says,

the hour is coming when all who are in their graves
will hear his voice and will come out —

those who have done good, to the resurrection of life,
and those who have done evil, to the resurrection of judgment

The first two lines refer to the hour that "is coming," rather than the time that has already arrived. In it Jesus focuses on those who are physically dead and in their graves. The new life they receive is a resurrection that is yet to come. At present Jesus calls people to faith, which is life in relationship with God. And this passage gives faith a future. The believer's relationship with God is not terminated by bodily death. The same Jesus who has already called them to faith will, in the future, call them to the resurrection of life.

The second two lines develop the connection between faith and action. The Gospel has already indicated that what people do expresses what they really believe (cf. 3:16-21). Accordingly, to say that those who *believe* have life now, and those who *do what is good* will have life in the future, is to understand that faith shapes action. People may say one thing and do another. But for John, the faith that people truly hold is the faith by which they live. The faith that is operative in life now holds within it the promise of life in the future. Similarly, present alienation from God places a person under judgment and carries within it the prospect of alienation from God in the future; that is the resurrection of judgment.

Of central importance for John is that the present and future are seen relationally. This differs from popular depictions of the future judgment, which often emphasize the places to which people go. Good people are said to go to a good place, which is usually pictured in pleasant terms, where they keep doing whatever they most enjoyed in life. In contrast, bad people go to a bad place, usually pictured as a realm of fiery torment. John, however, speaks of the future in terms of the relationships that have been formed in the present. If people find life in relationship with God now, that will be true in the future. If people want nothing to do with God now, that will also be true in the future. Judgment, from John's perspective, means letting the human rejection of God take its course. God sent the Son to bring life and love, and if people do not want that, then final judgment means accepting their refusal. The most unsettling form of divine judgment is for God to say, "Have it your way," and to let human estrangement from God take its course.

So what is Jesus' role in judgment? Sometimes he says that the Father has given him responsibility for judgment and that he judges according to

God's will (5:22, 30). Elsewhere the Gospel says that Jesus was not sent to judge but to save (3:17). Paradoxically, Jesus can say that he does and yet does not judge (8:15-16, 26). From John's perspective, Jesus brings the light of truth and life into the world and this means that judgment will occur, since people will respond to Jesus in some way. Those who receive the light and life he brings are not condemned, while those who reject him place themselves under judgment. By judging Jesus, people judge themselves (12:47-48).

John's understanding of judgment is dynamic rather than static. The Gospel does not suggest that unbelief and faith are two fixed categories with no movement from one to the other. The word that Jesus brings continues to call people to faith and life. As long as the light is with them, people are urged to believe and to become children of light (12:36). The Gospel also recognizes that discerning the difference between unbelief and belief must finally be left to God. After telling of the unbelief that seemed so pervasive at the end of Jesus' public ministry, the evangelist nevertheless repeats Jesus' invitation to believe, an invitation that remains open until "the last day" (12:44-50).

Present and Future of Life

The theme of resurrection leads to questions about the nature of life in the future. John's Gospel is unequivocal in its conviction that true life is a present reality for those who believe. What is more, it promises that those who eat the bread that Jesus offers will live forever and that those who keep his word will never see death (6:50; 8:51). The claim that believers do not die seems ludicrous, of course, and it exasperates those who hear Jesus. They retort with the obvious objection that people of faith do die. In the past, Abraham and the prophets died, and death continues to stalk the followers of Jesus (8:52-53). There is no reason to think that the faithful will escape dying any more than Jesus does.

The Gospel recognizes that death is an intruder. It approaches through the sickness that threatens the life of a child, and the violent actions that bring death to Jesus and others (4:47, 49; 5:18; 16:2; 18:32). Even Peter and the Beloved Disciple fall prey to it (21:19, 23).[13] Therefore, when addressing the problem of death the Gospel will do two things: First, it will acknowledge that death is real and not illusory. There is no attempt to mask it;

death's power is evident. Second, the Gospel will make clear that death is real but not final. Jesus died and Jesus rose, and what happened to him will happen to those who follow him.[14]

The problem of death is most vividly treated in the story of Lazarus of Bethany, as noted above. The man's two sisters, Martha and Mary, send this message to Jesus: "Lord, the one whom you love is ill" (11:3). Their poignant words underscore the painful truth that those who are loved by Jesus do become seriously ill. The Gospel does not attempt to explain the cause of the illness or the death that it brings. Sickness and death are simply a given. Upon receiving the message Jesus replies, "This illness does not lead to death; rather it is for God's glory" (11:4). He does not say that God caused the illness in order to provide an occasion for revealing his power. He takes the illness as a starting point and works forward to reveal God's glory. He does not attempt to explain why the illness occurred in the first place. The same approach was taken with the man born blind. Rather than looking back, in order to explain how the physical problem originated, Jesus begins with the problem as it exists and looks ahead to what might be done from that point on (see pp. 57-59). In what follows, the Gospel responds by exploring the significance of resurrection, since resurrection does not mean avoiding death but going through death to life.

Jesus' encounter with Martha helps define the resurrection hope. He tells her, "Your brother will rise again" (11:23). Jesus assumes that Lazarus has now died and will rise in the future. Death affects the whole person, not simply a part of a person. The whole person dies and the whole person is raised to new life. This differs from the common idea that a person can be neatly divided into a body and soul. According to this dualistic approach, death separates the body from the soul. The body dies and the soul ascends to spiritual life in heaven. Jesus could have expressed the dualistic perspective by telling Martha, "Your brother's soul is now in heaven," but he does not do so. Jesus' words treat Lazarus as a whole person, who has now died and who has the promise of rising to new life.[15]

Martha responds, "I know that he will rise again in the resurrection at the last day," and Jesus tells her, "I Am the resurrection" (11:24-25a). What Jesus himself experiences defines what resurrection means. The Gospel makes clear that he dies and rises as a whole person. There is no suggestion that his body dies while his soul ascends to heaven. By going the way of death and resurrection he comes to embody the promise of resurrection (see pp. 209-14). What this means for others is that those "who believe in me, even though they die, will live" (11:25b). Throughout this episode, the assumption is that death affects Lazarus as a whole person. Jesus bluntly tells the disciples, "Lazarus is dead" (11:11-14). For burial, Lazarus is wrapped in grave cloths, and when Jesus arrives in Bethany, Lazarus has already been in the tomb for four days (11:17). The passing of so much time emphasizes that death is real and complete.

A theology of resurrection means confessing without qualification that death is real. It also means believing that death is not final.[16] The Gospel understands that neither Jesus nor his followers are exempted from death. For all of them resurrection means fully experiencing death and then overcoming it. By dying Jesus gave himself completely, not partially, for the sake of others. By rising he also defines the promise of life in a way that is complete, not partial.

The raising of Lazarus is a sign of a resurrection that is yet to come. It points to the future life rather than fully bringing it about. The way Jesus calls Lazarus out of the tomb anticipates "the last day," when "all who are in their graves will hear his voice and will come out" (11:44; 5:28-29). The difference is that Lazarus is restored to bodily life — and the prospect of dying again — whereas the final resurrection involves the transformation of bodily life. Jesus died and rose as a whole person, an embodied person, but as one no longer subject to the constraints of death (see pp. 130-32). Resurrection is the corollary to creation. It means that the God who created people, body and soul, through his Word, has a future for them. Resurrection means that God is unwilling to limit his work to a purely spiritual form of salvation. God's Word comes to people in embodied form and offers an embodied future, a transformed future, in Jesus who is the resurrection.[17]

As Jesus extends the hope of resurrection, he also brings the promised future into the present. Having said, "I Am the resurrection," he adds, "and the life" (11:25). Then he says that everyone who "lives and believes in me will never die" (11:26; cf. 6:50; 8:51). The connotations of life and death change at a bewildering pace. Having made clear that people of faith do die in the ordinary bodily sense, he can say that there is another sense in which they do not die. We have seen that life and death have relational as well as physical aspects. Those who come to believe in Jesus enter a relationship with him and his Father that is true life. This relationship does not end with the person's final breath. The person remains in relationship with God and in this sense does not "die." The relationship will extend into the future through resurrection. The closest the Gospel comes to picturing this is through the metaphor of sleep (11:11, 13). Someone who falls asleep can remain in the care of someone else until he or she is awakened. By analogy, those who sleep in death remain in the care of God until they are awakened to life in Christ on the last day (6:39-40, 44, 54).

Present and Future of Jesus

Time changed, for the author of John's Gospel, when the Word of God became flesh. Since the coming of Jesus, things have not been the same. Yet at the end of his ministry, Jesus tells the disciples that he is returning to the Father and will no longer be visibly among them (14:28; 16:5, 28). In an ordinary story one might imagine the hero dying and his friends lamenting that they will not see him any longer, but in John's Gospel there is a twist: Jesus dies, then rises and appears to his followers before going away. Common sense would say that people no longer see Jesus because he is dead, but according to John, people no longer see him because he is alive and with the Father. It is the risen Jesus who says, "I am ascending to my Father and your Father, to my God and your God" (20:17). Readers may wait for John to tell them about Jesus being visibly taken up to heaven on the clouds, but the Gospel does not do so. This raises the question: How does anyone know that the risen Jesus is with the Father?

Jesus told the disciples that if he did not go away, the Advocate, the Holy Spirit, would not come, but by going to the Father, he would send the Spirit to them (16:7). This is how people know that Jesus is with the Father, according to John. The Spirit discloses the presence of the risen Christ to them (see pp. 149-57). Through the Spirit and the witness of the disciples, the risen Christ continues to be at work, calling people to faith and life in community. For the writer of John's Gospel, the conviction that Jesus is with the Father is not an attempt to explain Jesus' apparent absence. Just the opposite. It is the result of Jesus' continued presence and action in the world. John recognizes that no amount of explaining creates faith. People come to believe in the risen and unseen Christ when he himself draws them through the Spirit and the witness of his people (pp. 127-30).

The relationship that people now have with God and the risen Christ is real, but its form is not final, according to John. Having spoken about going to the Father, Jesus also speaks of coming again to take the disciples to his Father's house. At the last supper he says, "Do not let your hearts be troubled. Believe in God, believe also in me. In my Father's house there are many dwelling places. If it were not so, would I have told you that I go to prepare a place for you?" (14:1-2). The disciples are troubled because Jesus has told them that he is going away and they will not be able to follow (13:33). This threat of separation from Jesus is the backdrop for his promise to prepare a place for them.

The words "my Father's house" give a vivid sense of what future life means. The language is both spatial and relational. The Father's house is where the Father is present, and those who belong to God have a place in his household. As the Son of God, Jesus receives life from his Father, does the work of his Father, and has a permanent place in the house of his Father (5:19, 26; 8:35-36). Those who trust Jesus become his brothers and sisters. As members of his family they too can call God their Father (20:17; see pp. 51-52). The force of the promise would be different if Jesus had said, "In heaven there are many dwelling places." In the Gospel heaven is closely associated with God (6:33; 12:28; 17:1). Yet in popular imagination heaven can take on a life of its own, being pictured as a dreamy place in which God may or may not have much of a role. But the promise in John's Gospel centers on person more than place, on being with Jesus and his Father more than on being in a certain location.

The assurance that the Father's house has many rooms or dwelling places continues the relational emphasis. The word for a dwelling place *(monē)* can best be translated "abiding place," since it is connected to the verb "abide" *(menō)*, which is repeatedly used for enduring relationships. The Father abides in Jesus and Jesus abides in the Father's love. Jesus' words abide in the disciples and the disciples abide in his word and love (14:10; 15:4-10). As Jesus goes to prepare an abiding place or *monē* for the disciples, he and his Father come to make their abiding place or *monē* within the community of faith (14:23). This occurs through the Spirit that abides (14:17; see pp. 149-51). No details are given about the design or size of these abiding places, no comments about their splendor or ornamentation. John's Gospel leaves details aside, focusing on the sense of abiding relationship with God and those who belong to God.

Then Jesus says, "I will come again and will take you to myself, so that where I am you may be also" (14:3). Jesus' promise to come again is part of the Christian hope that what Christ has begun will be brought to completion in the future. It was a belief that was held by John's earliest readers, who were evidently shaken when the Beloved Disciple died before Jesus came again (21:22-23).[18] The belief in Jesus' return was also shared by other New Testament writers (Acts 1:11; 1 Thess. 4:13-18; Rev. 19:11-16). John, however, refrains from any attempt to describe it. His Gospel includes no scenes of heaven opening and Christ coming down on the clouds. For John, Jesus' departure to the Father is known by the coming of the Spirit, and his coming again will be known when the community is with Jesus where he is. The language is striking. Where one would expect Jesus to say, "I will come again and will take you to heaven," he says, "I will take you to *myself*." The focus is on being with Jesus, who is with the Father.

Jesus brings people to himself through resurrection. He already is the resurrection and the life, and by coming again he will extend the resurrection to others. Throughout the Gospel, Jesus is the one who embodies the hope of resurrection and who brings it about on the last day (John 6:39-40, 44, 54). John does not suggest that Jesus' promise to come again means that he will call a person's soul to heaven whenever the person dies. His own death and resurrection shape the believer's hope for the future. The Jesus who dies and rises also promises to bring others who die to life in his Father's house. His own story defines the future for others.

Jesus' promise to come again in the future is supported by his promise to come to the disciples at Easter. The language used for these two comings is so similar that it is not always easy to tell when Jesus speaks about his own resurrection and when he points to his future coming and the believer's resurrection.[19] At the last supper he says (14:18-19),

> I will not leave you orphaned; I am coming to you.
> In a little while the world will no longer see me,
> but you will see me; because I live, you also will live.

Many think that all of these lines refer to Jesus coming to the disciples at Easter. From this perspective the message is that Jesus' death will not result in the disciples being abandoned or orphaned, since Jesus will come to them again at Easter, when they will see him again. This happens when the risen Jesus comes to the disciples and is seen by them (20:20).[20]

Others think that the last two lines refer to Jesus' resurrection and that the first line pictures the time after his resurrection and return to the Father. When Jesus is no longer visibly present, his disciples will feel orphaned or abandoned in a conflicted world.[21] When read in this way, the first line repeats Jesus' promise to come again and take the disciples to himself (14:3, 28). Then, in the next two lines, he brings this future hope into the present by the assurance that he will see the disciples again at Easter. His resurrection to life will be the basis for their future hope. The Spirit, whom the risen Jesus sends from the Father, will disclose his presence to the disciples as they look to the future (see pp. 130-32).

The same interpretive difficulties occur when Jesus says, "A little while and you will no longer see me, and again a little while, and you will see me" (16:16). His cryptic words are confusing, and the disciples flatly say, "We do not know what he is talking about" (16:18). So Jesus continues (16:20-22),

> 20you will weep and mourn, but the world will rejoice;
> you will have pain, but your pain will turn into joy.
>
> 21When a woman is in labor, she has pain, because her hour has come.
> But when her child is born, she no longer remembers the anguish
> because of the joy of having brought a human being into the world.
>
> 22So you have pain now;
> but I will see you again, and your hearts will rejoice,
> and no one will take your joy from you.

Many interpreters relate Jesus' description of the disciples' pain and the world's rejoicing to the crucifixion, which will happen "a little while" after the last supper. At his death the disciples will mourn, but Jesus will come to them "a little while" afterwards through his resurrection. Then they will rejoice. From this perspective Good Friday is like the pain of a woman in labor, while Easter brings the joy of new life. This fits the narrative, for Mary Magdalene's tears end and the disciples rejoice when they see the risen Jesus (20:15-16, 19-20).

Others find that this passage also fits the experience of Christians after Easter. In "a little while" the disciples will no longer see Jesus because after his resurrection he will go to the Father. Note that Jesus does not go to the Father by dying but by ascending after his resurrection (16:17; 20:17). It is the ascension that begins the period in which his disciples will no longer see him. While Jesus is with the Father, his disciples will experience pain because of their conflict with the unbelieving world. Jesus' resurrection does not make Christians immune from sorrow. Grief is an ongoing part of

Christian life. Jesus says that the woman who has come to joy at the end of her labor no longer remembers her affliction. The evangelist, however, recognizes that believers know affliction all too well. To be sure, the paradox of Christian experience is that joy can come in the face of sorrow, and peace in the presence of conflict (15:11; 16:33; 17:13). But the joy that comes now, in the face of suffering, anticipates a final joy that will be unmarred by suffering.[22]

Jesus' prayer before his passion presses the tension between present reality and future hope toward its resolution. Before going to his death, Jesus asks that he might soon return to heavenly glory: "Father . . . I glorified you on earth by finishing the work that you gave me to do. So now, Father, glorify me in your own presence with the glory that I had in your presence before the world existed" (17:1-5). The vision is majestic, pointing to what awaits Jesus after his resurrection and return to the Father. The prayer lifts readers to a realm they cannot see, to a glory that can be affirmed in words but not perceived by the eye.

Jesus' unseen glory in the Father's presence sharply contrasts with the situation of his followers on earth. The disciples are protected in God's name, yet they experience ongoing conflict with the world. The world hates them because of their relationship to Jesus, and the evil one seeks their harm (17:14-15). Jesus may have come to heavenly glory but his followers have not. Yet Jesus did extend God's glory to them while he was on earth (17:22). It was given in the manner of a seed that falls to the earth and dies, of a Lord who gives himself through betrayal and crucifixion (12:23-24; 13:30-32). The glory of divine love, which the Son now shares in his Father's presence, has its present form in the self-sacrificing love of the Crucified.

The dissonance of the present time then moves toward resolution when Jesus prays, "Father, I desire that those also, whom you have given me, may be with me where I am, to see my glory, which you have given me because you loved me before the foundation of the world" (17:24). This looks to a future in which the faithful will no longer need to confess that Jesus is present despite his apparent absence. They will be with him where he is. Glory will no longer be given under the cloak of suffering; love will no longer be manifested through sacrifice and death. Instead, the glory of divine love, which Jesus shares with the Father, will come unopposed as the faithful share it in the presence of God. Such a future is beyond the present experience of the Christian community, but Jesus' prayer gives readers a glimpse of it. He points them to the final outcome of the love that has already been given.

CHAPTER 8

Discipleship in Community and World

Jesus' first words in John's Gospel are a question, "What are you looking for?" and an invitation, "Come and see" (1:38-39). The two people who hear this go with him, and a relationship is formed. At the end of the Gospel, when Jesus speaks for the last time, he says, "Follow me," and the implication is the same (21:22). To relate to Jesus is to go with him. The call to faith is a call to a way of life. Throughout the Gospel this path is shaped by the encounter with Jesus. The life of a disciple is not discussed in abstract terms, because it is so thoroughly bound up with Jesus himself. People are not given a set of teachings that can easily be separated from the Teacher. For the Fourth Evangelist, the questions of discipleship are, "What impact has Jesus had on you?" and "What is he calling you to do?"

Readers might expect the answers to such questions to be rather straightforward. Jesus gives people an example and others are to follow (13:15). That much seems clear enough. Yet the Gospel recognizes that those who believe often fail to understand what Jesus is doing. Jesus may see that the fields of Samaria are ripe for a harvest of faith, but the disciples see only the need for a quick bite of lunch (4:31-38). And Martha may have heard that Jesus is the resurrection and the life, but she advises against opening Lazarus's tomb (11:25, 39). Moreover, those who believe are called into community, yet unbelief remains a problem for individuals and the community as a whole. Peter's bold declarations of loyalty to Jesus all too readily give way to his emphatic denials (13:36-38; 18:15-18, 25-27). And when Jesus compares the community of faith to a vine with many branches, he assumes that some will fail to bear fruit and that others will need to be pruned (15:1-2; see pp. 39-41). As faith yields fruit in the living of life, it must do so despite the forces that impede it.

Jesus was sent to communicate God's love to a world alienated from its Creator, and the Gospel assumes that discipleship means continuing to engage the world in this way. Jesus calls people out of the world and into the believing community, but then he sends them back into the world as his witnesses (17:14-18; 20:21). As we consider the dynamics of following Jesus, according to John, we will begin with what it says about the path to which each person is called. Then we will explore the shape of community life, and finally what it might mean for Jesus to be called "the way" in a world of varied and often conflicting truth claims.

Discipleship

John's Gospel uses word pictures to give readers a way of seeing themselves in relation to God, Jesus, and other people.[1] They also find that the Gospel gives them remarkably few specific commands about what to do or not do. There is no list of virtues and vices, no detailed manual on how to act in each situation. When Jesus does give a command he makes comprehensive claims in very few words: "Love one another as I have loved you" (15:12). Studies of John's perspective on discipleship, moral formation, and ethics usually focus on this command to love, which does have a central place. But the Gospel also includes other images, which help readers work out the implications of what Jesus' command might mean.[2]

Walking in the Light

The image of light characterizes Jesus' ministry and the path of those who follow him. He says, "I am the light of the world. Whoever follows me will not walk in darkness but will have the light of life" (8:12). Walking is a vivid metaphor for a way of life that involves the whole person and is dynamic rather than static. The saying assumes that all people will live or "walk" in some way — the question is whether it will be in light or darkness. According to John, people do not live in a neutral space but in a world where both light and darkness are present. In ordinary life, people walk in daylight since they can see where they are going and are less likely to fall. By way of contrast, those walking in darkness can lose their way, stumble, and injure themselves (9:4; 11:9-10; 12:35). So one might assume that everything is clear: light is better than darkness. Yet the Gospel recognizes that darkness has its allure. There are those who prefer to work under the cloak of darkness in order to escape detection. If people do not want their deeds to be seen, then darkness provides protection from the scrutiny of others. For them, the light threatens their way of life (3:19-21).[3]

Light and darkness are forces that shape a person's actions, according to John. They pull people in different directions. As people live or "walk," they are drawn toward the light or drawn toward the darkness. The light is what comes into the world in Jesus; and light is associated with God, faith, truth, and life. As the light, Jesus calls people to himself. In contrast, darkness is the power that seeks to "overcome" the light. Although it cannot overcome Jesus (1:5), it threatens to overcome others, much as night engulfs travelers walking along a road (12:35). In John's Gospel, the darkness connotes sin, evil, falsehood, and death. All of these are forces that influence people and seek to hold them captive. In changing situations people must set a course of action, and they will find themselves drawn in different directions. The issue is whether it will be light or darkness that draws them.

This contrast between light and darkness can, of course, seem simplistic. When flattened out, the images might suggest that each situation can be reduced to clear alternatives that eliminate ambiguity. The world becomes black and white, the choices either/or. But John's use of the imagery is more complex. The Gospel assumes that actions are shaped by basic commitments. These commitments do not eliminate complexity but *operate as people cope with complexity.* Since the situations described in the Gospel are anything but simple for Jesus, who is the giver of the light, we can infer that they will not be simpler for those who follow him. The contrast between light and darkness identifies different directions of action without eliminating the need for discernment.

Consider how this is played out in the Gospel. Light can connote the truth of God that is revealed in Jesus. Receiving the light brings understanding, and walking in the light means doing what is true (3:21). By way of contrast, darkness connotes untruth and concealment. Someone walks in the light by speaking the truth in the face of untruth. The man born blind exemplifies this. Jesus is the light of the world, who opens the man's eyes, and the man tenaciously tells the truth when others question him (9:17, 24-34). But that does not mean that everything is clear to the man or anyone else. The authorities are at loggerheads. Some wonder if Jesus might be from God, since he performed a miraculous healing. Others argue that he must be a sinner, since he violated the law by healing on the Sabbath (9:16). The man himself acknowledges that he does not know where Jesus is, and he cannot even say whether or not Jesus is a sinner. But the man's sense of Jesus' identity progressively deepens as the conflict continues. His perception is not static. He also persists in telling the truth to the extent that he understands it, and he refuses to suppress the fact that Jesus healed him (9:12, 25). In exasperation the authorities confess that they really do not know where Jesus is from, and they put their ignorance into action by sending the man Jesus healed out of the synagogue (9:29, 34). The man born blind speaks in the light of what he knows even when this costs him his place in the community (9:31-34).

Other aspects of light also include tensions. Note that the prologue identifies light with God and his Word (1:4). Accordingly, walking in the light means living in relationship with God and Jesus. People do this by believing, which involves both trust and faithfulness (12:36). If this is how one relates to God, then the implication is that walking in the light means fostering trust and faithfulness in other relationships as well. People are also to love the light rather than hating it (3:19-20). In John's Gospel, neither love nor hate is simply an emotion. Love can include intimacy and depth of feeling, but it is primarily a bond of commitment. God's love for the world is his commitment to the world that has become alienated from him (3:16), and love for the Father is the bond that moves the Son to carry out his Father's will (14:31). Similarly, love is the bond that Jesus' followers share with each other. By way of contrast, hate is primarily a movement away from or in opposition to someone. If the light of love characterizes one's relationship to God, then walking in the light means putting love into practice with others. The critical edge is that this means resisting the darkness of sin and evil. Given the presence of powers that oppose God, believing in Jesus is an act of defiance, a refusal to be co-opted. Living in the light of love has a militant quality; it asserts itself against the forces of hostility at work in the world.

Finally, light is identified with life (1:4; 8:12). In practice, Jesus is the light who gives life in a physical sense by healing a blind man, and he gives life in relationship with God by enabling people to believe (12:44-46). If those who receive the light have life, they walk in the light by promoting life for others, whereas those allied with darkness work to diminish life.

The most vivid example is Judas, who hands Jesus over for execution under the cloak of night (13:30). By way of contrast, those who walk in the light are allied with life over against death. They resist those who seek to take away physical life or to damage the life that comes from faith.

A Seed Falling to the Earth

Another pattern for discipleship is presented in the saying, "Unless a grain of wheat falls into the earth and dies it remains alone, but if it dies it bears much fruit" (12:24). On one level this image describes Jesus himself. He uses it at the end of his public ministry, when crowds welcome him with palm branches and accolades. To all appearances he is not "alone" *(monos)* but surrounded by admirers. Yet in a profound sense he is alone in the crowd, since no one can comprehend him. When God speaks from heaven, no one can understand it, and when Jesus tells of being lifted up in death, the crowd is incredulous. He remains profoundly alone (12:27-36). Jesus' ministry will come to fruition through his death, for in being lifted through crucifixion he will draw people to himself. By laying down his life his work will bear fruit by creating a community of faith.

On another level the seed depicts what it means for people to follow Jesus. The implications appear in two couplets, which must be read together as a commentary on the image of the seed (12:25-26):

> He who loves his life *(psychē)* loses it, and
> He who hates his life *(psychē)* in this world
>   will keep it for eternal life.
> Whoever serves me must follow me,
>   and where I am, there will my servant be also.
> Whoever serves me the Father will honor.

In the first line the word translated as "life" is *psychē*, which typically refers to the soul or self. Those who make themselves the focus of their love are like the seed in Jesus' saying. They are alone. Their love is self-directed. Moreover, in centering love on themselves they actually lose themselves. To have life — to truly be oneself — is to be in relationship with God and others. The more intently love is focused on oneself, the more surely the person loses what it means to be himself or herself. The person remains alone.

The second line moves to hating one's life in this world. Here hatred is not an emotion but a movement away from the preoccupation with oneself. It corresponds to the death of the seed that Jesus spoke about. Jesus is like the seed in that he gives himself up to die by crucifixion. Those who follow him are like the seed in that they die to a life in which their love is focused on themselves. This begins the movement that leads to eternal life, which in John's Gospel is life in relationship with God. To be clear, there are forms of dying to oneself and hating oneself that are destructive, not life-giving. Like self-love, self-hatred can become an isolating preoccupation with oneself — and a debilitating self-loathing makes relationship impossible. But Jesus speaks of a movement from love *of* oneself through a hatred or turning *from* oneself into the faith relationship with God that is eternal life.

The movement is completed in the final lines, where true life is found in service: "Whoever serves me must follow me, and where I am, there will my servant be also" (12:26). Hatred or turning from oneself is not the goal. It is the transition from love of self into the service of Christ. All people will lose themselves and their lives — death is a given for everyone — but those who relinquish themselves in service to Christ remain in a relationship that bears fruit and brings them life. In this context they are no longer alone. They are with Jesus, sharing in community with him and his Father. And this relationship has a future through the promise of resurrection. What it means to "serve" Jesus is suggested by the scenes that surround this passage. Martha serves by providing a meal for Jesus and others. Mary anoints Jesus' feet, much as Jesus washes feet and directs others to do the same (12:2-3; 13:14). To serve is to convey extraordinary love in the contexts of ordinary life.

Those who serve are honored by Jesus' Father (12:26). To honor is to ascribe value to someone. All people need to know they are valued. The question is where their sense of value comes from.[4] Most often honor is sought from other people. A person may be honored because of family, professional status, education, and personal achievements. Yet public opinion is fickle, an unreliable measure of a person's worth. Praise fades quickly and honor seekers often compromise their principles in order to make others happy (12:43). Genuine honor comes from God. This was true for Jesus, who carried out the work of his Father despite public opposition, knowing that he was valued by his Father (8:50, 54). It is also true for those who follow Jesus. Taking the role of a servant may not be honored by the public, but it is valued by God. When the claims of faith conflict with those of society, it requires courage to follow one's convictions. The assurance

that God honors faithfulness and service helps people live with integrity in
the present and to face the future with hope.

I Have Washed Your Feet — Wash One Another's Feet

Footwashing is one of the Gospel's most memorable images for discipleship. Jesus washes the feet of his disciples and then asks, "Do you know
what I have done to you?" (13:12). The question centers first on what Jesus
has done for the disciples. Throughout the first half of the chapter Jesus is
the one who does the action, and the opening verse discloses the meaning
to the readers: "Jesus knew that his hour had come to depart from this
world and go to the Father," so having "loved his own who were in the
world, he loved them to the end" (13:1).

Showing love "to the end" *(eis telos)* means showing the full extent of
love, and footwashing is an arresting way to do this. We noted earlier that
free people washed their own feet but not the feet of others. A good host
would offer guests a basin of water so they could cleanse the dust from
their feet as they entered his home, but he would not do the washing for
them. Sometimes a slave would wash other people's feet, and anyone who
did this assumed the role of a slave. Jesus' action is not that of a host showing hospitality to his guests. He does the work of a slave. And the only reason a free person would assume the slave's role by washing the feet of others was to show utter devotion to them.[5] This is what Jesus does by laying
down his outer garments, wrapping himself with a towel, washing feet, and
wiping the feet with the towel he wears. The stunning impropriety of this
elicits Peter's refusal to let Jesus proceed, but Jesus insists that he must do
this for the disciples to be in relationship with him: "Unless I wash you,
you have no share with me" (13:8). We might paraphrase: "Unless I love
you completely, you will not be in relationship with me." The love Jesus
gives here through footwashing anticipates the consummate gift of love,
which he gives by laying down his life (see pp. 110-12).

What Jesus does for the disciples is the source and norm for what they
do for each other. If "I, your Lord and Teacher, have washed your feet, you
also ought to wash one another's feet. For I have set you an example, that
you also should do as I have done to you" (13:14-15). Love is the gift of Jesus.
By washing feet he gives extraordinary love in the sphere of ordinary life,
and he directs his followers to do the same. They are called to give them-

selves completely for others, even to the point of laying down their lives, as Jesus will say later (15:13). Yet the idea is not that disciples are to wait for a suitable occasion for martyrdom. Rather, if the claim of love extends up to the point of laying down one's life, then it also encompasses countless forms of less dramatic service. The need for footwashing is common, but to wash feet out of love is uncommon. A willingness to do this and similar types of service shows the impact of Jesus on a disciple's life.

The footwashing shows that love can be both giving and confrontational, as we have seen (see pp. 117-18). By washing feet, Jesus gives himself in service, yet he also counters evil rather than capitulating to it. The presence of evil is part of the footwashing episode. The Gospel says that the devil put betrayal into Judas's heart, yet Jesus washes his feet along with those of the other disciples. In so doing he confronts animosity with love (13:2, 10-12). For those who serve as Jesus does, love can take similarly militant forms. To serve in the presence of hostility challenges it. Service is a refusal to act on evil's terms.

Jesus sums up his point by saying, "I give you a new commandment, that you love one another. Just as I have loved you, you also should love one another" (13:34). The new commandment follows the pattern of the footwashing by identifying the love that Jesus gives to the disciples as the source and norm for the love they give to others. The importance of love is not new, of course. One of the most familiar commands in the Old Testament is, "You shall love your neighbor as yourself" (Lev. 19:18). This form of the commandment is widely cited in early Christian writings, where it is said to be central to the law of Israel (Matt. 22:39; Mark 12:31; Luke 10:27; Rom. 13:9; Gal. 5:14; Jas. 2:8). In John, however, the love command is reconfigured so that it becomes something new.

First, the basis and norm for love changes. The traditional commandment makes self-love the standard. People are to love others as they love themselves. In the new commandment, the basis and standard is the love that Jesus gives.[6] This is the cruciform love that disciples receive from Jesus and extend to others. The new commandment speaks about what it means to live out one's relationship with Jesus. Second, the direction of the love changes. The traditional commandment speaks of love for the neighbor, but the new commandment refers to love for one another. It envisions mutuality. It is a community-building commandment. As people give and receive love from one another, a community is formed. The new commandment recognizes that Jesus' followers need to continue receiving love even as they give love. The giving and receiving of love within the community enables them to continue on the path of discipleship.

One might wonder whether the new commandment is less radical than the command to love the neighbor or to love one's enemies (Matt. 5:44). When lifted out of its context in John's Gospel it can be turned into a rationale for creating a comfortable circle of like-minded people. In its context, however, the new commandment is not sentimental.[7] The love it commends is cruciform and serves as a commentary on the footwashing scene, which assumes that one's enemies may be within one's own community — recall the presence of Judas. Moreover, love within the community bears witness to those outside it. Jesus says, "By this everyone will know that you are my disciples, if you have love for one another" (John 13:35). The command to love one another means that Christians bring to the world not only a doctrine about love but an alternative society, a counterculture in which the message of Jesus takes lived form.[8] Christian community is not an end in itself. The love that is shared within it is a form of witness to those outside it, so that the world may know that the love of God is real (17:23).

Abiding in the Vine — Bearing Fruit for Others

The Christian community is perhaps most vividly depicted in the image of the vine and its branches (15:1-17). In this passage the Father tends the vineyard, Jesus is the vine, and the disciples are the branches. The term "abide" *(menō)* describes the connections between them. Abiding means wholeness in relationship. It points to a relationship that endures rather than one that is transient. To abide is to be present with and for someone. The Father abides in Jesus and Jesus abides with his Father in deep and enduring love (14:10; 15:10). Similarly, Jesus and his word abide in believers and they abide in him in love (15:4-10). The way that leafy branches are connected to the stalk of the vine is an apt description of what it means for believers to abide in Jesus.[9]

The word "abide" is pleasant enough on the surface, and it is repeated so often that the rhythms can lull readers into a feeling of complacency. Yet on closer inspection abiding is connected with fruitbearing. The image makes the jarring claim that love is manifested in obedience and that commitments are expressed in actions. The passage is based on the ordinary observation that a vine is cultivated for the fruit it bears. A vinegrower knows that branches produce fruit only when they have a healthy relationship with the stalk of the vine. Therefore, he tends the branches carefully — and sometimes sharply — as noted earlier (see pp. 39-41). But tending the branches is not an end in itself. The expectation is that branches will produce fruit for others (15:2, 4, 5, 8, 16). The same is true in Christian community. Branches are to abide in Jesus the vine because otherwise they bear no fruit. And if there is an absence of fruit, this reveals a lack of relationship.

Jesus' bond with the Father shows what it means to bear fruit. He abides in his Father's love and shows this by keeping his Father's commandments (15:10). His love is expressed in obedience. First, God commanded Jesus to lay down and take up his life for others (10:17-18). By going the way of the cross, Jesus keeps his Father's command. It is the consummate expression of his love. Second, God also commanded Jesus to speak a message to people (12:49). We have seen that Jesus' words are both confrontational and life-giving, for he tells the world the truth about itself and about the God who sent him. He identifies sin in order to turn people away from it and toward faith (see pp. 35-36). Jesus' obedience to these commands serves the same end: The love conveyed through his death and the truth expressed by his words call people to believe and have life (3:16; 12:50).

This sets the pattern for discipleship. The community of faith is called to abide in Jesus' love and words. As it does so, believers are called to bear fruit by obeying his commandments (15:7, 9). First, we have seen that they are commanded to love one another as Jesus has loved them. This was the new commandment, which was given after the footwashing, and is now repeated (15:12; cf. 13:34). Now Jesus adds, "No one has greater love than this, to lay down one's life for one's friends" (15:13). To abide in the vine is to bear the fruit of Jesus' love by giving of oneself for others. Second, the disciples are also to keep his words. Jesus said that a true disciple abides in his word and comes to know the truth about Jesus, his Father, and the world's bondage to sin (8:31-36; 14:23-24). Those who have been given this message are called to speak it in order that people might believe (15:27). By giving love and keeping Jesus' word, faith comes to fruition.

Christian Community

The faith of individuals is integrally connected to life in community, according to John. When disciples like Andrew and Philip come to believe that Jesus is the Messiah, they gather others into a circle of believers (1:40-46). When the Samaritan woman begins wondering whether Jesus might be the Messiah, she brings her townspeople to him, and her people confess together that he is the Savior of the world (4:39-42). Because of his faith, the man born blind is put out of the synagogue, yet he is given a place in the flock of Jesus the good shepherd (9:34–10:5). People become part of the community because they believe, and being part of the community also enables people to believe. Here we consider some aspects of that community.

Family, Friends, and Flock

The Gospel uses a number of expressions for the community of faith, all of which have theological significance. Those who follow Jesus are called "disciples." This term applies to those who knew Jesus during his ministry and those who come to faith after his resurrection. Everyone who continues in Jesus' word and bears the fruit of love can be considered a disciple (8:31; 13:35; 15:8). Significantly, the Gospel does not give the twelve in his inner circle the special title "apostle." The Greek word *apostolos* is used only once in a general sense for someone who is sent (13:16). Even the figure who is closest to Jesus is simply called the "disciple" whom he loved (13:23; 20:2; 21:20). This consistent preference for the term "disciple" rather than "apostle" gives an egalitarian quality to John's sense of Christian community.[10]

Relationships among believers are described by several metaphors. Some of these are taken from *the family*.[11] Believers are called children of God (1:12; 11:52), and after the resurrection Jesus identifies God as the Father of believers (20:17). We have seen that people become God's children by being brought to new birth or faith through the message of Jesus and the work of the Spirit. Those who call God their Father recognize that he is the source of life and love, and that their relationship is characterized by obedience and mutual honor (see pp. 51-52). Jesus himself is the Son of God, and those who follow him are his brothers and sisters (20:17; 21:23).

The familial aspect of Christian community is reflected in an evocative moment during the crucifixion. While hanging on the cross, Jesus sees his mother and the disciple whom he loves. He says to his mother, "Woman, here is your son," and to the disciple, "Here is your mother." Then the disciple takes her into his own home (19:26-27). Jesus' mother appears only twice in this Gospel — at the wedding at Cana and at Golgotha — and in both places Jesus addresses her as "woman" (2:4). He uses this term for other women, apparently without disrespect (4:21; 20:15), but it is a peculiar way for a son to address his mother. By speaking to his mother this way he makes clear that their relationship is not defined by biological kinship.[12] Moreover, he entrusts her to the care of his Beloved Disciple, whose relationship to Jesus is one of faithfulness and love. Jesus brings together a woman and a man, whose common bond is their relationship to him. They form the nucleus of a community that is created at the cross and continues after the resurrection, when Jesus begins addressing all of his disciples as his brothers and sisters.[13]

These metaphors create a way of seeing people. They are translated into a way of life when readers ask, "What does it mean to see other believers as my brothers and sisters?" Putting the question this way raises a host of issues. People do not ordinarily choose the members of their own families, and this is also true of the community of faith. All who acknowledge God as their Father and Jesus as their brother have a place in the family. Believers are connected to others whom they might or might not have chosen to be their brothers and sisters. Yet relating to Jesus creates relationships of faith, which are to be worked out on the basis of how one would treat a sister or brother. For example, the Gospel shows family members seeking help for those who are sick and grieving together in time of loss (4:47; 11:21, 32). The same is presumably true for members of the family of faith.

Friendship offers another perspective on community life. At the last supper Jesus tells the disciples, "I do not call you servants any longer," but "I have called you friends" (15:15). In ordinary terms, friendship arises out of common interests and values. Friends support each other, share each other's joys and sorrows, and maintain bonds of loyalty and affection. Some friendships are among social equals, while others involve someone of high social status befriending a person of lower status. Authentic friendship is based on trust and truthfulness rather than deception or empty flattery. By way of contrast, the disingenuous type of friendship is evident in Pilate, who considers himself a friend of Caesar. But to maintain that friendship — on which his career depends — Pilate abandons truth and crucifies a man he knows to be innocent. Here friendship is reduced to self-interest (19:12).[14]

Jesus chooses his disciples to be his friends and in so doing makes them friends with one another (15:14-16). This suggests that friendship with Jesus provides a sense of dignity. He gives his followers commands without treating them as slaves. This is important given the message of the footwashing. To wash the feet of others is to do the work of a slave, but this does not make someone into a slave. Jesus washes feet in his capacity as Teacher and Lord, and those who follow him do so in the dignity of friendship (13:14). Friendship with Jesus is also based on trust and truthfulness. A slave might not be told what the master is doing, but Jesus tells his followers what he has heard from the Father (15:15). When translated into community life this means that believers, as true friends, speak the truth with each other in order to maintain the integrity of their relationships. In the end, the highest form of love is to lay down one's life for one's friends (15:12). Jesus acts as the truest of friends when he goes to his death out of love for his disciples. By calling them to love one another as he loved them, he seeks to create a circle of friends in which his love can be expressed (see pp. 194-95).

Finally, the image of *the flock and sheepfold* pictures the community in terms of its center and boundaries. The center of the community is Jesus the good shepherd, who has the singular role of calling and leading. All who belong to the flock are simply sheep. Yet the flock has a sense of its center, since all the sheep depend on the one good shepherd and follow him (10:4). The community is also pictured as a sheepfold for which Jesus is the gate. This means there is a difference between the sheepfold and the world outside, where thieves and bandits threaten the well-being of the sheep (10:1, 8). The community has boundaries, and such boundaries function rightly when they provide protection for those who are most vulnerable. The world may operate on the basis of untruth or hatred, but these are destructive, and those within the sheepfold rightly seek to keep them outside the boundaries of their community. Boundaries play their proper role when they protect the sheep from the wolf, and create a sphere in which the faithful can support each other in the face of the forces that threaten to take away faith, life, and dignity.

Yet a gate defines the boundary without sealing the boundary. The gate allows the sheep to find protection within the community without closing them off from their surroundings. The implication is that those who are followers of Jesus find support in the gathered community, as the sheep do within the sheepfold, but they also live in the world. In the ordinary sense, sheep periodically come into the fold, where they are sheltered, but they do not spend their lives in the corral. They regularly go out into broader pastures. Similarly, Jesus' followers periodically come into the gathered community, where they find support and help, but then they go out into the world where life is lived. Coming into the gathered community and going out into the world are both aspects of "abundant life" (10:9-10).

The gate imagery also distinguishes Jesus' followers from others, while allowing for the entry and inclusion of newcomers. It is important for the circle of believers to have an identity that is distinct from the world; otherwise it has nothing to offer anyone. There is no reason to belong. Yet the community of faith must also provide for the inclusion of newcomers — after all, the Gospel anticipates that Jesus' followers will be sent into the world so that others might believe (17:18-21). As the gate, Jesus distinguishes the community from the world, but he also is the focus for faith, and faith is the way one enters his community. The gate creates a boundary, but it is a permeable boundary.

Unity Among Believers

Unity among believers is a well-known theme in John's Gospel.[15] Before his passion Jesus prays for "those who will believe in me" through the word of the disciples, asking "that they may all be one" (17:20-21). The prayer looks to life within an expanding circle of believers, which will be created through the work of his followers after his resurrection. The concern of the prayer is that a common faith might bring about genuine community. In contemporary church life this portion of the prayer has been a prominent theme for Christian ecumenism. Strategies for promoting oneness among Christians have ranged from occasional ecumenical prayer services to the mergers of denominations and proposals for interchurch cooperation. Our task here is to consider what Jesus' statement about unity might look like within the context of John's Gospel. Several points are significant:

First, oneness among believers comes about through the work of Jesus and his Father. It is the fruit of divine action. Jesus pictures himself as the good shepherd calling the sheep, who come and follow him (10:3-4). Then he adds, "I have other sheep that are not from this fold. I must bring them also, and they will listen to my voice; and there will be one flock, one shepherd" (10:16). Since Jesus is speaking to Jewish listeners, the "other sheep" are presumably non-Jews. Jesus will "bring" people of various ethnic backgrounds into one flock by calling them to a common faith.

Later Jesus is the one who will "gather into one" the dispersed children of God by dying on their behalf (11:52). The context of this comment is the Jewish authorities' plan to have Jesus executed in order to prevent his followers from embarking on a revolt against Rome (11:50-51). The evangelist comments that Jesus' death indeed brings deliverance — not from Rome but from sin — and his death is not just for Jewish people but for all the children of God, including non-Jews. Although the authorities assume that putting Jesus to death will end his popularity and disperse his followers, the result is the opposite. The crucified Jesus draws people from many backgrounds to himself (12:32). This clearly does not mean that Jesus will draw his followers into a single geographical location. They will remain visibly dispersed, and their oneness must be understood in another way. The point is that people become children of God through faith (1:12-13), and Jesus' death gathers them into one by fostering this faith. It is a shared faith that unites them, even as they remain visibly separated.

Second, focusing oneness on Jesus and his Father, rather than on anyone else, is essential for the community's well-being. Jesus is the good shepherd, who calls and leads the flock. He entrusts Peter and others with the responsibility of caring for the flock, while recognizing that no one else can take his place (21:15-17). The Gospel recognizes that human leadership is fallible, and when failure occurs the community can be put in jeopardy. Jesus contrasts himself with the hired hand, who abandons the flock under his charge in order to save his own life (10:11-14). The hired hand exemplifies fallible leadership, and the image is broad enough to fit the many situations in which those charged with tending the flock fall short. To focus the community's oneness on someone other than Jesus puts it at risk when leadership falters. Jesus is the "one shepherd" in whom the community finds its life and cohesion (10:16).

Similarly, oneness means being kept in the Father's name (17:11). The Father's name conveys his identity and character.[16] He entrusted his name to Jesus, who kept his followers in relationship with God throughout his earthly ministry. But after his death and resurrection, the faith relationship will be tended by the Father himself (17:10, 12). The prayer recognizes that the world is not a neutral place. The powers at work within it will seek to draw the faithful away from the Father and the Son whom he sent (17:14-15). Therefore, the Father sends the Spirit, who discloses his presence and that of the risen Christ to the community (see pp. 149-51). The community's oneness comes from God and is expressed as its members bear witness to the Father and Son who are at its center.

Third, Christian unity is not an end in itself. It is a form of witness to those outside the community.[17] When Jesus prays, he asks that those who come to faith "may all be one . . . *in order that the world may believe* that you have sent me" (17:21). Again, he asks "that they may become completely one, *in order that the world may know* that you have sent me and have loved them even as you have loved me" (17:23). This recognizes that the Father and Son relate to each other in love and extend their love to others. God communicates his love by sending the Son into the world to bring the world back into relationship (3:16). Those in the Christian community share this bond of love, and their relationships with each other bear witness that the love they receive from God is real. Yet love within the community is not an end in itself, for by living out the love of God in oneness with each other, the faithful call the wider world to know the love of God.

So how is this unity expressed within the context of John's Gospel? The oneness of the Father and Son is grounded in love and expressed in giving for the sake of others. Jesus makes this strikingly plain as he washes the disciples' feet out of love for them and then goes to his death out of love and obedience to the Father (13:1; 14:31). Here is where believers find the basis and pattern of unity within their community (17:11, 21, 23). Visible unity occurs when Christians bear witness to the love of God by their words and by serving one another. The footwashing is emblematic of Christian unity. Jesus told his followers to wash one another's feet and to love one another in order that others might know of that love (13:34-35). Later, he prays that they might be one in order that the world might know of the love that comes from God (17:23). Jesus' new commandment and his prayer for unity point to the same thing. *Oneness is made visible in the common witness Christians make to Christ through their words and in the kind of service exemplified by footwashing.*

Community Organization

John's Gospel does not link Christian unity to a specific pattern of organization. It does not translate the oneness of the Father and the Son into unified structures of church governance or administration. Other Christian writings may refer to apostles, bishops, and deacons, while elders are mentioned in the Johannine Epistles and other texts (e.g., 2 John 1; 3 John 1). But the Gospel itself does not include a specific pattern for church order.[18]

What the Gospel does picture is a group of "disciples" accompanying Jesus. What they are called to do is true for the community as a whole. When Jesus tells them to love one another, to wash feet, and to bear witness, the assumption is that this is the calling of every follower of Jesus. The disciples contribute to Christian unity by bearing witness to Jesus and exemplifying the kind of love and service he commends.

The images for the community that were considered above stress the importance of each person's connection to Jesus. They are brothers and sisters, friends, sheep in the same flock, and branches of the one true vine. Even when the Gospel focuses on specific disciples, it emphasizes each person's relationship to Jesus.[19] The Beloved Disciple represents the ideal follower of Jesus. He is known for his closeness to Jesus at the last supper, his place at the cross where he is entrusted with the care of Jesus' mother, and his faith at the empty tomb (13:22-26; 19:26-27; 20:8). Yet he is simply called a "disciple," and his role is that of a faithful witness to Jesus (21:24).

Peter also fits this pattern. Sometimes he is pictured as the spokesperson for the disciples (6:68), and elsewhere he has the Beloved Disciple speak to Jesus for him, as at the last supper (13:24). He sometimes voices his faith but later denies his relationship to Jesus three times, and is slow to believe after the resurrection (18:15-18, 25-27; 20:3-10). Peter is finally asked three times about his love for Jesus, and he affirms it each time. Such a bond of love is central not only for Peter but for all disciples. The principal command Jesus gives Peter is "Follow me," and this same call is given to all members of Jesus' flock (10:4; 21:19, 22). The commands to feed and tend the sheep are the specific forms that his discipleship will take, yet Peter does not become the center of the community. The flock belongs to Jesus, who calls them "my lambs" and "my sheep" (21:15-19).

The Fourth Gospel leaves the question of community organization open. The Gospel centers the common life of believers in Jesus and emphasizes the common callings of loving service and witness. As the faith community develops various patterns and structures, John's Gospel calls it to consider its life in light of this centered and egalitarian vision.[20]

The Worship of God in Jesus

Worship is integral to the community of faith. John's Gospel does not give detailed directives for worship but emphasizes its focus. Worship is directed toward God the Father, who is made known in Jesus his Son. In the prologue, Jesus is pictured as the sanctuary in which God is present. In him God's Word became flesh and dwelt or made his tent *(eskēnōsen)* among people (1:14). This makes Jesus analogous to the dwelling or tent *(skēnē)* that was the focus for worship in ancient Israel. The second half of the book of Exodus describes the tent-sanctuary in which God used to reveal his glory (Exod. 40:34). Now his glory has been revealed in the life, death, and resurrection of Jesus, so that divine glory is centered in a person rather than a structure.

The human response to what God has done takes the form of a corporate confession of faith: "we beheld his glory" (John 1:14, 16). If the community's sanctuary is Jesus, then worship means confessing what God gives in Jesus: "from his fullness we have all received grace upon grace" (1:16). Many people saw Jesus, but not all saw the glory of God in him. Many also saw him crucified, but they did not discern the glory of divine love or grace there. To confess that in giving himself Jesus gives the fullness of divine love and grace — this is central to the community's worship, according to John's prologue.

Temple imagery also contributes to a sense of worship. Jesus calls the Jerusalem temple his Father's house (2:16). Although God was not confined to the temple, it was there that he made his name to dwell (1 Kings 8:27-30). The Jerusalem temple was first built by Solomon, then rebuilt after the exile, and eventually remodeled in Roman times, but it always stood at the same location. There were not to be different sanctuaries situated throughout the country, for the temple was uniquely the place of God's presence. The temple was also where sacrifices were made. John's description of the cattle, sheep, and doves being marketed in the outer court reminds readers that the temple was the one place in Israel where sacrifices could be offered (John 2:14). When atonement for sin was needed, people were to come to the sanctuary. In a dramatic action, Jesus drives the merchants out of the temple. When bystanders demand a sign to show his authority for doing this, he replies, "Destroy this temple and in three days I will raise it up" (John 2:19). The narrator explains that Jesus speaks about "the temple of his body" (2:21).

For John, the body of the crucified and risen Jesus takes on the functions of the temple, and this has several implications for worship: First, those who seek God are now pointed to a person rather than a building.[21] By turning to the crucified and risen Jesus, people turn to God his Father

(12:45; 14:9). Second, we have already noted that Jesus is the sacrificial Lamb, who takes away the sin of the world (1:29; see pp. 112-17). Now he is portrayed as the temple in which the sacrifice is made. The result, however, is the same. Sin is removed through the crucified and risen Jesus. The implication is that the worshiping community attests to what Jesus has done by directing those in need of atonement to put their faith in him. Third, there was only one temple in Israel. The same is true of the Christian community. Jesus is the temple in whom true worship of God is centered.

Jesus' conversation with the Samaritan woman continues the theme. The woman recalls that Jews and Samaritans traditionally differed on the location of worship. She asks whether true worship is to be lodged in Jerusalem, following Jewish practice, or on the mountain in Samaria, where her fathers worshiped (4:20). Jesus, however, reframes the question. Rather than defining worship by the tradition of "the fathers" as the woman does, Jesus shifts the focus. He speaks about worship of "the Father," who seeks people to worship him (4:21, 23). Worship is defined by its center.

The new dimension in this conversation is the Spirit. Jesus says that in the hour that is coming, worship will not be tied to Jerusalem or the Samaritan mountain. Rather, it will be characterized by "Spirit and truth" (4:23). Jesus does not say that the drawback to worship in Jerusalem or Samaria is that people in those places are preoccupied with outward ceremonies. He does not argue that true worship is a purely inward matter that has nothing to do with externals. The point is that true worship comes about through God's Spirit, which will be sent by the crucified and risen Jesus.[22] Therefore, we might capitalize the word "Spirit" in Jesus' conversation with the Samaritan woman, because he speaks of the worship that God's Spirit brings about. If the word "spirit" remains in the lower case in Jesus' remarks to the woman, then it points to the faith that the Spirit of God evokes. What is born of God's Spirit is the new "spirit" that is faith (3:6). According to John, true worship expresses the spirit of faith that is given by the Spirit of God.

Jesus does not describe the form that such worship should take. Instead, his words present a criterion by which forms of worship can be assessed. Worship that is true bears witness to the God who is true. Jesus refers to worshiping "the Father," and throughout the Gospel those who know God as Father do so through Jesus his Son. God is not known as Father in isolation. He is identified this way in relation to the Son whom he sent. The spiritual — or Spiritual — aspect of worship brings people to the center of faith. Where worship directs people to the God made known in Jesus it is consistent with the Spirit's action and can be called "true."

Baptism and Lord's Supper

Baptism is one of the specific practices of the Christian community. We have already explored some of its theological dimensions. For the Fourth Evangelist, baptism is associated with the work of the Spirit and it binds people to Jesus (see pp. 140-41). Traditionally, baptism is also identified with cleansing. This may play a theological role in John's Gospel, but if so it comes indirectly. The evangelist links cleansing most directly to the death of Jesus. This is evident in the opening scenes, where John the Baptist's use of water is the occasion for revealing Jesus as the Lamb of God who takes away sin (1:26).

The Gospel later notes that purification was a concern for Jewish people. The jars at Cana held water for Jewish cleansing rites, and purification was a topic of debate (2:6; 3:25). People could be made unclean by bodily emissions and contact with unclean things. Although being unclean did not necessarily arise from sin according to this tradition, the Fourth Gospel reframes the issue. The water used for cleansing is transformed into the wine that reveals Jesus' glory (2:11). The debates about purification thus lead to the idea that people receive baptism from the disciples of the Christ, who comes from above (3:26-30). This takes the question of cleansing to a different level. The issue is not physical uncleanness but separation from God. And the response is not simply washing, but God acting through Jesus and the Spirit. If baptism is understood to cleanse, it does so because it binds people to Jesus, the one in whom relationships with God are restored.

The footwashing scene develops this idea. We have seen that the footwashing is an act of love and that it anticipates the crucifixion, when Jesus will give his love fully by giving his life (see pp. 110-12). The footwashing points primarily to Jesus' crucifixion rather than to baptism. This is also reflected in Jesus' cryptic comment, "One who has bathed does not need to wash, except for his feet, but is entirely clean. And you people are clean, but not every one of you" (13:10). This verse assumes that the disciples have bathed with water prior to the meal, as was customary, so the need for footwashing must point to a different kind of cleansing. This is the cleansing that comes from divine love. The disciples do not need another bath, but they do need the sacrificial love of Jesus, which the footwashing signifies. Connections with baptism are perhaps suggestive, but are not made explicit.[23]

Cleansing is finally linked to Jesus' death by the water flowing from his side at his crucifixion (19:34). The evangelist observes that the Jewish authorities want the bodies of Jesus and the others removed from the crosses before sundown, presumably because their corpses threaten to defile people (19:31; Deut. 21:22-23). When a soldier pierces Jesus' side, however, water and blood come out, giving the scene an ironic turn. Instead of defiling, the water suggestively identifies Jesus as a source of cleansing. An earlier passage also identified the water flowing from Jesus as an image of the Spirit (John 7:37-39). The scene at the cross is evocative and not explicitly baptismal.[24] What might be said is that its connection to the themes of water and Spirit suggests that baptism becomes significant through the Spirit that binds people to Jesus, who was lifted up in death (3:5, 14-15, 22-30).

The *Lord's Supper* plays an important role in most Christian communities, but what John's Gospel says about it is disputed. The other gospels and Paul say that during the last supper Jesus gave his disciples bread saying, "This is my body," and a cup of wine saying, "This is my blood" (Matt. 26:26-28; Mark 14:22-24; Luke 22:19-20; 1 Cor. 11:23-25). Many find it surprising that John's account of the last supper does not include this sharing of the bread and cup. Earlier, however, Jesus feeds the five thousand with bread and fish, identifies himself as the bread of life, and then says,

> Very truly I tell you, unless you eat the flesh of the Son of Man and drink his blood, you have no life in you. Those who eat my flesh and drink my blood have eternal life, and I will raise them up on the last day; for my flesh is true food and my blood is true drink. Those who eat my flesh and drink my blood abide in me, and I in them (John 6:53-56).

The question is whether this passage relates to the Lord's Supper and if so, what it might mean.[25]

Interpretation can best be done by identifying primary and secondary levels of meaning. On a primary level this passage points to the need to partake of the crucified Jesus through faith. After calling himself the bread of life Jesus adds, what "I will give for the life of the world is my flesh"

(6:51). He gives his flesh by dying, and he does this "for" the world by laying down his life as the good shepherd does (10:11, 15; 11:50). He goes on to speak not only of his flesh but also of his blood, which is given for others in his crucifixion (6:53; 19:34).

People partake of the crucified Jesus through faith. On a primary level to eat is to believe, and the centrality of faith is clear in the discourse. Jesus says that the work of God is that people believe, that those who believe in the bread of life do not hunger or thirst, and that those who believe have eternal life and will be raised at the last day (6:29, 35, 40, 47). He repeats this same idea by using the image of eating, saying that those who eat of him have eternal life and will be raised on the last day (6:54). Eating is a vivid way to speak about believing in the crucified Jesus.

On a secondary level, many interpreters connect this passage with the words that Jesus spoke over the bread and cup at the last supper according to other New Testament writers. Although John does not recount the words over the bread and cup in his passion narrative, he might have expected his readers to be familiar with that tradition. Hints of this might be apparent in his account of the feeding the five thousand, which says that Jesus took bread, gave thanks, and gave it to the people, much as Jesus did with the bread at the last supper according to the other gospels (6:11). Moreover, the idea that people are to eat his flesh and drink his blood is absolutely horrific unless one is used to hearing that Christians eat and drink of Jesus' body and blood through bread and wine. So when read in light of the broader tradition, the words in John 6 seem to affirm that partaking of Jesus through the bread and cup brings eternal life.

The passage also critiques the idea that simply eating bread, apart from faith, brings eternal life. Note that Jesus says that those who eat of his flesh and blood have eternal life and abide in him. Yet it seems clear that this does not happen automatically by partaking of a meal. In this chapter Jesus takes bread, gives thanks, and gives it to a group of people. They eat it, to be sure, yet they do not abide in Jesus as one would expect. By the end of the chapter they are offended by Jesus and turn away from him (6:60, 66). Moreover, John specifically says that Judas receives bread from Jesus at the last supper, but when Judas takes the bread, Satan enters him and he departs into the night (13:18-30). Again, simply sharing in the meal does not mean abiding in Jesus.

Theological coherence requires keeping faith as the primary level of meaning and questions about the Lord's Supper as the secondary level. At the primary level, the bread of life is Jesus, who gives his flesh for the world through crucifixion. The implications concerning the Lord's Supper constitute a secondary level that requires moving beyond the literary context of John's Gospel. When it is read in light of the wider tradition, one can say that eating the bread in the Lord's Supper is meaningful because it presents the crucified Jesus to people. At the primary level, eating is a vivid way to speak about believing. By extension, eating the bread in the Lord's Supper is life-giving as an act of faith.[26]

Jesus as the Way in a Pluralistic World

Jesus calls people out of the world and into the faith community, then sends them back into the world. This interplay between separation from the world and engagement with the world stems from the work of Jesus himself. John speaks of a world that is hostile to its Creator and of God sending his Son into the world to bear witness to the truth. Jesus encounters the world as someone "other," who can speak to the world precisely because he is different (see pp. 27-29). The same is true of his disciples. Jesus calls people out of the world, bringing them to the faith that sets them apart (15:19; 17:14-16). Yet he also sends them into the world in order to call others to faith (17:18; 20:21). Separation from the world is the basis for engagement with the world, just as love within the community is a form of witness to those outside it — in order that the world may believe (13:34-35; 17:20-23).[27]

Following Jesus in the world is complex, despite the apparent simplicity of sayings such as "I am the way, and the truth, and the life. No one comes to the Father except through me" (14:6). For many, this is one of Christianity's most essential teachings. It is heard as the good news that through Jesus Christ one may relate rightly to God. But for others the idea that Jesus is the way is uncomfortably narrow. It is heard as an expression of Christian exclusivity that is awkward at best and dangerous at worst in a pluralistic world.[28] A large part of the problem arises from the repeated use of the word "the" in Jesus' statement. Many objections presumably would fade if the passage read, "I am a way, and a truth, and a life." For Jesus to be "a way" among other ways and "a truth" among other truths would be a modest claim that would probably elicit little opposition from those outside the Christian fold. Moreover, referring to Jesus as "a way" would ease the discomfort of those within the Christian community who want to avoid the impression that Christianity is exclusivistic. The difficulty is that the word "the" stubbornly appears before each of the three terms "way," "truth," and "life," in Greek as well as in English. Understanding the passage involves coming to terms with its particularity, and the best way to do this is to think it through in the context of John's Gospel itself.

Human Context

Jesus identifies himself as the way in John 14:6a, then explains what this means by making a statement about the human condition: "no one comes to the Father" (14:6b). This comment is in a sense one of the Gospel's most inclusive claims, since the context makes clear that "no one" actually includes everyone. The assumption is that all people are separated from God. To say that "no one comes to the Father" assumes that all people are separated from the Father — otherwise there would be no need to come to him. This separation from God arises from human sin, and sin figures into the condition of every human being. To say that no one comes to the Father means that sin separates everyone from the Father.

Humanity's separation from God is a persistent theme in John's Gospel. When speaking of God's word, the prologue declares that "he was in the world, and the world came into being through him, yet the world did not know him" (1:10). Throughout the Gospel Jesus addresses listeners who do not know God, who have never heard God's voice and have never seen God's form (5:27; 7:28; 8:19). Jesus says to his opponents, "You are from below, I am from above; you are of this world, I am not of this world," and "I told you that you would die in your sins" (8:23-24). Therefore, when the Son of God crosses the divide and enters the world, the world hates him because he testifies that its works are evil (7:7). The statement that "no one comes to the Father" (14:6b) points to humanity's estrangement from God.

Because separation from God is a fundamentally *human* problem, it affects Jesus' followers as well as his foes. The disciples do not show the same kind of animosity that Jesus' opponents do, but the context reveals that separation from God is an issue for all people. Jesus addresses his followers in the same way that he previously addressed his adversaries when he tells them, "as I said to the Jews" who have shown opposition, "so now I say to *you*" who belong to the inner circle: "Where I am going, *you* cannot come" (13:33). At a fundamental level the disciples are in the same position as the Pharisees and temple police who tried to arrest Jesus (7:34; 8:21): none of them has any innate ability to go where Jesus goes.

The portrayal of individual disciples at the last supper reinforces the sense that Jesus addresses a fundamentally human problem. Peter protests, "Lord, why can I not follow you now? I will lay down my life for you" (13:37). In reply Jesus discloses that Peter will deny him three times (13:37-38). When Peter, in the high priest's courtyard, denies that he is Jesus' disciple, he shows that he shares the condition that manifests itself in Jesus' Jewish opponents. Earlier in the Gospel some of the Jewish leaders were asked whether they wanted to be included among Jesus' disciples, and they denied it, as Peter did (9:27-28). Next, Thomas interrupts Jesus by declaring, "Lord, we do not know where you are going. How can we know the way?" (14:5). Jesus was going to God, and Thomas's inability to understand this recalls the incomprehension that Jesus' adversaries showed earlier when they asked, "Where does this man intend to go that we will not find him?" and "What does he mean by saying . . . 'Where I am you cannot come?'" (7:35-36; 8:22). Finally Philip says, "Lord, show us the Father, and we will be satisfied" (14:8). His words echo previous scenes in which Jesus' Jewish opponents demanded to know, "Where is your Father?" (8:19). Accordingly, Jesus' response is poignant: "Have I been with you all this time, Philip, and you still do not know me?" (14:9).

The words "no one comes to the Father" (14:6b) level the distinctions between people by directing attention to the separation from God that all human beings share. This negative assessment of humanity's situation underlies the Gospel's positive presentation of Jesus as the way. John does not identify Jesus as the way in order to close off relationships with God, but to open up relationships with God where sin has created separation (14:6a). The word "except" in the phrase "except by me" (14:6c) means that the categorical judgment that "no one comes to the Father" is not the last word (14:6b). "Except" is like a window that lets light into a closed room. It fits what the Gospel says about Christ coming as light into a world of darkness (1:5, 9; 3:19) and serving as the door or gate that enables people to enter God's sheepfold (10:7-10). Rather than restricting access to God the word "except" creates access to God.

Jesus as the Way

Calling Jesus "the way" can best be understood by noting that Jesus spoke about *going the way* himself before he spoke about *being the way* for others. Jesus' own journey is mentioned repeatedly in John 13–14, and his words can be taken on two levels. First, we can consider the destination. During his public ministry Jesus speaks of going to the one who sent him (7:33-34). Bystanders in the story find these remarks opaque, but John gives readers enough information to know that God sent Jesus (5:23-24; 6:38-39). Therefore, when Jesus speaks of going to the one who sent him, readers understand that he refers to his return to the Father. Similarly, the comments that introduce John's account of the last supper repeat that Jesus has come from God and is going to God (13:1, 3). After piquing the disciples' curiosity about where he is going, Jesus tells of preparing a place for them in his Father's house with its many rooms (14:2-4). Readers who follow these cues will respond to the question, "Where is Jesus going?" (13:36; 14:5) by saying, "He is going to God."

Second, we must note the route that Jesus will take. He speaks about where he is going in contexts that mention the prospect of arrest and the coming "hour" of the passion (7:30, 34; 8:20-21). When the evangelist later tolls the hour of Jesus' return to the Father, readers learn that the path Jesus follows will pass through betrayal (13:1-2). After Judas leaves the company of disciples and plunges into the night in order to carry out the betrayal, Jesus speaks about glorification and going where no one else can go (13:30-33). According to John's Gospel, Jesus' glorification and return to the Father take place through his dying and rising (12:23-24). These cues in the text enable readers to respond to the question, "Where is Jesus going?" by saying, "He is going the way of the cross."[29]

John 14 begins by identifying Jesus' destination as his Father's house, but when Jesus introduces the term "way" in the statement "You know the way where I am going" (14:4), he focuses attention on the way of crucifixion and resurrection that will lead to that destination. As the narrative unfolds, Jesus goes to the garden where he is arrested, then to the high priest's house where he is questioned, and then to the headquarters of the Roman governor where he is scourged. He follows the way out of the city, bearing his own cross, and is crucified at Golgotha. Death and entombment are followed by resurrection — and all of this belongs to the way by which he returns to the Father (20:17). Jesus says "I am the way" (14:6) after he has spoken about going the way himself (14:4). By going the way of the cross and resurrection he comes to embody the way of the cross and resurrection. To call Jesus "the way" is to call him "the Crucified and Risen One."

Asking "For whom is Jesus the way?" means considering the prior question, "For whom did Jesus go the way?" or more pointedly, "For whom did Christ die?" According to John's Gospel, Jesus went the way of the cross for all people, not just for some people. In the opening chapter John the Baptist announces "the way of the Lord" (1:23) by pointing to "the Lamb of God who takes away the sin of the world" (1:29). Using the term "world" emphasizes the scope of Christ's mission. Christ sacrificed himself for all because sin, which separates people from God, is part of the human condition. And the conviction that Christ dies for the sake of the world is underscored by the sign above the cross, which proclaims Christ's identity in Hebrew, Latin, and Greek for all the world to see (19:20).

The way of the cross is the way of divine love. It was because "God so loved the world that he gave his only Son" to suffer, die, and rise, "so that whoever believes in him might not perish but have eternal life" (3:16). When Jesus reveals God by going the way of the cross, he manifests God's love for a world alienated from its Creator. Love takes this particular form because the greatest expression of love is to lay down one's life on behalf of someone else (15:13). Accordingly, Jesus went to the cross not only to show his own love for his followers (13:1) but also to reveal the love of the God who sent him in order that the world's relationship with God might be restored (3:16).

The particular and the universal aspects of the Gospel's message are counterparts to each other and must be heard together. On the universal side, the Gospel assumes that sin separates all people from God. This is understood to be a basic dimension of the human condition. Given only human capacities, "no one comes to the Father." And in such a situation, the action needed to restore relationships must be taken from God's side. No one has any innate ability to overcome the separation and go to the Father, but the Father can do what human beings cannot by providing the way.

This is where the particular aspect of the message comes in. When Jesus says, "I Am the way and the truth and the life," he speaks of a gift that God extends to human beings through Jesus' death and resurrection. Jesus can be called "the way" for others because he has gone the way of death and resurrection himself. This is central to John's theological vision. Jesus does not become the way by offering information about God but by conveying the love that comes *from* God. It is not a general idea of love but God's particular act of love that is at the heart of this Gospel. And God's act of love reaches its goal when it evokes faith, for faith is the restoration of relationship with God.

The Fourth Gospel presents a particular message with a universal scope. At the beginning of our study we noted that the evangelist wrote in a world of varied religious traditions. The people depicted in this Gospel have different ideas about God, and their viewpoints often conflict. John is no stranger to interreligious controversy (see pp. 25-26). In this context, he seeks to show that God is known in a definitive way through what God has done in Jesus. John can speak to the pluralistic world in which his readers live because he has something particular to offer. To make the message less particular would mean making the love of God less radical, since the evangelist understands that divine love is definitively conveyed through the crucified and risen Messiah. At the same time, John understands that God's love is given in this particular way for the sake of the world (3:16). This means that the Gospel writer cannot say, "Jesus is the way for me but not for you." To say that would to be to say that "the love of God is for me but not for you," or that "Jesus went the way of the cross and resurrection for me but not for you." The Jesus of John's Gospel sends his followers into the world. There they meet human beings who, like themselves, have no innate ability to generate relationships with God. What the followers of Jesus bring is what they themselves have received: the message of the cruciform love of God that calls any and all to faith and life. This is the purpose for which John's Gospel was written (20:31).

Notes

Notes to Chapter 1

1. On the authorship and date of the Gospel see Raymond E. Brown, *An Introduction to the Gospel of John* (ed. Francis J. Moloney; New York: Random House, 2003), pp. 189-99, 206-15.

2. On John's relationship to the Synoptic Gospels see D. Moody Smith, *John Among the Gospels: The Relationship in Twentieth-Century Research,* 2nd ed. (Columbia: University of South Carolina, 2001).

3. See Marianne Meye Thompson, "The Historical Jesus and the Johannine Christ," in *Exploring the Gospel of John: In Honor of D. Moody Smith* (ed. R. Alan Culpepper and C. Clifton Black; Louisville: Westminster John Knox, 1996), pp. 21-42.

4. Richard Bauckham, *God Crucified: Christology and Monotheism in the New Testament* (Grand Rapids: Eerdmans, 1999).

5. For an overview of the issue see Robert Martin-Achard and George W. E. Nickelsburg, "Resurrection" in *ABD* vol. 5 (1992), pp. 680-91.

6. On the approach to the setting of the Gospel taken here see Craig R. Koester, *Symbolism in the Fourth Gospel: Meaning, Mystery, Community,* 2nd ed. (Minneapolis: Fortress, 2003), pp. 18-24, 247-57.

7. David Rensberger, *Johannine Faith and Liberating Community* (Philadelphia: Westminster, 1988), pp. 87-106; Craig R. Koester, "'The Savior of the World' (John 4:42)," *JBL* 109 (1990): 665-80; Bill Sailer, "Jesus, the Emperor, and the Gospel of John," in *Challenging Perspectives on the Gospel of John* (ed. John Lierman; WUNT 2/219; Tübingen: Mohr Siebeck, 2006), pp. 284-301.

8. See J. Louis Martyn, *History and Theology in the Fourth Gospel,* 3rd ed. (Louisville: Westminster John Knox, 2003), pp. 136-43; Sandra M. Schneiders, *The Revelatory Text: Interpreting the New Testament as Sacred Scripture,* 2nd ed. (Collegeville, Minn.: Liturgical, 1999), pp. 72-75.

9. See Koester, *Symbolism in the Fourth Gospel,* pp. 1-32.

10. Kurt Rudolph, *Gnosis: The Nature and History of Gnosticism* (San Francisco: Harper & Row, 1983), pp. 53-59.

11. See Elaine H. Pagels, *The Gospel of John in Gnostic Exegesis: Heracleon's Commentary on John* (Nashville and New York: Abingdon, 1973); Kyle Keefer, *The Branches of the Gospel of John: The Reception of the Fourth Gospel in the Early Church* (London: T. & T. Clark, 2006), pp. 21-43. On the question of how widespread the Gnostic use of John was, see Charles Hill, *The Johannine Corpus in the Early Church* (Oxford: Oxford University, 2004).

12. Irenaeus, *Against Heresies* 1.9.1-3; 5.6.1. See further Pagels, *Gospel of John,* pp. 36-50.

13. Mark A. Noll, *Turning Points: Decisive Moments in the History of Christianity* (Grand Rapids: Baker Academic, 2000), pp. 47-64.

14. For the texts of the creeds and commentary see Noll, *Turning Points,* pp. 57-58,

15. On the setting and outlook of 1 John see Raymond E. Brown, *The Epistles of John* (Anchor Bible 30; Garden City, N.Y.: Doubleday, 1982), pp. 69-79.

16. See Ronald E. Heine, "The Role of the Gospel of John in the Montanist Controversy," *Second Century* 6 (1987): 1-18.

17. Iain Gardner, *The Kephalaia of the Teacher: The Edited Coptic Manichaean Texts in Translation with Commentary* (Leiden: Brill, 1995), pp. xi-xv, 20-21.

18. An early Islamic identification of Muhammad as the Paraclete is made in Ibn Ishaq's biography of the prophet. See A. Guillaume, *The Life of Muhammad: A Translation of Sirat Rasul Allah* (Karachi and Oxford: Oxford University, 1955), pp. 103-4. For an early Christian response see "The Apology of Timothy the Patriarch before the Caliph Mahdi," in *Woodbrooke Studies* vol. 12 (ed. A. Mingana; Cambridge: W. Heffer & Sons, 1928), pp. 1-162, esp. 33-35. On the nature of the debate see Sidney H. Griffith, "Arguing from Scripture: The Bible in the Christian/Muslim Encounter in the Middle Ages," in *Scripture and Pluralism: Reading the Bible in the Religiously Plural Worlds of the Middle Ages and Renaissance* (ed. Thomas J. Heffernan and Thomas E. Burman; Leiden and Boston: Brill, 2005), pp. 29-58, esp. 40-42.

19. On Baptism in the early church see Jaroslav Pelikan, *The Emergence of the Catholic Tradition (100-600)* (Chicago and London: University of Chicago, 1971), pp. 163-66, 304.

20. Quotations are from *The Rites of the Catholic Church,* vol. 1 (Collegeville, Minn.: Liturgical, 1990), p. 384; *The Book of Common Prayer* (New York: Church Hymnal Corporation and Seabury, 1979), p. 307; *Evangelical Lutheran Worship* (Minneapolis: Augsburg Fortress, 2006), p. 227.

21. John Calvin, *The Gospel According to St. John 1–10* (Grand Rapids: Eerdmans, 1959), pp. 64-65; idem, *Institutes of the Christian Religion* 4.16.25.

22. John Wesley, *Sermons* 18 and 45. See *The Works of John Wesley,* vols. 1-2 (ed. Albert C. Outler; Nashville: Abingdon, 1984, 1985), vol. 1, pp. 417-30; vol. 2, pp. 186-201.

23. George Whitefield, *Journals* (Carlisle, Penn.: Banner of Truth, 1960), p. 47.

24. Billy Graham, *How to Be Born Again* (Waco: Word, 1977).

25. Johann Arndt, *True Christianity* (New York: Paulist, 1979), pp. 79, 177.

26. Ernst Troeltsch, *Christian Thought: Its History and Application* (New York: Meridian, 1957), p. 63.

27. John Hick, *God Has Many Names* (Philadelphia: Westminster, 1980), pp. 124-26.

28. Karl Barth, *Church Dogmatics* II/1 (New York: Scribner's, 1957), pp. 172-78.

Notes to Chapter 2

1. On the theme see Marianne Meye Thompson, *The God of the Gospel of John* (Grand Rapids: Eerdmans, 2001); C. K. Barrett, "Christocentric or Theocentric? Observations on the Theological Method of the Fourth Gospel," in *Essays on John* (London: SPCK, 1982), pp. 1-18. For a survey of older research see Tord Larsson, *God in the Fourth Gospel: A Hermeneutical Study of the History of Interpretations* (ConBNT 35; Stockholm: Almqvist & Wiksell, 2001).

2. On proposed backgrounds of the *logos* idea see Craig S. Keener, *The Gospel of John*, vol. 1 (Peabody, Mass.: Hendrickson, 2003), pp. 339-63.

3. D. Moody Smith, *The Theology of the Gospel of John* (Cambridge: Cambridge University, 1995), p. 75; Thompson, *The God of the Gospel of John*, pp. 7-8, 46.

4. D. François Tolmie, "The Characterization of God in the Fourth Gospel," *JSNT* 69 (1998): 57-75.

5. See the summary of the discussion in Marianne Meye Thompson, *The Humanity of Jesus in the Fourth Gospel* (Philadelphia: Fortress, 1988), pp. 13-52.

6. Thompson, *The God of the Gospel of John*, pp. 228-29.

7. John Painter, "Inclined to God: The Quest for Eternal Life — Bultmannian Hermeneutics and the Theology of the Fourth Gospel," in *Exploring the Gospel of John: In Honor of D. Moody Smith* (ed. R. Alan Culpepper and C. Clifton Black; Louisville: Westminster John Knox, 1996), pp. 346-68.

8. Some think that John the Baptist ceases speaking at 3:30, but literary context suggests that he continues speaking in 3:31-36. See Gail R. O'Day, *The Gospel of John* (*NIB* 9; Nashville: Abingdon, 1995), p. 558.

9. On the sending motif see Paul W. Meyer, "'The Father': The Presentation of God in the Fourth Gospel," in *Exploring the Gospel of John: In Honor of D. Moody Smith* (ed. R. Alan Culpepper and C. Clifton Black; Louisville: Westminster John Knox, 1996), pp. 255-73; Thompson, *The God of the Gospel of John*, pp. 92-98; Paul N. Anderson, "The Having-Sent-Me Father: Aspects of Agency, Encounter, and Irony in the Johannine Father-Son Relationship," in *God the Father in the Gospel of John* (ed. Adele Reinhartz; *Semeia* 85; Atlanta: Society of Biblical Literature, 1999), pp. 33-57.

10. On symbolic language see Craig R. Koester, *Symbolism in the Fourth Gospel: Meaning, Mystery, Community,* 2nd ed. (Minneapolis: Fortress, 2003), pp. 1-32. On metaphors see Jan G. van der Watt, *Family of the King: Dynamics of Metaphor in the Gospel of John* (BibIntSer 47; Leiden: Brill, 2000), pp. 1-24. On the significance of a figure or *paroimia* in John see Ruben Zimmermann, *Christologie der Bilder im Johannesevangelium: Die*

Christopoetik des vierten Evangeliums unter besonderer Berücksichtigung von Joh 10 (WUNT 171; Tübingen: Mohr Siebeck, 2004), pp. 29-59.

11. Jesus says that the hour is coming when he will speak *(apangellō)* plainly of the Father (16:25). But this does not mean that figurative language will then become unnecessary. Rather, it anticipates that the Spirit will disclose *(anangellō)* the meaning of what Jesus has said within the community of faith, after his death and resurrection (16:13-15; cf. 14:26). See Ruben Zimmermann, "Imagery in John: Opening Up Paths into the Tangled Thicket of John's Figurative World," in *Imagery in the Gospel of John: Terms, Forms, Themes, and Theology of Johannine Figurative Language* (ed. Jörg Frey, Jan G. van der Watt, and Ruben Zimmermann; WUNT 200: Tübingen: Mohr Siebeck, 2006), pp. 1-43, esp. 12-15.

12. C. H. Dodd, "A Hidden Parable in the Fourth Gospel," in *More New Testament Studies* (Grand Rapids: Eerdmans, 1968), pp. 30-40.

13. Keener, *The Gospel of John,* vol. 1, p. 668.

14. Marianne Meye Thompson, "'Every Picture Tells a Story': Imagery for God in the Gospel of John," in *Imagery in the Gospel of John* (ed. Jörg Frey, Jan G. van der Watt, and Ruben Zimmermann; WUNT 200; Tübingen: Mohr Siebeck, 2006), pp. 259-77.

15. Jesus' "hour" is linked to his arrest (7:30; 8:20), his departure to the Father (13:1), and his glorification, which would be accomplished through his death and resurrection (12:23, 27; 17:1). In 11:9 he comments that there are twelve hours in the day. Since the day was divided into twelve parts or hours, this means that there was a fixed span of time in which he could work.

16. Craig R. Koester, "Why Was the Messiah Crucified? A Study of God, Jesus, Satan, and Human Agency in Johannine Theology," in *The Death of Jesus in the Gospel of John* (ed. Gilbert Van Belle; BETL 200; Leuven: Leuven University and Peeters, 2007), pp. 163-80.

17. On the issues see the essays in Adele Reinhartz, ed., *God the Father in the Gospel of John* (*Semeia* 85; Atlanta: Society of Biblical Literature, 1999); Dorothy Lee, *Flesh and Glory: Symbol, Gender, and Theology in the Gospel of John* (New York: Crossroad, 2002), pp. 123-32; Mark Stibbe, "Telling the Father's Story: The Gospel of John as Narrative Theology," in *Challenging Perspectives on the Gospel of John* (ed. John Lierman; WUNT 2/219; Tübingen: Mohr Siebeck, 2006), pp. 170-93.

18. Thompson, *The God of the Gospel of John,* p. 58.

19. Lee, *Flesh and Glory,* p. 113.

20. Thompson, *The God of the Gospel of John,* pp. 78-79.

21. Christopher Cowan argues that the "subordination" fits aspects of John's Christology ("The Father and the Son in the Fourth Gospel: Johannine Subordination Revisited," *JETS* 49 [2006]: 115-35). Thompson argues that this term implies a degree of hierarchy that does not fit John's overall portrayal of the relationship (*The God of the Gospel of John,* p. 94).

22. van der Watt, *Family of the King,* pp. 304-33.

23. O'Day, *The Gospel of John,* pp. 748-50.

Notes to Chapter 3

1. On John's anthropology see Rudolf Bultmann, *Theology of the New Testament* (2 vols.; New York: Scribner's, 1951, 1955), vol. 1, p. 191; vol. 2, pp. 15-21; Udo Schnelle, *The Human Condition: Anthropology in the Teachings of Jesus, Paul, and John* (Minneapolis: Fortress, 1996); Craig R. Koester, "What Does It Mean to Be Human? Imagery and the Human Condition in John's Gospel," in *Imagery in the Gospel of John: Terms, Forms, Themes, and Theology of Johannine Figurative Language* (ed. Jörg Frey, Jan G. van der Watt, and Ruben Zimmermann; WUNT 200; Tübingen: Mohr Siebeck, 2006), pp. 403-20.

2. On representative figures see R. Alan Culpepper, *Anatomy of the Fourth Gospel: A Study in Literary Design* (Philadelphia: Fortress, 1983), pp. 101-4; Craig R. Koester, *Symbolism in the Fourth Gospel: Meaning, Mystery, Community,* 2nd ed. (Minneapolis: Fortress, 2003), pp. 33-39; Raymond F. Collins, *These Things Have Been Written: Studies in the Fourth Gospel* (Leuven: Peeters and Grand Rapids: Eerdmans, 1990), pp. 1-45; Colleen M. Conway, *Men and Women in the Fourth Gospel: Gender and Johannine Characterization* (SBLDS 167; Atlanta: Scholars, 1999); James L. Resseguie, *The Strange Gospel: Narrative Design and Point of View in John* (BibIntSer 56; Leiden: Brill, 2001), pp. 109-68.

3. For another perspective on the different levels of John's narrative see Adele Reinhartz, *The Word in the World: The Cosmological Tale in the Fourth Gospel* (SBLMS 45; Atlanta: Scholars, 1992), pp. 1-15.

4. On John's anthropological terms see Jaime Clark-Soles, "'I Will Raise [Whom?] Up on the Last Day': Anthropology as a Feature of Johannine Eschatology," in *New Currents Through John: A Global Perspective* (ed. Francisco Lozada Jr. and Tom Thatcher; Atlanta: Society of Biblical Literature, 2006), pp. 29-53, esp. 31-41.

5. On creation and John's anthropology see Bultmann, *Theology of the New Testament,* vol. 2, pp. 17-20; John Painter, "Inclined to God: The Quest for Eternal Life — Bultmannian Hermeneutics and the Theology of the Fourth Gospel," in *Exploring the Gospel of John: In Honor of D. Moody Smith* (ed. R. Alan Culpepper and C. Clifton Black; Louisville: Westminster John Knox, 1996), pp. 346-68.

6. Connecting 9:3 with 9:4 fits Johannine style. The same pattern appears in 1:31: "I myself did not know him, but in order that [*all' hina*] he might be revealed to Israel, for this I came baptizing with water." Another example is 14:30-31: "I will no longer speak much with you . . . but in order that [*all' hina*] the world may know that I love the Father, and just as the Father commanded me, thus I do."

7. Bultmann, *Theology of the New Testament,* vol. 2, pp. 26-27; Painter, "Inclined to God," pp. 353-54.

8. On thirst see Jan G. van der Watt, *Family of the King: Dynamics of Metaphor in the Gospel of John* (BibIntSer 47; Leiden: Brill, 2000), pp. 217-18; Dorothy Lee, *Flesh and Glory: Symbol, Gender, and Theology in the Gospel of John* (New York: Crossroad, 2002), pp. 71-77. On the theme see Bultmann, *Theology of the New Testament,* vol. 2, pp. 26-27; Painter, "Inclined to God," pp. 350-54. Both Painter and Bultmann recall Augustine's words, "You have made us for yourself, and our hearts are restless until they rest in you" (*Confessions* 1.1).

9. On Samaritan worship see Craig R. Koester, "'The Savior of the World' (John 4:42)," *JBL* 109 (1990): 665-80, esp. pp. 672-74. On Jewish perspectives on Jewish and Samaritan worship see also Raimo Hakola, *Identity Matters: John, the Jews, and Jewishness* (NovTSup 118; Leiden: Brill, 2005), pp. 87-115.

10. The ceremony is described in *m. Sukkah* 3:1–4:10. See also Larry Paul Jones, *The Symbol of Water in the Gospel of John* (JSNTSup 145; Sheffield: JSOT, 1997), pp. 151-55; Francis J. Moloney, *Signs and Shadows: Reading John 5–12* (Minneapolis: Fortress, 1996), pp. 65-70, 84-88.

11. On darkness and light see Koester, *Symbolism in the Fourth Gospel*, pp. 141-73; van der Watt, *Family of the King*, pp. 235-39, 245-60; Lee, *Flesh and Glory*, pp. 166-96.

12. On sin in John see D. Moody Smith, *The Theology of the Gospel of John* (Cambridge: Cambridge University, 1995), pp. 81-82; Rainer Metzner, *Das Verständnis der Sünde im Johannesevangelium* (WUNT 122; Tübingen: Mohr Siebeck, 2000); Martin Hasitschka, *Befreiung von Sünde nach dem Johannesevangelium: Eine bibeltheologische Untersuchung* (Innsbruck: Tyrolia, 1989); Hasitschka, "Befreiung von Sünde nach dem Johannesevangelium," in *Sünde und Erlösung im Neuen Testament* (ed. Hubert Frankenmölle; Freiburg: Herder, 1996), pp. 92-107.

13. Metzner, *Das Verständnis der Sünde*, p. 216.

14. On referring capital cases to the Romans see Raymond E. Brown, *The Death of the Messiah: From Gethsemane to the Grave*, vol. 1 (New York: Doubleday, 1994), pp. 363-72, 747-49. On John's portrayal of the Jews see Reimund Bieringer, D. Pollefeyt, and F. Vandecasteele-Vanneuville, eds., *Anti-Judaism and the Fourth Gospel* (Louisville: Westminster John Knox, 2001); Andrew T. Lincoln, *Truth on Trial: The Lawsuit Motif in the Fourth Gospel* (Peabody, Mass.: Hendrickson, 2000), pp. 397-404.

15. On the political implications of *lēstēs* in John see Lincoln, *Truth on Trial*, p. 130; Francis J. Moloney, *Glory Not Dishonor: Reading John 13–21* (Minneapolis: Fortress, 1998), p. 138; David Rensberger, *Johannine Faith and Liberating Community* (Philadelphia: Westminster, 1988), p. 96.

16. Roman emperors were formally deified at their deaths, but the imperial cults sometimes included the living emperors in divine honors. See S. R. F. Price, *Rituals and Power: The Roman Imperial Cult in Asia Minor* (Cambridge: Cambridge University Press, 1984).

17. On the portrayal of Pilate see Helen K. Bond, *Pontius Pilate in History and Interpretation* (SNTSMS 100; Cambridge: Cambridge University, 1998); Warren Carter, *Pontius Pilate: Portraits of a Roman Governor* (Collegeville, Minn.: Liturgical, 2003).

18. Evil is defeated but not eliminated through Jesus' death. See Ronald A. Piper, "Satan, Demons and the Absence of Exorcisms in the Fourth Gospel," in *Christology, Controversy and Community: New Testament Essays in Honour of David R. Catchpole* (ed. David G. Horrell and Christopher M. Tuckett; NovTSup 99; Leiden, Brill, 2000), pp. 253-78.

19. Some take 13:2 to mean that the devil put betrayal into the devil's own heart (Francis J. Moloney, *The Gospel of John* [SP 4; Collegeville, Minn.: Liturgical, 1998], p. 378; Gail R. O'Day, *The Gospel of John* [NIB 9; Nashville: Abingdon, 1995], p. 722). But the use

of the expression "put into the heart" in other sources indicates that the devil put the idea into Judas's heart, which is how it is usually understood.

20. On various positions on this issue see Robert Kysar, *John, the Maverick Gospel,* 2nd ed. (Louisville: Westminster John Knox, 1993), pp. 70-74.

21. Leander E. Keck, "Derivation as Destiny: 'Of-ness' in Johannine Christology, Anthropology, and Soteriology," in *Exploring the Gospel of John: In Honor of D. Moody Smith* (ed. R. Alan Culpepper and C. Clifton Black; Louisville: Westminster John Knox, 1996), pp. 274-88. On questions of predestination in John's anthropology see Schnelle, *Human Condition,* pp. 125-28.

22. Smith, *The Theology of the Gospel of John,* pp. 80-85.

23. Some assume that John narrows "the world" to essentially mean Judaism. See Bruce J. Malina and Richard L. Rohrbaugh, *Social-Science Commentary on the Gospel of John* (Minneapolis: Fortress, 1998), pp. 245-46. But the Gospel works with a broader notion of the world. For a survey of various positions and a proposal for understanding the broader view of the world see Lars Kierspel, *The Jews and the World in the Fourth Gospel: Parallelism, Function, and Context* (WUNT 2/220; Tübingen: Mohr Siebeck, 2006).

Notes to Chapter 4

1. On creative tensions in John's thought see D. Moody Smith, *The Theology of the Gospel of John* (Cambridge: Cambridge University, 1995), pp. 91-92; Paul N. Anderson, *The Christology of the Fourth Gospel: Its Unity and Disunity in the Light of John 6* (WUNT 2.78; Tübingen: Mohr Siebeck, 1996), p. 263; Larry W. Hurtado, *Lord Jesus Christ: Devotion to Jesus in Earliest Christianity* (Grand Rapids: Eerdmans, 2003), pp. 392-96.

2. Some argue that John's emphasis on Jesus' divinity diminishes the sense of humanity. See Ernst Käsemann, *The Testament of Jesus According to John 17* (Philadelphia: Fortress, 1968). Others argue that John emphasizes Jesus' humanity at points. See Udo Schnelle, *Antidocetic Christology in the Gospel of John: An Investigation of the Place of the Fourth Gospel in the Johannine School* (Minneapolis: Fortress, 1992). The approach taken here is that the Gospel does not argue for Jesus' humanity but presupposes it. See Marianne Meye Thompson, *The Humanity of Jesus in the Fourth Gospel* (Philadelphia: Fortress, 1988), pp. 121-22. On different aspects of the issue see Robert Kysar, *Voyages with John: Charting the Fourth Gospel* (Waco, Tex.: Baylor University, 2005), pp. 121-24.

3. Francis J. Moloney, *Signs and Shadows: Reading John 5–12* (Minneapolis: Fortress, 1996), p. 56.

4. Rudolf Bultmann, *The Gospel of John* (Philadelphia: Westminster, 1971), p. 659; Thompson, *The Humanity of Jesus,* p. 108.

5. The nature of Jesus' emotions in this passage is disputed. See Raymond E. Brown, *The Gospel According to John* (2 vols.; AB 29-29A; Garden City, N.Y.: Doubleday, 1966, 1970), vol. 1, pp. 425-26; Stephen Voorwinde, *Jesus' Emotions in the Fourth Gospel: Human or Divine?* (JSNTSup 284; London: T. & T. Clark, 2005), pp. 139-86. I understand Jesus to respond sympathetically to Mary.

6. See the summary of the discussion in Thompson, *The Humanity of Jesus*, pp. 13-52.

7. Smith, *The Theology of the Gospel of John*, p. 91; Andreas Köstenberger, "Jesus the Rabbi in the Fourth Gospel," in *Studies in John and Gender: A Decade of Scholarship* (New York: Lang, 2001), pp. 65-98.

8. On the bread imagery see Craig R. Koester, *Symbolism in the Fourth Gospel: Meaning, Mystery, Community*, 2nd ed. (Minneapolis: Fortress, 2003), p. 101.

9. On a student washing the teacher's feet see the *Mekilta*, "Nezikin" 1.56-63. On footwashing generally see Koester, *Symbolism in the Fourth Gospel*, pp. 127-31.

10. J. Louis Martyn, *History and Theology in the Fourth Gospel*, 3rd ed. (Louisville: Westminster John Knox, 2003), pp. 101-23; Smith, *The Theology of the Gospel of John*, pp. 125-27; Richard Bauckham, "Messianism According to the Gospel of John," *Challenging Perspectives on the Gospel of John* (ed. John Lierman; WUNT 2/219; Tübingen: Mohr Siebeck, 2006), pp. 34-68, esp. 40-53; in the same volume see John Lierman, "The Mosaic Pattern of John's Christology," pp. 210-34.

11. Cf. *Psalms of Solomon* 17:32; 18:6-8. On the range of messianic expectations in Jewish sources of the period see Emil Schürer et al., *The History of the Jewish People in the Age of Jesus Christ*, vol. 2 (Edinburgh: T. & T. Clark, 1979), pp. 488-513. On the importance of the messianic theme in John's Gospel see John Ashton, *Understanding the Fourth Gospel* (Oxford: Clarendon, 1991), pp. 238-79; Richard Bauckham, "Messianism According to the Gospel of John," pp. 54-67.

12. Craig R. Koester, "Messianic Exegesis and the Call of Nathanael (John 1.45-51)," *JSNT* 39 (1990): 23-34.

13. Paul D. Duke, *Irony in the Fourth Gospel* (Atlanta: John Knox, 1985), pp. 66-67.

14. On crowds going out to meet a visiting dignitary see Josephus, *Jewish War* 3.459; 4.112-13. On palms as a victory symbol see 1 Maccabees 13:51; 2 Maccabees 10:7.

15. On "son of man" as a human being see Ezekiel 2:1. On its use as a circumlocution meaning "I" see Matthew 8:20. On issues surrounding this expression see Delbert R. Burkett, *The Son of Man Debate: A History and Evaluation* (Cambridge: Cambridge University, 1999).

16. Francis J. Moloney, "The Johannine Son of Man Revisited," in *The Gospel of John: Text and Context* (Leiden: Brill, 2005), pp. 66-92.

17. The NRSV can translate 1:14 as "a father's only son," because the definite article "the" does not appear before the word "father" in Greek. It also takes the word "as" to mean that God's glory is being compared to human glory. The context makes it preferable to translate it "the Father's only Son." A noun can be definite even if it lacks the article. In 1:6, for example, John the Baptist is sent from "God" not "a god," even though the definite article is not used. In 1:18 the word "Father" has the definite article. The word "as" can indicate identity rather than comparison. Jesus comes "as" one who serves (Luke 22:27).

18. Brown, *The Gospel According to John*, vol. 1, pp. 216-17.

19. On ironic judgment see Duke, *Irony in the Fourth Gospel*, pp. 126-37; Andrew T. Lincoln, *Truth on Trial: The Lawsuit Motif in the Fourth Gospel* (Peabody, Mass.: Hendrickson, 2000), pp. 123-38.

20. Marianne Meye Thompson, *The God of the Gospel of John* (Grand Rapids: Eerd-

mans, 2001), pp. 87-92, 232-35; Robert Kysar, *John: The Maverick Gospel,* 2nd ed. (Louisville: Westminster John Knox, 1993), pp. 45-49; David Mark Ball, *"I Am" in John's Gospel* (JSNTSup 124; Sheffield: Sheffield Academic, 1996).

21. William Loader, *The Christology of the Fourth Gospel: Structure and Issues,* 2nd ed. (Frankfurt: Lang, 1992), p. 171.

22. On light imagery see Koester, *Symbolism in the Fourth Gospel,* pp. 152-56.

23. Margaret Daly-Denton, *David in the Fourth Gospel: The Johannine Reception of the Psalms* (Leiden: Brill, 2000), pp. 309-14.

24. Thomas Söding, "'Ich und der Vater sind eins' (Joh 10,30): Die johanneische Christologie vor dem Anspruch das Hauptgebotes (Dtn 6,4f)," *ZNW* 93 (2002): 177-99.

Notes to Chapter 5

1. Cicero, *In Defense of Rabirius* 4.13.

2. On the centrality of these motifs in John's narrative see Udo Schnelle, "Cross and Resurrection in the Gospel of John," in *The Resurrection of Jesus in the Gospel of John* (ed. Craig R. Koester and Reimund Bieringer; WUNT 222; Tübingen: Mohr Siebeck, 2008), pp. 127-52. On recent approaches to the question of Jesus' death in John see John Dennis, "Jesus' Death in John's Gospel: A Survey of Research from Bultmann to the Present with Special Reference to the Johannine Hyper-Texts," *Currents in Biblical Research* 4 (2006): 331-63; Gilbert Van Belle, ed., *The Death of Jesus in the Fourth Gospel* (BETL 200; Leuven: Peeters, 2007); Roy A. Harrisville: *Fracture: The Cross as Irreconcilable in the Language and Thought of the Biblical Writers* (Grand Rapids: Eerdmans, 2006), pp. 203-33. On the cross as the point on which the Gospel's many revelatory images focus see Harold W. Attridge, "The Cubist Principle in Johannine Imagery: John and the Reading of Images in Contemporary Platonism," in *Imagery in the Gospel of John: Terms, Forms, Themes, and Theology of the Johannine Figurative Language* (ed. Jörg Frey, Jan G. van der Watt, and Ruben Zimmermann; WUNT 200; Tübingen: Mohr Siebeck, 2006), pp. 47-60.

3. These four dimensions are summarized in Craig R. Koester, "Why Was the Messiah Crucified? A Study of God, Jesus, Satan, and Human Agency in Johannine Theology," in *The Death of Jesus in the Fourth Gospel* (ed. Gilbert Van Belle; BETL 200; Leuven: Peeters, 2007), pp. 163-80.

4. See Craig R. Koester, "The Death of Jesus and the Human Condition: Exploring the Theology of John's Gospel," *Life in Abundance: Studies of John's Gospel in Tribute to Raymond E. Brown, S.S.* (ed. John R. Donahue; Collegeville, Minn.: Liturgical Press, 2005), pp. 141-57.

5. Plato, *Symposium* 179b; Aristotle, *Nicomachean Ethics* 9.8 1169a; Seneca, *Moral Epistles* 9.10; Diogenes Laertius, *Lives* 10.120; Romans 5:7.

6. Craig R. Koester, *Symbolism in the Fourth Gospel: Meaning, Mystery. Community,* 2nd ed. (Minneapolis: Fortress, 2003), pp. 127-34.

7. Raymond F. Collins, *These Things Have Been Written* (Leuven: Peeters and Grand Rapids: Eerdmans, 1990), pp. 217-56. On the problems that arise from a diminished sense

of Jesus' humanity or a truncated view of Christian love, see Raymond E. Brown, *The Epistles of John* (AB 30; Garden City, N.Y.: Doubleday, 1982), pp. 73-86.

8. Those who downplay the sacrificial imagery include John Ashton, *Understanding the Fourth Gospel* (Oxford: Clarendon, 1991), p. 491; J. Terence Forestell, *The Word of the Cross* (AnBib 57; Rome: Biblical Institute, 1974), pp. 157-66. See also Esther Straub, *Kritische Theologie ohne ein Wort vom Kreuz* (FRLANT 203; Göttingen: Vandenhoeck & Ruprecht, 2003). Those who develop the sacrificial aspects include Thomas Knöppler, *Die theologia crucis des Johannesevangeliums* (WMANT 69; Neukirchen-Vluyn: Neukirchener, 1994), pp. 67-101; Jörg Frey, "Die 'theologia crucifixi' des Johannesevangeliums," in *Kreuzestheologie im Neuen Testament* (ed. Andreas Dettwiler and Jean Zumstein; Tübingen: Mohr Siebeck, 2002), pp. 169-238, esp. 200-19.

9. Exodus 12:46; Numbers 9:12. Similar words are used for the righteous sufferer of Psalm 34:20, whose legs were not broken, but the connection with the Passover lamb is primary. See Raymond E. Brown, *The Death of the Messiah: From Gethsemane to the Grave* (2 vols.; New York: Doubleday, 1994), vol. 2, pp. 1185-86. The link with Passover is stressed and the atoning aspect of Jesus' death is minimized by Christine Schlund, *"Kein Knochen Soll Gebrochen Werden"* (WMANT 107; Neukirchen-Vluyn: Neukirchener, 2005). John, however, transforms traditional Passover imagery.

10. On the various associations connected with the Lamb of God imagery see Raymond E. Brown, *The Gospel According to John* (2 vols.; AB 29-29A; Garden City, N.Y.: Doubleday, 1970), vol. 1, pp. 60-63; Koester, *Symbolism in the Fourth Gospel*, pp. 219-24.

11. John uses the verb *airein* in a physical sense for removing doves from the temple (2:16), a stone from a tomb door (11:41; 20:1), a branch from a vine (15:2), and a body from its burial place (20:2). In an extended sense it entails taking away life or joy (10:18; 16:22). The verb does not suggest that the Lamb took sin upon himself, but that he took it away (Forestell, *Word of the Cross*, pp. 160-65). On the role of faith in taking away sin see R. Alan Culpepper, *Anatomy of the Fourth Gospel* (Philadelphia: Fortress, 1983), p. 88.

12. Gerhard O. Forde, *Theology Is for Proclamation* (Minneapolis: Fortress, 1990), pp. 129-33.

13. For a nuanced case for a substitutionary view that makes use of legal categories see Andrew T. Lincoln, *Truth on Trial: The Lawsuit Motif in the Fourth Gospel* (Peabody, Mass.: Hendrickson, 2000), p. 203. On atonement theories see Colin Gunton, *The Actuality of Atonement: A Study of Metaphor, Rationality, and the Christian Tradition* (Grand Rapids: Eerdmans, 1989), pp. 83-141.

14. For a vicarious interpretation of 10:11-15 and 11:50 see Knöppler, *Die theologia crucis*, pp. 201-16. This approach is unlikely. See Frank J. Matera, "'On Behalf of Others,' 'Cleansing,' and 'Return': Johannine Images for Jesus' Death," *LS* 13 (1988): 161-78, esp. 164-70.

15. Peter Abelard in *A Scholastic Miscellany: Anselm to Ockham* (ed. and trans. Eugene R. Fairweather; Library of Christian Classics 10; Philadelphia: Westminster, 1956), p. 284.

16. Forde, *Theology Is for Proclamation*, p. 131.

17. On conflict, victory, and the crucifixion see Judith L. Kovacs, "'Now Shall the

Ruler of This World Be Driven Out': Jesus' Death as Cosmic Battle in John 12:20-36," *JBL* 114 (1995): 227-47.

18. Roman emperors were formally deified at their deaths, but the imperial cults sometimes included the living emperors in divine honors. See S. R. F. Price, *Rituals and Power: The Roman Imperial Cult in Asia Minor* (Cambridge: Cambridge University, 1984).

19. Gail R. O'Day, *The Gospel of John* (*NIB* 9; Nashville: Abingdon, 1995), p. 830. The title "Savior of the world" was sometimes used for the Roman emperors. See Craig R. Koester, "'The Savior of the World' (John 4:42)," *JBL* 109 (1990): 665-80.

20. See John Painter, "Inclined to God: The Quest for Eternal Life — Bultmannian Hermeneutics and the Theology of the Fourth Gospel," in *Exploring the Gospel of John. In Honor of D. Moody Smith* (ed. R. Alan Culpepper and C. Clifton Black; Louisville: Westminster John Knox, 1996), pp. 346-68.

21. Marianne Meye Thompson, *The Humanity of Jesus in the Fourth Gospel* (Philadelphia: Fortress, 1988), pp. 87-115.

22. C. H. Dodd, *The Interpretation of the Fourth Gospel* (Cambridge: Cambridge University, 1953), pp. 207-8.

23. Forestell, *Word of the Cross*, pp. 73-74.

24. On the literary and theological dimensions of the resurrection in the Fourth Gospel see the essays in Craig R. Koester and Reimund Bieringer, eds., *The Resurrection of Jesus in the Gospel of John* (WUNT 222; Tübingen: Mohr Siebeck, 2008).

25. C. K. Barrett, *The New Testament Background* (New York: Harper & Row, 1956), p. 15.

26. O'Day, *The Gospel of John*, p. 841.

27. Dorothy Lee, *Flesh and Glory: Symbolism, Gender and Theology in the Gospel of John* (New York: Crossroad, 2002), pp. 223-26.

28. Francis J. Moloney, *Glory Not Dishonor: Reading John 13–21* (Minneapolis: Fortress, 1998), p. 175.

29. The importance of "drawing" has been emphasized by Brown, *Gospel According to John,* vol. 2, p. 1097.

30. Sandra M. Schneiders, "The Resurrection (of the Body) in the Fourth Gospel: A Key to Johannine Spirituality," in *Life in Abundance* (ed. John R. Donahue; Collegeville, Minn.: Liturgical, 2005), pp. 168-98; Schneiders, "Touching the Risen Jesus: Mary Magdalene and Thomas the Twin in John 20," in *The Resurrection of Jesus in the Gospel of John* (ed. Craig R. Koester and Reimund Bieringer; WUNT 222; Tübingen: Mohr Siebeck, 2008), pp. 153-76.

31. Moloney, *Glory Not Dishonor*, 161.

Notes to Chapter 6

1. Studies that trace the Spirit theme throughout the Gospel include Gary M. Burge, *The Anointed Community: The Holy Spirit in the Johannine Tradition* (Grand Rapids: Eerdmans, 1987); Tricia Gates Brown, *Spirit in the Writings of John: Johannine Pneuma-*

tology in Social-Scientific Perspective (London and New York: T. & T. Clark, 2003); Cornelius Bennema, *The Saving Power of Wisdom: An Investigation of Spirit and Wisdom in Relation to the Soteriology of the Fourth Gospel* (WUNT 2/148; Tübingen: Mohr Siebeck, 2002).

2. Marianne Meye Thompson, *The God of the Gospel of John* (Grand Rapids: Eerdmans, 2001), pp. 156-65. A different view is that of Bennema, who thinks that the Spirit endows Jesus with wisdom (*The Saving Power of Wisdom,* pp. 160-67). But since the prologue has already identified Jesus as the incarnate logos, this view seems unlikely.

3. Cornelius Bennema, "Spirit-Baptism in the Fourth Gospel: A Messianic Reading of John 1,33," *Bib* 84 (2003): 35-60.

4. Jörg Frey, *Die johanneische Eschatologie,* vol. 3, *Die eschatologische Verkündigung in den johanneischen Texten* (WUNT 117; Tübingen: Mohr Siebeck, 2000), pp. 248-61.

5. Francis Moloney, *The Gospel of John* (SP 4; Collegeville, Minn.: Liturgical, 1998), pp. 91-92; Gail R. O'Day, *The Gospel of John* (*NIB* 9; Nashville: Abingdon, 1995), pp. 549-50.

6. Karl Olav Sandness, "Whence and Whither: A Narrative Perspective on Birth ἄνωθεν (John 3,3-8)," *Bib* 86 (2005): 153-73.

7. Gary M. Burge, *The Anointed Community: The Holy Spirit in the Johannine Tradition* (Grand Rapids: Eerdmans, 1987), pp. 169-71.

8. For a survey of positions see Matthew Vellanickal, *The Divine Sonship of Christians in the Johannine Writings* (AnBib 72; Rome: Biblical Institute, 1977), pp. 181-86.

9. On the water theme in John see Craig R. Koester, *Symbolism in the Fourth Gospel: Meaning, Mystery, Community,* 2nd ed. (Minneapolis: Fortress, 2003), pp. 175-206; Larry Paul Jones, *The Symbol of Water in the Gospel of John* (JSNTSup 145; Sheffield: JSOT, 1997).

10. R. Alan Culpepper, *Anatomy of the Fourth Gospel: A Study in Literary Design* (Philadelphia: Fortress, 1983), p. 193; Rudolf Schnackenburg, *The Gospel According to St John,* vol. 1 (New York: Herder, 1968), pp. 369-70.

11. John 3:34 seems to speak of God giving the Spirit to Jesus, making Jesus the bearer of the Spirit. See Burge, *The Anointed Community,* pp. 81-84; Thompson, *The God of the Gospel of John,* pp. 170-79.

12. Burge, *The Anointed Community,* p. 163.

13. For helpful reflections on the variety in the Gospel see Marianne Meye Thompson, "When the Ending Is Not the End," in *The Endings of Mark and the Ends of God: Essays in Memory of Donald Harrisville Juel* (ed. Beverly Roberts Gaventa and Patrick D. Miller; Louisville: Westminster John Knox, 2005), pp. 65-75.

14. For a positive reading of Nicodemus's faith see Francis J. Moloney, *Glory Not Dishonor: Reading John 13–21* (Minneapolis: Fortress, 1998), p. 149. For a negative assessment see Andreas J. Köstenberger, *John* (Grand Rapids: Baker Academic, 2004), pp. 118-19. On the ambiguity see Jouette M. Bassler, "Mixed Signals: Nicodemus in the Fourth Gospel," *JBL* 108 (1989): 635-46; Gabi Renz, "Nicodemus: An Ambiguous Disciple? A Narrative Sensitive Investigation," in *Challenging Perspectives on the Gospel of John* (ed. John Lierman; WUNT 2/219; Tübingen: Mohr Siebeck, 2006), pp. 255-83.

15. On the living water as word or revelation and Spirit see Raymond E. Brown, *The*

Gospel According to John (AB 29-29A; Garden City, N.Y.: Doubleday, 1966-70), vol. 1, pp. 178-80.

16. Translations that have the water flow from the believer include the ESV, NAB, NIV, and NRSV. For detailed discussion of the translation given here see Burge, *The Anointed Community*, pp. 88-93.

17. The Greek verbs in 7:37b-38 are in the present tense. This indicates ongoing action: continued thirsting, coming, believing, and drinking.

18. Raymond E. Brown, *The Death of the Messiah: From Gethsemane to the Grave* (New York: Doubleday, 1994), vol. 2, pp. 1082-83; Moloney, *The Gospel of John*, pp. 505, 508-9.

19. See Koester, *Symbolism in the Fourth Gospel*, pp. 201-3.

20. On the word *paraklētos* and its functions in John see Raymond E. Brown, *The Gospel According to John*, vol. 2, pp. 1135-37; David Pastorelli, *Le paraclet dans le corpus Johannique* (BZAW 142; Berlin: de Gruyter, 2006), pp. 40-104.

21. Burge, *The Anointed Community*, p. 141.

22. Thompson, *The God of the Gospel of John*, pp. 181-82.

23. Rudolf Bultmann, *The Gospel of John* (Philadelphia: Westminster, 1971), p. 616.

24. O'Day, *The Gospel of John*, pp. 774-78.

25. Burge, *The Anointed Community*, p. 147.

26. The verb *elenchō* can mean to convict someone in the sense of convincing the person that he or she has done wrong. This does not seem to be the point here. The world does not recognize its own guilt. See O'Day, *The Gospel of John*, p. 772; Moloney, *The Gospel of John*, 440.

27. M. Eugene Boring, *The Continuing Voice of Jesus: Christian Prophecy and the Gospel Tradition* (Louisville: Westminster John Knox, 1991), pp. 160-61, 179.

28. Some argue that the Spirit does predict the future, according to John. See Crinisor Stefan, "The Paraclete and Prophecy in the Johannine Community," *Pneuma* 27 (2005): 273-96; George Johnston, *The Spirit-Paraclete in the Gospel of John* (SNTSMS 12; Cambridge: Cambridge University, 1970), p. 39.

29. On the broader sense of declaring meaning see Fernando F. Segovia, *The Farewell of the Word: The Johannine Call to Abide* (Minneapolis: Fortress, 1991), p. 239; O'Day, *The Gospel of John*, p. 773.

30. The way 3:11-21 reflects a post-resurrection perspective has led some to suggest that Jesus stops speaking at 3:15, making 3:16-21 a post-resurrection commentary by the evangelist. See, e.g., Köstenberger, *John*, p. 128; Schnackenburg, *The Gospel According to St John*, pp. 380-409.

31. See Raymond E. Brown, *The Gospel According to John*, vol. 2, pp. 1039-45.

32. Rainer Metzner, *Das Verständnis der Sünde im Johannesevangelium* (WUNT 122; Tübingen: Mohr Siebeck, 2000), pp. 262-82; Martin Hasitschka, *Befreiung von Sünde nach dem Johannesevangelium: Eine bibeltheologische Untersuchung* (Innsbruck: Tyrolia, 1989), pp. 378-422.

Notes to Chapter 7

1. On John's vocabulary of faith see John Painter, *The Quest for the Messiah: The History, Literature and Theology of the Johannine Community* (Edinburgh: T. & T. Clark, 1991), pp. 327-33. On characters as exemplars of belief and unbelief see R. Alan Culpepper, *Anatomy of the Fourth Gospel: A Study in Literary Design* (Philadelphia: Fortress, 1983), p. 104.

2. See further, Craig R. Koester, "Hearing, Seeing, and Believing in the Gospel of John," *Bib* 70 (1989): 327-48.

3. On signs and resurrection appearances see Gilbert Van Belle, "The Meaning of the σημεῖα in Jn 20,30-31," *ETL* 74 (1998): 300-25; Craig R. Koester, "Jesus' Resurrection, the Signs, and the Dynamics of Faith in the Gospel of John," in *The Resurrection of Jesus in the Gospel of John* (ed. Craig R. Koester and Reimund Bieringer; Tübingen: Mohr Siebeck, 2008), pp. 47-74.

4. For a critical interpretation of signs see Rudolf Bultmann, *The Gospel of John* (Philadelphia: Westminster, 1971), p. 696. For a positive interpretation of signs see Marianne Meye Thompson, *The Humanity of Jesus in the Fourth Gospel* (Philadelphia: Fortress, 1988), pp. 63-64; Udo Schnelle, *Antidocetic Christology in the Gospel of John: An Investigation of the Place of the Fourth Gospel in the Johannine School* (Minneapolis: Fortress, 1992), pp. 173-75. On signs producing an initial faith see Robert Kysar, *John: The Maverick Gospel*, 2nd ed. (Louisville: Westminster John Knox, 1993), pp. 78-86.

5. Gail R. O'Day, *The Gospel of John* (*NIB* 9; Nashville: Abingdon, 1995), p. 575.

6. J. Louis Martyn, *History and Theology in the Fourth Gospel*, 3rd ed. (Louisville: Westminster John Knox, 2003), pp. 36, 40.

7. Philip F. Esler and Ronald Piper, *Lazarus, Martha, and Mary: Social-Scientific Approaches to the Gospel of John* (Minneapolis: Fortress, 2006), pp. 108-11.

8. Rudolf Schnackenburg, *The Gospel According to St John*, vol. 2 (New York: Seabury, 1980), p. 329.

9. See Raymond E. Brown, *The Death of the Messiah: From Gethsemane to the Grave*, vol. 2 (New York: Doubleday, 1994), p. 1268.

10. For a positive reading of the Samaritan woman see Sandra M. Schneiders, *The Revelatory Text: Interpreting the New Testament as Sacred Scripture*, 2nd ed. (Collegeville, Minn.: Liturgical, 1999), pp. 180-99. For a less positive reading see Francis J. Moloney, *Belief in the Word: Reading John 1–4* (Minneapolis: Fortress, 1993), pp. 157-58.

11. Marianne Meye Thompson, "When the Ending Is Not the End," in *The Endings of Mark and the Ends of God: Essays in Memory of Donald Harrisville Juel* (ed. Beverly Roberts Gaventa and Patrick D. Miller; Louisville: Westminster John Knox, 2005), pp. 65-75.

12. For a survey of discussion on John's eschatology see Jörg Frey, "Eschatology in the Johannine Circle," in *Theology and Christology in the Fourth Gospel* (ed. Gilbert Van Belle, Jan G. van der Watt, and Petrus J. Maritz; BETL 184; Leuven: Leuven University and Peeters, 2005), pp. 47-82. On present and future dimensions in John see Raymond E. Brown, *An Introduction to the Gospel of John* (ed. Francis J. Moloney; New York: Doubleday, 2003), pp. 234-48; Gail R. O'Day, *The Gospel of John* (*NIB* 9; Nashville:

Abingdon, 1995), p. 784; R. Alan Culpepper, "Realized Eschatology in the Experience of the Johannine Community," in *The Resurrection of Jesus in the Gospel of John* (ed. Craig R. Koester and Reimund Bieringer; WUNT 222; Tübingen: Mohr Siebeck, 2008), pp. 253-78.

13. Some argue that for John the present reality of life makes death irrelevant. See Jaime Clark-Soles, "'I Will Raise [Whom?] Up on the Last Day": Anthropology as a Feature of Johannine Eschatology," in *Currents Through John: A Global Perspective* (ed. Francisco Lozada and Tom Thatcher; Atlanta: Society of Biblical Literature, 2006), pp. 29-53, esp. 50-51. But this is unlikely. The Gospel writer is aware of the continuing problem of death for believers. See Frey, "Eschatology in the Johannine Circle," pp. 79-80.

14. Andrew T. Lincoln, "'I Am the Resurrection and the Life': The Resurrection Message of the Fourth Gospel," in *Life in the Face of Death: The Resurrection Message of the New Testament* (ed. Richard N. Longenecker; Grand Rapids and Cambridge: Eerdmans, 1998), pp. 122-44, esp. 139-42; N. T. Wright, *The Resurrection of the Son of God* (Minneapolis: Fortress, 2003), pp. 440-48. On the tensions in the Gospel's treatment of resurrection see Harold W. Attridge, "From Discord Rises Meaning: Resurrection Motifs in the Fourth Gospel," in *The Resurrection of Jesus in the Gospel of John* (ed. Craig R. Koester and Reimund Bieringer; WUNT 222; Tübingen: Mohr Siebeck, 2008), pp. 1-19.

15. On the wholistic dimension of resurrection see Sandra Schneiders, "Touching the Risen Jesus: Mary Magdalene and Thomas the Twin," in *The Resurrection of Jesus in the Gospel of John* (ed. Craig R. Koester and Reimund Bieringer; WUNT 222; Tübingen: Mohr Siebeck, 2008), pp. 153-76.

16. Sandra M. Schneiders, "Death in the Community of Eternal Life: History, Theology, and Spirituality in John 11," *Int* 41 (1987), pp. 44-56, esp. p. 50.

17. See Sandra M. Schneiders, "The Resurrection (of the Body) in the Fourth Gospel: A Key to Johannine Spirituality," in *Life in Abundance: Studies of John's Gospel in Tribute to Raymond E. Brown* (ed. John R. Donahue; Collegeville, Minn.: Liturgical, 2005), pp. 168-98

18. Jörg Frey, *Die johanneische Eschatologie*, vol. 3, *Die eschatologische Verkündigung in den johanneischen Texten* (WUNT 117; Tübingen: Mohr Siebeck, 2000), pp. 14-22.

19. C. K. Barrett, *The Gospel According to St. John,* 2nd ed. (Philadelphia: Westminster, 1978), p. 464.

20. Jean Zumstein, "Jesus' Resurrection in the Farewell Discourses," in *The Resurrection of Jesus in the Gospel of John* (ed. Craig R. Koester and Reimund Bieringer; WUNT 222; Tübingen: Mohr Siebeck, 2008), pp. 103-26.

21. Frey, *Die johanneische Eschatologie*, pp. 165-66; Udo Schnelle, "Die Abschiedsreden im Johannesevangelium," *ZNW* 80 (1989), pp. 64-79, esp. 68-69.

22. Frey, *Die johanneische Eschatologie*, pp. 204-22.

Notes to Chapter 8

1. For an overview of discussion on discipleship in John's Gospel see Rekha M. Chennattu, *Johannine Discipleship as a Covenant Relationship* (Peabody, Mass.: Hendrickson, 2006), pp. 1-22.

2. For helpful discussion on the various moral and ethical dimensions of John's Gospel see Jan G. van der Watt, "Ethics Alive in Imagery," in *Imagery in the Gospel of John* (ed. Jörg Frey, Jan G. van der Watt, and Ruben Zimmermann; WUNT 200; Tübingen: Mohr Siebeck, 2006), pp. 421-48; van der Watt, "Ethics and Ethos in the Gospel According to John," *ZNW* 97 (2006): 147-76. Richard A. Burridge, *Imitating Jesus: An Inclusive Approach to New Testament Ethics* (Grand Rapids: Eerdmans, 2007), pp. 285-346.

3. On light imagery see Craig R. Koester, *Symbolism in the Fourth Gospel: Meaning, Mystery, Community*, 2nd ed. (Minneapolis: Fortress, 2003), pp. 141-73.

4. On the concept of honor see David A. deSilva, *The Hope of Glory: Honor Discourse and New Testament Interpretation* (Collegeville, Minn.: Liturgical, 1999), pp. 1-33; Bruce Malina and Jerome H. Neyrey, "Honor and Shame in Luke-Acts: Pivotal Values in the Mediterranean World," in *The Social World of Luke-Acts* (ed. Jerome H. Neyrey; Peabody, Mass.: Hendrickson, 1991), pp. 25-65.

5. On footwashing see Koester, *Symbolism in the Fourth Gospel*, pp. 127-34; John Christopher Thomas, *Footwashing in John 13 and the Johannine Community* (JSNTSup 61; Sheffield: JSOT, 1991), pp. 44-46.

6. Wolfgang Schrage, *The Ethics of the New Testament* (Philadelphia: Fortress, 1988), pp. 297-319.

7. Richard B. Hays, *The Moral Vision of the New Testament: A Contemporary Introduction to New Testament Ethics* (San Francisco: HarperSanFrancisco, 1996), pp. 144-46.

8. David Rensberger, *Johannine Faith and Liberating Community* (Philadelphia: Westminster, 1988), p. 150.

9. Dorothy Lee, *Flesh and Glory: Symbol, Gender, and Theology in the Gospel of John* (New York: Crossroad, 2002), pp. 88-109.

10. Raymond E. Brown, *The Churches the Apostles Left Behind* (New York: Paulist, 1984), pp. 84-101.

11. Jan G. van der Watt, *Family of the King: Dynamics of Metaphor in the Gospel According to John* (Leiden: Brill, 2000), pp. 161-65.

12. On the term "woman" see Craig R. Keener, *The Gospel of John*, vol. 1 (Peabody, Mass.: Hendrickson, 2003), pp. 504-5.

13. Francis J. Moloney, *Glory Not Dishonor: Reading John 13–21* (Minneapolis: Fortress, 1998), pp. 144-45; Gail R. O'Day, *The Gospel of John* (*NIB* 9; Nashville: Abingdon, 1995), p. 832. On the various interpretations of this scene in Roman Catholic and Protestant exegesis see Rudolf Schnackenburg, *The Gospel According to St John*, vol. 3 (New York: Crossroad, 1982), pp. 274-82.

14. On friendship see Keener, *The Gospel of John*, vol. 2, pp. 1004-15.

15. Mark L. Appold, *The Oneness Motif in the Fourth Gospel* (WUNT 2/1; Tübingen: Mohr Siebeck, 1976).

16. Gail R. O'Day, *The Gospel of John* (*NIB* 9; Nashville: Abingdon, 1995), p. 791.

17. R. Alan Culpepper, "Inclusivism and Exclusivism in the Fourth Gospel," in *Word, Theology, and Community in John* (ed. John Painter, R. Alan Culpepper, and Fernando F. Segovia; St. Louis: Chalice, 2002), pp. 85-108, esp. 94-95.

18. On the issues see Raymond E. Brown, *An Introduction to the Gospel of John* (ed. Francis J. Moloney; New York: Doubleday, 2003), pp. 221-28.

19. Brown, *The Churches the Apostles Left Behind*, p. 93.

20. Brown, *The Churches the Apostles Left Behind*, pp. 94-101.

21. Mary L. Coloe, *God Dwells with Us: Temple Symbolism in the Fourth Gospel* (Collegeville, Minn.: Liturgical, 2001), pp. 65-84.

22. Gary M. Burge, *The Anointed Community: The Holy Spirit in the Johannine Tradition* (Grand Rapids: Eerdmans, 1987), pp. 190-97.

23. On the baptismal interpretation see the survey of scholars in Thomas, *Footwashing in John 13*, pp. 12-13.

24. On the baptismal interpretations in patristic writings see Raymond E. Brown, *The Gospel According to John*, vol. 2 (Garden City, N.Y.: Doubleday, 1970), p. 951. On thematic connections to baptism in John see John Paul Heil, *Blood and Water: The Death and Resurrection of Jesus in John 18–21* (CBQMS 27; Washington, D.C.: Catholic Biblical Association, 1995), pp. 105-9.

25. For sacramental interpretations see Udo Schnelle, *Antidocetic Christology in the Gospel of John: An Investigation of the Place of the Fourth Gospel in the Johannine School* (Minneapolis: Fortress, 1992), pp. 201-8; David Rensberger, *Johannine Faith and Liberating Community* (Philadelphia: Westminster, 1988), pp. 70-81. For a survey of other viewpoints on the Lord's Supper in John, together with balanced discussion of the question, see Martin J. J. Menken, "John 6:51c-58: Eucharist or Christology?" in *Critical Readings of John 6* (ed. R. Alan Culpepper; Leiden: Brill, 1997), pp. 183-204.

26. See further Koester, *Symbolism in the Fourth Gospel*, pp. 301-9.

27. On engaging the world see Teresa Okure, *The Johannine Approach to Mission* (WUNT 2/31; Tübingen: Mohr Siebeck, 1988).

28. On the differing perspectives see D. Moody Smith, "Prolegomena to a Canonical Reading of the Fourth Gospel," in *"What Is John?": Readers and Readings of the Fourth Gospel* (ed. Fernando F. Segovia; Atlanta: Scholars Press, 1996), pp. 169-82, esp. 175-76; R. Alan Culpepper, "The Gospel of John as a Document of Faith in a Pluralistic Culture," in *"What Is John?,"* pp. 107-27, esp. 121-25. For a negative assessment of 14:6 see James H. Charlesworth, "The Gospel of John: Exclusivism Caused by a Social Setting Different from That of Jesus (John 11:54 and 14:6)," in *Anti-Judaism and the Fourth Gospel* (ed. Reimund Bieringer, Didier Pollefeyt, and Frederique Vandecasteele-Vanneuville; Louisville: Westminster John Knox, 2001), pp. 247-78.

29. Moloney, *Glory Not Dishonor*, p. 36. John Painter, *John: Witness and Theologian* (London: SPCK, 1975), pp. 41, 47.

Bibliography of Works Cited

Anderson, Paul N. *The Christology of the Fourth Gospel: Its Unity and Disunity in the Light of John 6.* WUNT 2/78. Tübingen: Mohr Siebeck, 1996.

―――. "The Having-Sent-Me Father: Aspects of Agency, Encounter, and Irony in the Johannine Father-Son Relationship." Pages 33-57 in *God the Father in the Gospel of John.* Edited by Adele Reinhartz. *Semeia* 85. Atlanta: Society of Biblical Literature, 1999.

Appold, Mark L. *The Oneness Motif in the Fourth Gospel: Motif Analysis and Exegetical Probe into the Theology of John.* WUNT 2/1. Tübingen: Mohr Siebeck, 1976.

Arndt, Johann. *True Christianity.* New York: Paulist, 1979.

Ashton, John. *Understanding the Fourth Gospel.* Oxford: Clarendon, 1991.

Attridge, Harold W. "The Cubist Principle in Johannine Imagery: John and the Reading of Images in Contemporary Platonism." Pages 47-60 in *Imagery in the Gospel of John: Terms, Forms, Themes, and Theology of the Johannine Figurative Language.* Edited by Jörg Frey, Jan G. van der Watt, and Ruben Zimmermann. WUNT 200. Tübingen: Mohr Siebeck, 2006.

―――. "From Discord Rises Meaning: Resurrection Motifs in the Fourth Gospel." Pages 1-19 in *The Resurrection of Jesus in the Gospel of John.* Edited by Craig R. Koester and Reimund Bieringer. WUNT 222. Tübingen: Mohr Siebeck, 2008.

Ball, David Mark. *"I Am" in John's Gospel.* JSNTSup 124. Sheffield: Sheffield Academic, 1996.

Barrett, C. K. "Christocentric or Theocentric? Observations on the Theological Method of the Fourth Gospel." Pages 1-18 in *Essays on John.* London: SPCK, 1982.

―――. *The Gospel According to St. John.* 2nd ed. Philadelphia: Westminster, 1978.

————. *The New Testament Background: Selected Documents.* New York: Harper & Row, 1956.

Barth, Karl. *Church Dogmatics* II/1. New York: Scribner's, 1957.

Bassler, Jouette M. "Mixed Signals: Nicodemus in the Fourth Gospel." *JBL* 108 (1989): 635-46.

Bauckham, Richard. *God Crucified: Christology and Monotheism in the New Testament.* Grand Rapids: Eerdmans, 1999.

————. "Messianism According to the Gospel of John." Pages 34-68 in *Challenging Perspectives on the Gospel of John.* Edited by John Lierman. WUNT 2/219. Tübingen: Mohr Siebeck, 2006.

Bennema, Cornelius. *The Saving Power of Wisdom: An Investigation of Spirit and Wisdom in Relation to the Soteriology of the Fourth Gospel.* WUNT 2/148. Tübingen: Mohr Siebeck, 2002.

————. "Spirit-Baptism in the Fourth Gospel: A Messianic Reading of John 1,33." *Bib* 84 (2003): 35-60.

Bieringer, Reimund, D. Pollefeyt, and F. Vandecasteele-Vanneuville, eds. *Anti-Judaism and the Fourth Gospel.* Louisville: Westminster John Knox, 2001.

Bond, Helen K. *Pontius Pilate in History and Interpretation.* SNTSMS 100. Cambridge: Cambridge University, 1998.

Boring, M. Eugene. *The Continuing Voice of Jesus: Christian Prophecy and the Gospel Tradition.* Louisville: Westminster John Knox, 1991.

Brown, Raymond E. *The Churches the Apostles Left Behind.* New York: Paulist, 1984.

————. *The Death of the Messiah: From Gethsemane to the Grave.* 2 vols. New York: Doubleday, 1994.

————. *The Epistles of John.* AB 30. Garden City, N.Y.: Doubleday, 1982.

————. *The Gospel According to John.* 2 vols. AB 29-29A. Garden City, N.Y.: Doubleday, 1966, 1970.

————. *An Introduction to the Gospel of John.* Edited by Francis J. Moloney. New York: Random House, 2003.

Brown, Tricia Gates. *Spirit in the Writings of John: Johannine Pneumatology in Social-Scientific Perspective.* JSNTSup 235. London and New York: T. & T. Clark, 2003.

Bultmann, Rudolf. *The Gospel of John.* Philadelphia: Westminster, 1971.

————. *Theology of the New Testament.* 2 vols. New York: Scribner's, 1951, 1955.

Burge, Gary M. *The Anointed Community: The Holy Spirit in the Johannine Tradition.* Grand Rapids: Eerdmans, 1987.

Burkett, Delbert R. *The Son of Man Debate: A History and Evaluation.* SNTSMS 107. Cambridge: Cambridge University, 1999.

Burridge, Richard A. *Imitating Jesus: An Inclusive Approach to New Testament Ethics.* Grand Rapids: Eerdmans, 2007.

Calvin, John. *The Gospel According to St. John 1–10.* Grand Rapids: Eerdmans, 1959.

Carter, Warren. *Pontius Pilate: Portraits of a Roman Governor*. Collegeville, Minn.: Liturgical, 2003.

Charlesworth, James H. "The Gospel of John: Exclusivism Caused by a Social Setting Different from That of Jesus (John 11:54 and 14:6)." Pages 247-78 in *Anti-Judaism and the Fourth Gospel*. Edited by Reimund Bieringer, Didier Pollefeyt, and Frederique Vandecasteele-Vanneuville. Louisville: Westminster John Knox, 2001.

Chennattu, Rekha M. *Johannine Discipleship as a Covenant Relationship*. Peabody, Mass.: Hendrickson, 2006.

Clark-Soles, Jaime, " 'I Will Raise [Whom?] Up on the Last Day': Anthropology as a Feature of Johannine Eschatology." Pages 29-53 in *New Currents Through John: A Global Perspective*. Edited by Francisco Lozada Jr. and Tom Thatcher. Atlanta: Society of Biblical Literature, 2006.

Collins, Raymond F. *These Things Have Been Written: Studies in the Fourth Gospel*. Leuven: Peeters and Grand Rapids: Eerdmans, 1990.

Coloe, Mary L. *God Dwells with Us: Temple Symbolism in the Fourth Gospel*. Collegeville, Minn.: Liturgical, 2001.

Conway, Colleen M. *Men and Women in the Fourth Gospel: Gender and Johannine Characterization*. SBLDS 167. Atlanta: Scholars, 1999.

Cowan, Christopher. "The Father and the Son in the Fourth Gospel: Johannine Subordination Revisited." *JETS* 49 (2006): 115-35.

Culpepper, R. Alan. *Anatomy of the Fourth Gospel: A Study in Literary Design*. Philadelphia: Fortress, 1983.

———. "The Gospel of John as a Document of Faith in a Pluralistic Culture." Pages 107-27 in *"What Is John?" Readers and Readings of the Fourth Gospel*. Edited by Fernando F. Segovia. Atlanta: Scholars, 1996.

———. "Inclusivism and Exclusivism in the Fourth Gospel." Pages 85-108 in *Word, Theology, and Community in John*. Edited by John Painter, R. Alan Culpepper, and Fernando F. Segovia. St. Louis: Chalice, 2002.

———. "Realized Eschatology in the Experience of the Johannine Community." Pages 253-78 in *The Resurrection of Jesus in the Gospel of John*. Edited by Craig R. Koester and Reimund Bieringer. WUNT 222. Tübingen: Mohr Siebeck, 2008.

Daly-Denton, Margaret. *David in the Fourth Gospel: The Johannine Reception of the Psalms*. AGAJU 46. Leiden: Brill, 2000.

Dennis, John. "Jesus' Death in John's Gospel: A Survey of Research from Bultmann to the Present with Special Reference to the Johannine Hyper-Texts." *Currents in Biblical Research* 4 (2006): 331-63.

deSilva, David A. *The Hope of Glory: Honor Discourse and New Testament Interpretation*. Collegeville, Minn.: Liturgical, 1999.

Dodd, C. H. "A Hidden Parable in the Fourth Gospel." Pages 30-40 in *More New Testament Studies*. Grand Rapids: Eerdmans, 1968.

————. *The Interpretation of the Fourth Gospel.* Cambridge: Cambridge University, 1953.

Duke, Paul D. *Irony in the Fourth Gospel.* Atlanta: John Knox, 1985.

Esler, Philip F., and Ronald Piper. *Lazarus, Martha, and Mary: Social-Scientific Approaches to the Gospel of John.* Minneapolis: Fortress, 2006.

Forde, Gerhard O. *Theology Is for Proclamation.* Minneapolis: Fortress, 1990.

Forestell, J. Terence. *The Word of the Cross.* AnBib 57. Rome: Biblical Institute, 1974.

Frey, Jörg. "Eschatology in the Johannine Circle." Pages 47-82 in *Theology and Christology in the Fourth Gospel.* Edited by Gilbert Van Belle, Jan G. van der Watt, and Petrus J. Maritz. BETL 184. Leuven: Leuven University and Peeters, 2005.

————. *Die johanneische Eschatologie,* vol. 3. *Die eschatologische Verkündigung in den johanneischen Texten.* WUNT 117. Tübingen: Mohr Siebeck, 2000.

————. "Die '*theologia crucifixi*' des Johannesevangeliums." Pages 169-238 in *Kreuzestheologie im Neuen Testament.* Edited by Andreas Dettwiler and Jean Zumstein. WUNT 151. Tübingen: Mohr Siebeck, 2002.

————, Jan G. van der Watt, and Ruben Zimmermann, eds. *Imagery in the Gospel of John: Terms, Forms, Themes, and Theology of Johannine Figurative Language.* WUNT 200. Tübingen: Mohr Siebeck, 2006.

Gardner, Iain. *The Kephalaia of the Teacher: The Edited Coptic Manichaean Texts in Translation with Commentary.* NHMS 37. Leiden: Brill, 1995.

Graham, Billy. *How to Be Born Again.* Waco: Word, 1977.

Griffith, Sidney H. "Arguing from Scripture: The Bible in the Christian/Muslim Encounter in the Middle Ages." Pages 29-58 in *Scripture and Pluralism: Reading the Bible in the Religiously Plural Worlds of the Middle Ages and Renaissance.* Edited by Thomas J. Heffernan and Thomas E. Burman. SHCT 123. Leiden and Boston: Brill, 2005.

Guillaume, A. *The Life of Muhammad: A Translation of Sirat Rasul Allah* (Karachi and Oxford: Oxford University, 1955.

Gunton, Colin. *The Actuality of Atonement: A Study of Metaphor, Rationality, and the Christian Tradition.* Grand Rapids: Eerdmans, 1989.

Hakola, Raimo. *Identity Matters: John, the Jews, and Jewishness.* NovTSup 118. Leiden: Brill, 2005.

Harrisville, Roy A. *Fracture: The Cross as Irreconcilable in the Language and Thought of the Biblical Writers.* Grand Rapids: Eerdmans, 2006.

Hasitschka, Martin. "Befreiung von Sünde nach dem Johannesevangelium." Pages 92-107 in *Sünde und Erlösung im Neuen Testament.*" Edited by Hubert Frankenmölle; Freiburg: Herder, 1996.

————. *Befreiung von Sünde nach dem Johannesevangelium: Eine bibeltheologische Untersuchung.* Innsbrucker theologische Studien 27. Innsbruck: Tyrolia, 1989.

Hays, Richard B. *The Moral Vision of the New Testament: A Contemporary Introduction to New Testament Ethics.* San Francisco: HarperSanFrancisco, 1996.

Heil, John Paul. *Blood and Water: The Death and Resurrection of Jesus in John 18–21.* CBQMS 27. Washington, D.C.: Catholic Biblical Association, 1995.

Heine, Ronald E. "The Role of the Gospel of John in the Montanist Controversy." *Second Century* 6 (1987): 1-18.

Hick, John. *God Has Many Names.* Philadelphia: Westminster, 1980.

Hill, Charles E. *The Johannine Corpus in the Early Church.* Oxford: Oxford University, 2004.

Hurtado, Larry W. *Lord Jesus Christ: Devotion to Jesus in Earliest Christianity.* Grand Rapids: Eerdmans, 2003.

Johnston, George. *The Spirit-Paraclete in the Gospel of John.* SNTSMS 12. Cambridge: Cambridge University, 1970.

Jones, Larry Paul. *The Symbol of Water in the Gospel of John.* JSNTSup 145. Sheffield: JSOT, 1997.

Käsemann, Ernst. *The Testament of Jesus According to John 17.* Philadelphia: Fortress, 1968.

Keck, Leander E. "Derivation as Destiny: 'Of-ness' in Johannine Christology, Anthropology, and Soteriology." Pages 274-88 in *Exploring the Gospel of John: In Honor of D. Moody Smith.* Edited by R. Alan Culpepper and C. Clifton Black. Louisville: Westminster John Knox, 1996.

Keefer, Kyle. *The Branches of the Gospel of John: The Reception of the Fourth Gospel in the Early Church.* LNTS 332. London: T. & T. Clark, 2006.

Keener, Craig S. *The Gospel of John.* 2 vols. Peabody, Mass.: Hendrickson, 2003.

Kierspel, Lars. *The Jews and the World in the Fourth Gospel: Parallelism, Function, and Context.* WUNT 2/220. Tübingen: Mohr Siebeck, 2006.

Knöppler, Thomas. *Die theologia crucis des Johannesevangeliums.* WMANT 69. Neukirchen-Vluyn: Neukirchener, 1994.

Koester, Craig R. "The Death of Jesus and the Human Condition: Exploring the Theology of John's Gospel." Pages 141-57 in *Life in Abundance: Studies of John's Gospel in Tribute to Raymond E. Brown, S.S.* Edited by John R. Donahue. Collegeville, Minn.: Liturgical, 2005.

——."Hearing, Seeing, and Believing in the Gospel of John." *Bib* 70 (1989): 327-48.e

——. "Jesus' Resurrection, the Signs, and the Dynamics of Faith in the Gospel of John." Pages 47-74 in *The Resurrection of Jesus in the Gospel of John.* Edited by Craig R. Koester and Reimund Bieringer. WUNT 222. Tübingen: Mohr Siebeck, 2008.

——. "Messianic Exegesis and the Call of Nathanael (John 1.45-51)." *JSNT* 39 (1990): 23-34.

——. "'The Savior of the World' (John 4:42)." *JBL* 109 (1990): 665-80.

——. *Symbolism in the Fourth Gospel: Meaning, Mystery, Community.* 2nd ed. Minneapolis: Fortr ss, 2003.

————. "What Does It Mean to Be Human? Imagery and the Human Condition in John's Gospel." Pages 403-20 in *Imagery in the Gospel of John: Terms, Forms, Themes, and Theology of Johannine Figurative Language*. Edited by Jörg Frey, Jan G. van der Watt, and Ruben Zimmermann. WUNT 200. Tübingen: Mohr Siebeck, 2006.

————. "Why Was the Messiah Crucified? A Study of God, Jesus, Satan, and Human Agency in Johannine Theology." Pages 163-80 in *The Death of Jesus in the Gospel of John*. Edited by Gilbert van Belle. BETL 200. Leuven: Leuven University and Peeters, forthcoming.

————, and Reimund Bieringer, eds. *The Resurrection of Jesus in the Gospel of John*. WUNT 222. Tübingen: Mohr Siebeck, 2008.

Köstenberger, Andreas J. "Jesus the Rabbi in the Fourth Gospel." Pages 65-98 in *Studies in John and Gender: A Decade of Scholarship*. New York: Lang, 2001.

————. *John*. BECNT. Grand Rapids: Baker Academic, 2004.

Kovacs, Judith L. "'Now Shall the Ruler of This World Be Driven Out': Jesus' Death as Cosmic Battle in John 12:20-36." *JBL* 114 (1995): 227-47.

Kysar, Robert. *John, the Maverick Gospel*. 2nd ed. Louisville: Westminster John Knox, 1993.

————. *Voyages with John: Charting the Fourth Gospel*. Waco, Tex.: Baylor University, 2005.

Larsson, Tord. *God in the Fourth Gospel: A Hermeneutical Study of the History of Interpretations*. ConBNT 35. Stockholm: Almqvist & Wiksell, 2001.

Lee, Dorothy. *Flesh and Glory: Symbol, Gender, and Theology in the Gospel of John*. New York: Crossroad, 2002.

Lierman, John. "The Mosaic Pattern of John's Christology." Pages 210-34 in *Challenging Perspectives on the Gospel of John*. WUNT 2/219. Tübingen: Mohr Siebeck, 2006.

Lincoln, Andrew T. "'I Am the Resurrection and the Life': The Resurrection Message of the Fourth Gospel." Pages 122-44 in *Life in the Face of Death: The Resurrection Message of the New Testament*. Edited by Richard N. Longenecker. Grand Rapids: Eerdmans, 1998.

————. *Truth on Trial: The Lawsuit Motif in the Fourth Gospel*. Peabody, Mass.: Hendrickson, 2000.

Loader, William. *The Christology of the Fourth Gospel: Structure and Issues*. 2nd ed. Frankfurt: Lang, 1992.

Malina, Bruce, and Jerome H. Neyrey. "Honor and Shame in Luke-Acts: Pivotal Values in the Mediterranean World." Pages 25-65 in *The Social World of Luke-Acts*. Edited by Jerome H. Neyrey. Peabody, Mass.: Hendrickson, 1991.

————, and Richard L. Rohrbaugh. *Social-Science Commentary on the Gospel of John*. Minneapolis: Fortress, 1998.

Martin-Achard, Robert, and George W. E. Nickelsburg. "Resurrection" in *ABD* 5: 680-91. 6 vols. New York: Doubleday, 1992.

Martyn, J. Louis. *History and Theology in the Fourth Gospel.* 3rd ed. Louisville: Westminster John Knox, 2003.

Matera, Frank J. "'On Behalf of Others,' 'Cleansing,' and 'Return': Johannine Images for Jesus' Death." *LS* 13 (1988): 161-78.

Menken, Martin J. J. "John 6:51c-58: Eucharist or Christology?" Pages 183-204 in *Critical Readings of John 6.* Edited by R. Alan Culpepper. BibIntSer 22. Leiden: Brill, 1997.

Metzner, Rainer. *Das Verständnis der Sünde im Johannesevangelium.* WUNT 2/122. Tübingen: Mohr Siebeck, 2000.

Meyer, Paul W. "'The Father': The Presentation of God in the Fourth Gospel." Pages 255-73 in *Exploring the Gospel of John: In Honor of D. Moody Smith.* Edited by R. Alan Culpepper and C. Clifton Black. Louisville: Westminster John Knox, 1996.

Mingana, A., ed. *Woodbrooke Studies,* vol. 12. Cambridge: W. Heffer & Sons, 1928.

Moloney, Francis J. *Belief in the Word: Reading John 1–4.* Minneapolis: Fortress, 1993.

———. *Glory Not Dishonor: Reading John 13–21.* Minneapolis: Fortress, 1998.

———. *The Gospel of John.* SP 4. Collegeville, Minn.: Liturgical, 1998.

———. "The Johannine Son of Man Revisited." Pages 66-92 in *The Gospel of John: Text and Context.* BibIntSer 73. Leiden: Brill, 2005.

———. *Signs and Shadows: Reading John 5–12.* Minneapolis: Fortress, 1996.

Noll, Mark A. *Turning Points: Decisive Moments in the History of Christianity.* Grand Rapids: Baker Academic, 2000.

O'Day, Gail R. *The Gospel of John.* NIB 9. Nashville: Abingdon, 1995.

Okure, Teresa. *The Johannine Approach to Mission.* WUNT 2/31. Tübingen: Mohr Siebeck, 1988.

Outler, Albert, ed. *The Works of John Wesley.* Nashville: Abingdon, 1984.

Pagels, Elaine H. *The Gospel of John in Gnostic Exegesis: Heracleon's Commentary on John.* SBLMS 17. Nashville and New York: Abingdon, 1973.

Painter, John. "Inclined to God: The Quest for Eternal Life — Bultmannian Hermeneutics and the Theology of the Fourth Gospel." Pages 346-68 in *Exploring the Gospel of John: In Honor of D. Moody Smith.* Edited by R. Alan Culpepper and C. Clifton Black. Louisville: Westminster John Knox, 1996.

———. *John: Witness and Theologian.* London: SPCK, 1975.

———. *The Quest for the Messiah: The History, Literature and Theology of the Johannine Community.* Edinburgh: T. & T. Clark, 1991.

Pastorelli, David. *Le paraclet dans le corpus Johannique.* BZAW 142. Berlin: de Gruyter, 2006.

Pelikan, Jaroslav. *The Christian Tradition: A History of the Development of Doctrine,* vol. 1. *The Emergence of the Catholic Tradition (100-600)*. Chicago and London: University of Chicago, 1971.

Piper, Ronald A. "Satan, Demons and the Absence of Exorcisms in the Fourth Gospel." Pages 253-78 in *Christology, Controversy and Community: New Testament Essays in Honour of David R. Catchpole*. Edited by David G. Horrell and Christopher M. Tuckett. NovTSup 99. Leiden, Brill, 2000.

Price, S. R. F. *Rituals and Power: The Roman Imperial Cult in Asia Minor*. Cambridge: Cambridge University, 1984.

Reinhartz, Adele, ed. *God the Father in the Gospel of John*. Semeia 85. Atlanta: Society of Biblical Literature, 1999.

———. *The Word in the World: The Cosmological Tale in the Fourth Gospel*. SBLMS 45. Atlanta: Scholars, 1992.

Rensberger, David. *Johannine Faith and Liberating Community*. Philadelphia: Westminster, 1988.

Renz, Gabi. "Nicodemus: An Ambiguous Disciple? A Narrative Sensitive Investigation. Pages 255-83 in *Challenging Perspectives on the Gospel of John*. Edited by John Lierman. WUNT 2/219. Tübingen: Mohr Siebeck, 2006.

Resseguie, James L. *The Strange Gospel: Narrative Design and Point of View in John*. BibIntSer 56. Leiden: Brill, 2001.

Rudolph, Kurt. *Gnosis: The Nature and History of Gnosticism*. San Francisco: Harper & Row, 1983.

Sailer, Bill. "Jesus, the Emperor, and the Gospel of John." Pages 284-301 in *Challenging Perspectives on the Gospel of John*. Edited by John Lierman. WUNT 2/219. Tübingen: Mohr Siebeck, 2006.

Sandness, Karl Olav. "Whence and Whither: A Narrative Perspective on Birth ἄνωθεν (John 3,3-8)." *Bib* 86 (2005): 153-73.

Schlund, Christine. *"Kein Knochen Soll Gebrochen Werden": Studien zu Bedeutung des Pesachfests in Textes des frühen Judentums und im Johannesevangelium*. WMANT 107. Neukirchen-Vluyn: Neukirchener, 2005.

Schnackenburg, Rudolf. *The Gospel According to St. John*. 3 vols. New York: Herder/Seabury/Crossroad, 1968, 1980, 1982.

Schneiders, Sandra M. "Death in the Community of Eternal Life: History, Theology, and Spirituality in John 11." *Int* 41 (1987): 44-56.

———. "The Resurrection (of the Body) in the Fourth Gospel: A Key to Johannine Spirituality." Pages 168-98 in *Life in Abundance: Studies of John's Gospel in Tribute to Raymond E. Brown*. Edited by John R. Donahue. Collegeville, Minn.: Liturgical, 2005.

———. *The Revelatory Text: Interpreting the New Testament as Sacred Scripture*. 2nd ed. Collegeville, Minn.: Liturgical, 1999.

———. "Touching the Risen Jesus: Mary Magdalene and Thomas the Twin." Pages

153-76 in *The Resurrection of Jesus in the Gospel of John.* Edited by Craig R. Koester and Reimund Bieringer. WUNT 222. Tübingen: Mohr Siebeck, 2008.

Schnelle, Udo. *Antidocetic Christology in the Gospel of John: An Investigation of the Place of the Fourth Gospel in the Johannine School.* Minneapolis: Fortress, 1992.

———. "Cross and Resurrection in the Gospel of John." Pages 127-52 in *The Resurrection of Jesus in the Gospel of John.* Edited by Craig R. Koester and Reimund Bieringer. WUNT 222. Tübingen: Mohr Siebeck, 2008.

———. "Die Abschiedsreden im Johannesevangelium." *ZNW* 80 (1989): 64-79.

———. *The Human Condition: Anthropology in the Teachings of Jesus, Paul, and John.* Minneapolis: Fortress, 1996.

Schrage, Wolfgang. *The Ethics of the New Testament.* Philadelphia: Fortress, 1988.

Schürer, Emil, et al. *The History of the Jewish People in the Age of Jesus Christ.* 3 vols. Edinburgh: T. & T. Clark, 1973-87.

Segovia, Fernando F. *The Farewell of the Word: The Johannine Call to Abide.* Minneapolis: Fortress, 1991.

Smith, D. Moody. *John Among the Gospels: The Relationship in Twentieth-Century Research.* 2nd ed. Columbia: University of South Carolina, 2001.

———. "Prolegomena to a Canonical Reading of the Fourth Gospel." Pages 169-82 in *"What Is John?": Readers and Readings of the Fourth Gospel.* Edited by Fernando F. Segovia. Atlanta: Scholars, 1996.

———. *The Theology of the Gospel of John.* Cambridge: Cambridge University, 1995.

Söding, Thomas. "'Ich und der Vater sind eins' (Joh 10,30): Die johanneische Christologie vor dem Anspruch das Hauptgebotes (Dtn 6,4f)." *ZNW* 93 (2002): 177-99.

Stefan, Crinisor. "The Paraclete and Prophecy in the Johannine Community." *Pneuma* 27 (2005): 273-96.

Stibbe, Mark. "Telling the Father's Story: The Gospel of John as Narrative Theology." Pages 170-93 in *Challenging Perspectives on the Gospel of John.* Edited by John Lierman. WUNT 2/219. Tübingen: Mohr Siebeck, 2006.

Straub, Esther. *Kritische Theologie ohne ein Wort vom Kreuz: zum Verhältnis Joh 1–12 und 13–20.* FRLANT 203. Göttingen: Vandenhoeck & Ruprecht, 2003.

Thomas, John Christopher. *Footwashing in John 13 and the Johannine Community.* JSNTSup 61. Sheffield: JSOT, 1991.

Thompson, Marianne Meye. "'Every Picture Tells a Story': Imagery for God in the Gospel of John." Pages 259-77 in *Imagery in the Gospel of John: Terms, Forms, Themes, and Theology of Johannine Figurative Language.* Edited by Jörg Frey, Jan G. van der Watt, and Ruben Zimmermann. WUNT 200. Tübingen: Mohr Siebeck, 2006.

———. *The God of the Gospel of John.* Grand Rapids: Eerdmans, 2001.

———. "The Historical Jesus and the Johannine Christ." Pages 21-42 in *Exploring the Gospel of John: In Honor of D. Moody Smith.* Edited by R. Alan Culpepper and C. Clifton Black. Louisville: Westminster John Knox, 1996.

―――. *The Humanity of Jesus in the Fourth Gospel.* Philadelphia: Fortress, 1988.

―――. "When the Ending Is Not the End." Pages 65-75 in *The Endings of Mark and the Ends of God: Essays in Memory of Donald Harrisville Juel.* Edited by Beverly Roberts Gaventa and Patrick D. Miller. Louisville: Westminster John Knox, 2005.

Tolmie, D. François. "The Characterization of God in the Fourth Gospel." *JSNT* 69 (1998): 57-75.

Troeltsch, Ernst. *Christian Thought: Its History and Application.* New York: Meridian, 1957.

Van Belle, Gilbert, ed. *The Death of Jesus in the Fourth Gospel.* BETL 200. Leuven: Peeters, 2007.

―――. "The Meaning of the σημεῖα in Jn 20,30-31." *ETL* 74 (1998): 300-25.

van der Watt, Jan G. "Ethics Alive in Imagery." Pages 421-48 in *Imagery in the Gospel of John.* Edited by Jörg Frey, Jan G. van der Watt, and Ruben Zimmermann. WUNT 200. Tübingen: Mohr Siebeck, 2006.

―――. "Ethics and Ethos in the Gospel According to John." *ZNW* 97 (2006): 147-76.

―――. *Family of the King: Dynamics of Metaphor in the Gospel of John.* BibIntSer 47. Leiden: Brill, 2000.

Vellanickal, Matthew. *The Divine Sonship of Christians in the Johannine Writings.* AnBib 72. Rome: Biblical Institute, 1977.

Voorwinde, Stephen. *Jesus' Emotions in the Fourth Gospel: Human or Divine?* JSNTSup 284. London: T. & T. Clark, 2005.

Whitefield, George. *Journals.* Carlisle, Penn.: Banner of Truth, 1960.

Wright, N. T. *The Resurrection of the Son of God.* Minneapolis: Fortress, 2003.

Zimmermann, Ruben. *Christologie der Bilder im Johannesevangelium: Die Christopoetik des vierten Evangeliums unter besonderer Berücksichtigung von Joh 10.* WUNT 171. Tübingen: Mohr Siebeck, 2004.

―――. "Imagery in John: Opening Up Paths into the Tangled Thicket of John's Figurative World." Pages 1-43 in *Imagery in the Gospel of John: Terms, Forms, Themes, and Theology of Johannine Figurative Language.* Edited by Jörg Frey, Jan G. van der Watt, and Ruben Zimmermann. WUNT 200. Tübingen: Mohr Siebeck, 2006.

Zumstein, Jean. "Jesus' Resurrection in the Farewell Discourses." Pages 103-26 in *The Resurrection of Jesus in the Gospel of John.* Edited by Craig R. Koester and Reimund Bieringer. WUNT 222. Tübingen: Mohr Siebeck, 2008.

Index

Abide: believers in Jesus, 195-96; Jesus and his Father in the community, 183; Spirit in the community, 147-51, 183; Spirit on Jesus, 136

Advocate, 147-57; and term *paraklētos* or *paraclete*, 147; "another," 147-48. *See also* Holy Spirit

Arius and Arian controversy, 14

Arndt, Johann, 21

Ascension of Jesus, 11-12, 127-28, 175-76, 182, 185

Athanasius, 14

Atonement, 112-17

Augustine, 19

Baptism, 19, 40-41, 206-7

Barmen Declaration, 22

Barth, Karl, 22

Birth, new, 19-20, 137-43

Body: of Jesus, 103-7; and resurrection, 46-47, 109, 123-25, 130-32, 179-82; as temple, 204. *See also* Flesh; Incarnation

Born again experience, 19-20, 142-43

Calvin, John, 20

Church: as family, 197-98; as flock, 199-200; as friends, 198-99; love within, 52, 193-209; organization of, 202-3; Spirit within, 149-51; unity of, 200-202; witness of, 129-30, 133, 157-60

Clement of Alexandria, 4

Creed, Nicene-Constantinopolitan, 15-16

Crucifixion: and God, 41-46; as love in human terms, 110-12; problem of, 108-9; as revelation of divine glory, 120-23; as sacrifice for sin, 112-17; and sin, 70-72; and Spirit, 146; as victory over evil, 117-20

Cyprian, 19

Darkness, 63-65

Death, 56-65, 179-82

Determinism, 78-80

Devil: children of the, 76; traits of, 74-76. *See also* Evil; Satan

Ecclesiology. *See* Church

Eschatology, 175-86

Evil: God's restraint of, 41-44; Jesus' victory over, 117-20; problem of, 74-78

Faith: and action, 177-78, 187, 190, 193,